THE CINEMA OF ECONOMIC MIRACLES

POST-CONTEMPORARY INTERVENTIONS

Series Editors: Stanley Fish and Fredric Jameson

angelo restivo

THE CINEMA OF ECONOMIC MIRACLES

Visuality and Modernization in the Italian Art Film

DUKE UNIVERSITY PRESS   DURHAM AND LONDON   2002

© 2002 Duke University Press

All rights reserved

Printed in the United States of

America on acid-free paper ∞

Designed by Amy Ruth Buchanan

Typeset in Carter & Cone Galliard

by G&S Typesetters, Inc.

Library of Congress Cataloging-in-

Publication Data appear on the last

printed page of this book.

CONTENTS

The idea of undertaking this study came about after I read, in manuscript form, Marsha Kinder's study of Spanish cinema, *Blood Cinema*. Thus, I am most indebted to her; her enthusiasm for my project, her patient reading of the chapters as they progressed, and her always astute comments were invaluable. Lynn Spigel was especially helpful in working through issues of urban space. It was she who introduced me to Michael Dear, who generously gave of his time to introduce me to the geographer's point of view on postmodern space. I would also like to thank Michael Renov for our many long discussions of theory, and especially for the summer spent working through Lacan's Seminar VII.

James Hay has been supportive of my work ever since we first met at the Ohio Conference in 1994. I would also like to thank Peter Brunette for his enthusiastic support of this book, as well as for his sharp editorial comments. At the University of Iowa, Dudley Andrew, Rick Altman, and Lauren Rabinowitz brought me in as a visiting faculty specifically to teach the ideas I was developing in this book, and I am grateful for their having given me that opportunity. Working with the graduate students at Iowa was truly a wonderful experience, and their sharpness, seriousness, and commitment to theory helped refine my thinking on many of the issues raised in this book.

At the University of Michigan, Phillip Hallman went out of his way to track down videotapes unavailable in the United States. Abe Marcus Nornes also provided me with tapes of hard-to-find Taiwanese films. I also want to thank Alan Young, who set up a stand where I could make frame enlargements. Additional frame enlargements were made at the

Film Studies Center of the University of Chicago. I would like to thank Tom Gunning, Julia Gibbs, and the technicians at the center.

At Duke University Press, I must thank Ken Wissoker for his confidence in this project, Katie Courtland for her enthusiasm in overseeing the production, and Maura High for her perceptive and intelligent copyediting of the manuscript.

Finally, I would like to thank friends who—though we are now scattered in various institutions across the country—have always followed my intellectual development with interest: Cesare Casarino, Bhaskar Sarkar, Bishnu Ghosh, Amy Villarejo, and Virginia Wexman. Lastly, I must single out my friend, colleague, and collaborator Richard Cante. The eight years that have passed since we met have been an ongoing intellectual adventure of the rarest sort, one in which "life" and "theory" come to coincide.

Portions of part 2 of this manuscript appeared, in different form, in *Film Quarterly* and *The Road Movie Book*.

part I

NEOREALISM AND NATION

Of all the national cinemas outside of Hollywood, Italian cinema is probably the one most thoroughly researched and written about in English. Thus, the question that immediately confronts anyone who is attempting to traverse this seemingly familiar territory yet again is that agonizingly simply one, "Why?" Everyone, presumably, "knows" Italian cinema; and without important new material from the archive, or discoveries of new works or *auteurs,* are there any compelling reasons to go over such well-trodden ground, motivated "only" by aesthetic and theoretical questions? Two recent studies of canonical cinemas— P. Adams Sitney's *Vital Crises in Italian Cinema* and Dudley Andrew's *Mists of Regret* —have acknowledged the (at least partially) self-reflexive nature of the question posed. Sitney, for example, tells us that his decision to write about Italian cinema came out of a "passion," that particular Italian films played crucial roles in his development as a *cinéphile.*[1] The very title of Andrew's book, *Mists of Regret,* suggests a nostalgia for the lost object that is not simply a psychological event but also a mirror that reflects the tracing of history. As the philosophers of the Frankfurt school knew so well, it is never simply a question of acknowledging one's desire animating the work one is doing; for that desire is itself a mode of entry into history.

The starting point for this study was in some ways very close to that of Sitney's: namely, that postwar Italian cinema was profoundly connected, first, to the processes of political and economic reorganization that (re)constructed the nation into the Italy we know today; and second, to the larger and more "invisible" processes that have marked the transformation of global capitalism in the postwar period. Until recently, studies of Italian cinema have tended to adopt an overly simplistic "reflectionist" position regarding the relation between cinema and history, so that an analysis of, for example, Pier Paolo Pasolini's *Accattone* (1961) will begin by mentioning that Pasolini's material was taken from the lives of the Roman underclass in the slums generated by economic development, and then would proceed to analyze in a rather disconnected argument the painterly compositional style, the use of Bach, and so on. Clearly, from the point of view of critical theory, this reification of the formal is inadequate. Sitney's book marks an advance in the ways it attempts to connect political and economic transformation to the national cinema. Historiographically, Sitney adopts a rather traditional methodology, which nevertheless yields fruitful results: he relies on political and cultural documents of the period—or on the great Italian historians of the cinema, who deploy the same methodology—through which to trace the films' relationships to politics and culture.

This study is grounded in a different conception of historiography. If we admit the centrality of neocapitalism to the development of Italian cinema in the sixties, then certainly we know more today about the characteristics of this economic transformation than did those who were writing about it (or making films about it) then. The Italian cinema of the sixties thus becomes a highly charged historical conjuncture in which we may see, retroactively, the emergence of the most important concerns in contemporary theory today. In a sense, then, Italian cinema becomes the site for a "genealogy" of some of today's most pressing questions in critical theory, cultural studies, and theories of the image.

In this regard, Italian cinema's centrality in the canon becomes an advantage, for it has always been the privileged site for discourses on visuality, on the image as historical document, on the emergence of cinematic modernism, and on the possibilities of cinematic expression outside the "hegemonic" enunciative regime of classical Hollywood. From André Bazin to Gilles Deleuze, the history of cinema has been conceived as marked by a great break or divide—classical to modernist, or action-image to time-image—of which the postwar Italian cinema is the great exemplar. In fact, in his study of contemporary international cinema, Robert Kolker—in the chapter significantly titled "The Validity of the Image"—takes Italian neorealism as the fundamental point of reference not just for the European new waves that followed, but for cinematic developments across the globe.[2]

And yet this very "coincidence"—of a radical historical rupture and the emergence of an "aesthetic of reality"—presents us with a profound contradiction, a contradiction that, I will argue, manifests itself throughout the development of Italian cinema through the sixties. For this historical rupture is intimately connected to the postwar reorganization of capitalism around consumption, and to the emergence of a new technology of vision in the form of television. Ironically, perhaps, the great faith in the validity of the image emerges at exactly the moment when a technology emerges that would ultimately undermine, programmatically, that very validity. Richard Dienst has argued that the televisual—as an *idea* (of liveness, of instantaneous transmission, and thus, ultimately, of the abolition of that distance that is constitutive of "representation" itself)—has been always, already the conceptual "outside" of the cinema.[3] And yet Bazin's "Myth of Total Cinema," one of the foundational theoretical arguments for the realist image, also posits an "outside" of the cinema. We could say that Italian cinema, especially during the sixties, achieves its brilliance precisely because it pushes up against these two "outsides," both of which promise the impossible: nothing less than the end of representation.

In looking at Italian cinema in light of neocapitalism and the incipient postmodernity that accompanies it, we are able to formulate new questions about Italian cinema. Most prominent, from the point of view of this study, are questions of space and questions of the nation—questions that are central to what we call "postmodern theory" and yet were only in a nascent state in intellectual discourses of the sixties. Certainly, strong arguments have been made that, whether or not postmodern electronic culture has brought about the "end of history," it has nevertheless radically altered those "modernist" conceptions of space that undergird the theory of the cinema. Itineraries are now traversed in essentially different ways, whether one is in a shopping mall or in cyberspace. But more important, the media-specific movements through various postmodern spaces is profoundly connected to the material transformations of the urban space itself. This study takes as an assumption the proposition of Henri Lefebvre that space is always a heterogenous "superimposition" of concrete historical moments and practices. That said, the spaces of Italy provide a unique vantage point for the investigation of postmodern geographies, insofar as Italian space is subject simultaneously to the deformations of the new "global space" and to the "inertia" of an urban space overloaded with traces of the past. The question then becomes, how does cinema make visible the spatial tensions of the city at once deeply rooted in the old and fully plugged into the new?

Circulating within this diverse collection of spaces is a conceptual construction—the "nation"—which works in many ways to orchestrate these spaces into "coherences" or structures of meaning. If film and television have become privileged media for investigating the constructedness of the nation, it is because of the ways each is able to *create narrative space:* that is, to connect particular local spaces to the shared, public narrative that underpins the nation. Once again, Italy can be seen as a privileged site for looking at this process, given that its historically intense regionalism has always presented a stumbling block to the national project. While the particular problems of writing about national cinemas will be addressed in the next sections of this chapter, the point to be made here is that in cinema, the question of the nation is intimately bound up with questions of space, and that the nation—not as ossified myth but as dynamic "mediator"—is always (re)configuring spaces and trajectories through space.

Thus, theories of visuality and theories of space (and by extension, of the nation) are the central terrain upon which this study rests. It is by no means meant to be an exhaustive history of the Italian cinema, even during the years of the sixties that are its main focus. And yet it *is* the history of "a certain tendency in Italian cinema," and the uniqueness of this work lies precisely in this doubling of focus, between, on the one hand, theories of space and the image and, on the other hand, the particularities of the canonical Italian cinema. This is a problematic faced by Gérard Genette in his book *Narrative Discourse:* Is his book a reading of Proust or the elaboration of a theory? His answer can just as easily be my own: "What I propose here is essentially a method of analysis; I must therefore recognize that by seeking the specific I find the universal, and that by wishing to put theory at the service of criticism I put criticism, against my will, at the service of theory. This is the paradox of every poetics."[4] The emergence of the word "poetics" in Genette's statement brings to mind another overarching point about my own work: namely, that it is unapologetically engaged in aesthetics and aesthetic theory—something that has become somewhat unfashionable in current theory, though the current "buzz" about the "return of philosophy" may help to revitalize a much-needed mode of thought. Here, I am conceiving "aesthetics" in its broadest sense, as a certain way of thinking about the relation between subject and object. Thus conceived, aesthetics is not some reified, ahistorical "cult of genius," but rather, as the Frankfurt school knew well, a mode of apprehending the historical subject immersed in the historical "World."

Finally, a word should be said about psychoanalysis as a central methodological underpinning of this work—once again, because psychoanalysis, even more than aesthetics, has fallen upon hard times in recent theory. This is certainly not the place to write an intellectual history of film theory's appropriations of Lacanian theory; it should suffice to say that if even today much of Lacan's work remains unavailable (even in French), the situation was much worse in the late seventies and early eighties. Ironically, then, media theory has rejected its own "concoction" and misrecognized it as psychoanalysis, while recently published work by Lacan and others is indicating that the intellectual project of psychoanalysis—far from being dead—still has profound things to tell us.

In fact, recent work on Lacan can be seen as part of that "return of philosophy" alluded to earlier: for Lacan saw psychoanalysis as profoundly engaged with the most fundamental notions of philosophy— not only subject and object, but also representation, mediation, will (or agency), and pleasure. Thus, at its most fundamental level, psychoanalysis engages with an entire philosophical tradition, at the same time as it refigures it (perhaps deconstructing it, even) through the introduction of the crucial concept of the unconscious. This is certainly the way that, for example, Slavoj Žižek reads Lacan; and if Žižek's work is central to my own, it is because of the way in which this "philosophical turn" allows for a more complex understanding of the interaction of text, subject, and the social. Specifically, this book will explore such concepts (which have emerged from the encounter of psychoanalysis with philosophy) as the "ideological signifier," history as the Real, the postmodern superego (and its relation to social fragmentation), and the gaze-as-Other.

Where my work differs from Žižek's is in its attention to the *textual system* embedded within a history. In a certain sense, Žižek's view of textuality is thoroughly "postmodern"; his work is overloaded with cultural fragments—from jokes to film scenes to details of opera—which are usually wrenched from the particular textual economy from which they come. Of course, Žižek is doing this because—as he himself admits—he is using the cultural field to explain conceptual entities. The danger in this strategy is that of "wild interpretation": for just as the dream or symptom cannot be interpreted outside the context of a set of associations produced by the analysand, so might a particular film detail take on completely different resonances in light of the context in which it is situated. My work, then, posits at least a "strategic unity" to the text, and hopefully it will point the way toward an invigorated relationship between textual analysis and the encounter with theory.

Italian Cinema as Paradigm

In an excellent study of postwar Italian cinema, P. Adams Sitney takes for his title a phrase—"vital crisis"—first used by Pasolini in 1957 in an analysis of the problematic of neorealism. For Pasolini, the aesthetic project of neorealism was necessarily doomed to contradiction and ultimately failure, insofar as neorealism staked itself ultimately on a "complete reorganization of the culture." That is to say, for Pasolini, neorealism was a "superstructural" phenomenon that "outran"—and thus was in some essential way disconnected from—the real historical conditions of postfascist Italy: those conditions being both the promise of radical change through the Partita Communista Italiano led by Palmiro Togliatti, and the constellation of reactionary forces (both national and international) that by 1948 had decisively won control of the government. In Sitney's periodization of postwar Italian cinema (a periodization I'm largely in agreement with), he considers the cinema of the early sixties a manifestation of a second "vital crisis," one directly connected to the radical social transformation brought about by Italy's "economic miracle."[5]

This, then, will be a study of Italian cinema in the period of the second vital crisis, roughly from 1959 to 1968. But in changing the singular "miracle" into the plural "miracles" in the title, I am asserting, not only that the Italian cinema of this period must be conceived as intimately bound up with a profound historic conjuncture, but also that Italy's cinema of this period can in some ways be considered a paradigm. First, it was the most visible national cinema to confront the modernization to "late capitalism" outside the Hollywood enunciative regime.[6] Second, the peculiar cultural divisions within Italy made visible within the national space—in ways to be explored in depth in the following chapters—the kind of "uneven development" characteristic of neocapitalism. Thus, we might expect that certain strategies adopted within Italian cinema of this period will reappear later, in other countries undergoing economic miracles.

In the sixties, Italian cinema was extraordinarily robust, and the art films that defined the Italian cinema internationally were only a part of a thriving production industry. Besides the now canonical art films, there were the more popular comedies *all'italiana* which, while made for the national audience, began to find an international audience, with films such as *I soliti ignoti* (*Big Deal on Madonna Street*, 1958) and *Divorzio all'italiana* (*Divorce, Italian-Style*, 1961). In fact, the comedies were but the most respectable of a number of genres that flourished in the sixties, the most notable being horror (Dario Argento, Mario Bava) and the *peplum* films (the Hercules cycle, for example). In fact, this latter genre, with its easy-to-follow plots that celebrated masculinity as a kind of *mythos*, found international audiences among classes whose essentialist worldviews[7] were not yet modernized by the changing international economic structures; and in a sense, the niche created by the peplum films provided a ready-made audience for the spaghetti Westerns of Sergio Leone. Finally, by the late fifties, Hollywood had discovered "the sweet life" to be had in shooting films at Cinecittà, bringing that much more energy (and money) to an already vital filmmaking scene.[8]

Thus, the Italian art cinema of the sixties thrived in part because the Italian film industry as a whole had such a secure economic base. But it would be a mistake, I think, to view the Italian art film *solely* as a differentiated product defining "Italy" for an international elite.[9] One of the central premises of this study is that the Italian art film of the sixties differentiates itself from the "low art" of the period insofar as it self-consciously addresses itself to a national cinematic tradition: the tradition of neorealism, so crucial to the process of national reconstruction after the war.[10] Thus, while I do discuss one important (and I think neglected) comedy, as well as popular discourses and advertising from national magazines, my focus is largely on canonical art films. Not only that: I am restricting myself largely to the films of Pasolini and Michelangelo Antonioni, because I see in these two auteurs two paradigmatic responses to the project that *began*, at least, as a reinvention of neorealism.

What is at stake in the conjunction of the work of Pasolini and Antonioni is precisely the *reinsertion into history* of the Italian art cinema, whose films have too often been wrested from history by a process of reification of the work of art. Here, it is especially useful to note that André Bazin — our first and still our most valuable commentator on the neorealist project — saw that the neorealist films were stamped with their own historicity: the films were first and foremost "reportage," inseparable from the social context in which they were made.[11] Bazin traces this fact to the peculiarities of the Italian resistance and liberation as compared to the French experience: for the French, the resistance became immediately "legendary" as life returned to normalcy; for the Italians, in contrast, the postwar economic, social, and political reorganization was drawn out over a long period of time.[12] Implicit, then, in Bazin's view is the very same "vital crisis" Pasolini was later to delineate. That is, the "legend" (applicable to the French experience) implies a history already written, already occluded into some fixed meaning; the Italian experience of the immediate postwar was that of history that remained to be written, of meanings that remained to be fixed. For Italians, the postwar period was one of social antagonisms that existed at the level of the *Real* of history. And thus it is no surprise that history itself is a subject obsessively revisited by Italian cinema: the story of the Risorgimento and the unification of Italy in 1871 was told countless times in the cinema of the fifties and sixties, from *Senso* (1954) through *Vanina vanini* (1961) to *Il gattopardo* (*The Leopard*, 1963).[13]

But there is something else at stake in the conjunction of Pasolini and Antonioni: for once their work is reinscribed within the "crisis" that was the modernization of Italy in the sixties, what suddenly becomes apparent is a conflict that persists to the present day within the *metadiscourses* of film theory. If current film theory is riven by the competing claims of cultural context versus formal system, then we see in the work of Pasolini and Antonioni this very same "fault line," but articulated in relation to a historical conjuncture that allows us the potential to see these claims as inextricably linked. As Thomas Elsaesser has written, we see within current film theory "the conflicting paradigms of analysis and interpretation . . . rubbing against one another like architectonic plates,"[14] and what this study aims to do is to let the tension become productive so as to see more clearly the contours of the fault.

It is, in fact, this very tension that has fueled the recent attempts to rethink the entire project of writing about national cinemas. Until recently, much of the study of national cinemas borrowed their models from the study of national literatures. The most notable exceptions among the canonical film histories are Siegfried Kracauer's *From Caligari to Hitler* and Noel Burch's *To the Distant Observer*, insofar as both these works deploy concepts of the national in order to organize and explain the specificities of textual production in (Weimar) Germany or in Japan. It is for good reason that Philip Rosen isolates these two histories for special attention, since there is a way in which they provide us with a kind of "prolegomena" for the study of national cinema. Rosen begins his brief study of these two histories by setting forth three criteria that, for him, constitute the basic requirements for the study of a national cinema: "(1) not just a conceptualization of textuality, but one which describes how a large number of superficially differentiated texts can be associated in a regularized, relatively limited intertextuality in order to form a coherency, a 'national cinema'; (2) a conceptualization of a nation as a kind of minimally coherent entity which it makes sense to analyze in conjunction with (1); (3) some conceptualization of what is traditionally called 'history' or 'historiography.'"[15] Examining these requirements, one easily sees that they are rather deviously imbricated. We can see, for example, how the first requirement—that we have some coherent means to assign certain texts the status of "representatives" of the national cinema—by no means guarantees a stable body of films to look at. We might say that the traditional history conceives of textuality through predominantly aesthetic and thematic criteria: in regard to neorealism, for example, location shooting, natural light, ensemble acting, a concern with the everyday, and so on. But as soon as our conception of textuality is extended to include the possibility of symptomatic readings of the text—that is, once the notion of unconscious formations of meaning is accepted—then the list of texts comprising the national canon is immediately expanded, even as our conceptions of the older canonical texts become radically changed.

This is precisely where the second and third criteria come into play; for if the text is exhibiting "symptoms," it is only against some larger background from which we can read them as such. History, in the broadest sense, is that background. And of course that history is usually not only a "national" one, but one looked at from a particular "gaze." Kracauer, to give a specific example, is certainly an early proponent of the symptomatic reading of film texts, even if his notion of symptom is rather reductive. But the background against which the symptom takes meaning is the failure—within the German *nation*—of the middle classes to achieve the kind of economic security that would allow them to construct solid, democratic institutions. For both Kracauer and Burch, the national cinema is read through the lenses of certain historical conjunctures; this is the great value of their work, despite the criticisms leveled against them. As Rosen points out, both these historians implicitly conceive of the nation as an unstable, shifting entity, which the gaze of the historian perceives only against the background of particular historical trauma.[16]

The Nation in Postmodernity

Ultimately, though, the gazes of both Kracauer and Burch are "stained" by the master narratives of historicism, whether Marxist or otherwise. Central to postmodern thinking is precisely the great suspicion leveled toward master narratives of any kind. Taking once again Rosen's three criteria for a discourse on national cinema, we could say that postmodern thought turns each of the criteria into the plural: "histories" instead of "history," "subcultures" instead of (or in addition to) nation, and a notion of textuality that turns the entire field of cultural production into a vast intertextual network to be deciphered.

There is no doubt that this increasing heterogeneity of discourses (and discursive positions) has led historians to attend to marginalized subjects hitherto ignored; history itself must now be viewed as a site of a radical *écriture*, a project of the "redemption"—as Walter Benjamin might put it [17]—of the real lives and struggles until now consigned to oblivion. It is also true that this increasing heterogeneity is directly analogous to the deterritorialization characteristic of capitalism in its "late," consumption-driven stage. To say this is by no means to consign the discourses of plurality to a simple reflection of the economic "base": even someone as enthusiastic about postmodernity as Jean-François Lyotard links what he calls "the postmodern condition" to certain key economic and technological developments.[18] It is simply to point out, yet again, the seemingly irresolvable split within critical theory today.

In *Rethinking Media Theory*, Armand and Michèle Mattelart are quite lucid about this problem: as one after another conceptual apparatus for determining cause/effect connections between media and society falls, increasingly the very project itself is called into question. Against theoretical knowledge is pitted the claims of experience, or "the practice of everyday life." The reality of experience—in all of its variegated and circumscribed forms—takes precedence over any kind of conceptual reality. Following Lefebvre, the Mattelarts make from this an extremely fine philosophical point: one of the strongest points in Hegel's conception of history is the notion that conceptual reality derives its validity ultimately from the state (the state being the "concept of concepts," that which delineates nature from nonnature).[19] Thus, the very crisis of the nation-state—whose boundaries have become increasingly "formal" as the global and the local have become directly connected—this very crisis is the other side of the coin of the crisis in the concept.

While there is certainly a liberation (of sorts) that comes when conceptual reality gives way to the experiential, there are dangers: first, a "regression to positivism,"[20] and partly as a result of this, the "risk of *masking the emergence* of the new macrosubjects which are now taking over from the action of the state."[21] At this historical juncture, it seems that the only possibility is to *hold open* the contradiction between concept and experience, between structure and immediacy.

In light of this, how does film theory meet history in the study of national cinemas? To generalize rather broadly from two of the best recent histories of national cinema,[22] it seems that this "meeting" of film studies and history is manifested in four central areas: (1) subjectivity: How does the cinema participate in the construction of the national subject? (2) national discourse: How does the cinema work to discursively construct "the nation"? (3) cultural specificity: To what extent do particular films appropriate indigenous cultural forms or modes of apprehension? (4) intertextualities: What are the points of contact, not only among the films themselves, but between films and other cultural products? Before exploring these further, we should note that we see—yet again—the same theoretical tensions described earlier. The first two areas necessarily concern themselves with formal system, while the second two stress cultural studies and stand ready to challenge any mechanistic claims about "the" nation made by the first group of questions.

However much the psychoanalytic models of film spectatorship have been criticized—if not completely discredited by now—they have nevertheless left as their important legacy the notion that cinema (and media generally) has at least some role in the construction of subjectivity. What was unaccountable in the first wave of psychoanalytic film theory was the historical embeddedness of any particular spectator, a lack which becomes especially problematic when looking at the ways cinema addresses the spectator as a *national*. For Thomas Elsaesser, the New German Cinema shows us a way out of this impasse. Elsaesser notes that New German Cinema often presents us with characters who are "exhibitionistic," so that the mechanism of looking/being-looked-at is not elided or repressed, but rather foregrounded. And, Elsaesser argues, it is precisely in this "performativity" that the traces of a peculiarly German historicity can be found, insofar as the very mechanism of fascism is to "spectacularize" the relation of subject to Other.[23]

What is most remarkable about Elsaesser's argument is the way it anticipates some of the most recent rereadings of Lacan (by Žižek, especially). Elsaesser is implicitly invoking the Lacanian *doxa* of "seeing oneself being seen," which lies at the heart of Lacan's notion of the gaze as essentially an *abstraction*. The gaze—to put it in the cinema's terms—belongs neither to the spectator nor to the character on screen, but to the "Other": not a particular person, but the symbolic system itself. While theories of the gaze will be examined in great detail in part 3 of this work, we can note here that this attention to the gaze of the Other works to reinvigorate the issue of textual address, as it emerges in specific films. In Elsaesser's argument, for example, his perspective on the gaze ends up privileging a symbolic identification over an imaginary one, insofar as the Other or symbolic order is asking the characters (and by extension, the film spectators) to occupy a position that it, the (historically specific) symbolic order, has carved out for them. The characters either assume this position, or resist assuming it;[24] in either case, their performativity results from their being under this gaze.

Much of this "correction" of the Lacanian theory of the gaze (and its relation to symbolic identification) comes out of the work of Slavoj Žižek. Significantly, Žižek is from the former Yugoslavia, and his familiarity with discursive mechanisms specific to Stalinism (and its aftermath) puts him in a position similar to that of the directors of the New German Cinema. Perhaps because of this unique vantage point—where one sees in plain sight the shift from one symbolic order to another—Žižek has been able to establish the far-reaching political dimensions of Lacanian theory, dimensions that extend far beyond the analysis of totalitarian discourse. For when Lacan brings together Kant with Sade—and it is certainly one of Žižek's lasting achievements to have brought home the importance of this particular essay—he is making an argument about the construction of *modern subjectivity* at precisely the moment when that subjectivity becomes inextricably connected to a particular political/ideological structure: that of formal democracy, instituted under the banner of the nation-state.[25]

The French Revolution, as Peter Brooks wonderfully put it in his study of melodrama, in its shattering of the sacred, presents the West with one of its critical "epistemological moments." The revolution constantly forced the posing of the ethical question in terms of the radical binary of terror/virtue.[26] That is to say, how could anyone be convincing about the purity of his/her motives, about their freedom from "pathological interest"? This logic of the excluded middle produces the same paradox that begins Kant's ethical project; it is also the implacable logic of the modern superego, whose birth can be traced to this epistemological moment.

When, in the Eastern bloc nations, the long-standing communist regimes fell apart (and here "regimes" can be taken to mean not just institutional structures but also discursive, symbolic ones), something quite unexpected happened. The universalist claims of the nation were widely challenged by the seemingly "irrational" eruption of counterclaims of ethnicity (in other words, of particularity) leading to the fragmentation of what were previously constituted as "nations." The psychoanalytic view is that this contradiction is evident at the very moment of the emergence of the democratic nation, the moment of Kant and Sade. The prerequisite for the construction of the national subject was the suppression of all particularity (as remnants of the feudal past). This is a purely *formal* move, very much the same as the Kantian reformulation of the Cartesian subject as a purely contentless unknown quantity. In Kant's moral system, there is nothing to tell us whether any particular act is motivated by "pathological" interest. It is at this point, Lacan argues, that Sade uncovers the repressed truth of the Kantian universal, simply by showing how the categorical imperative can just as easily be applied to construct a world of radical evil. What Sade makes evident is that there always remains one thing—*jouissance* or enjoyment—that cannot be universalized without throwing the democratic project into contradiction. Formal democracy will always stumble over the issue of jouissance; and the nation-state has been, at least until very recently, the embodiment of this stumbling block, insofar as "the Rights of Man" are accorded only in relation to one's citizenship in the nation.[27]

If anything, postmodernity has aggravated this contradiction at the heart of the idea of the nation. In this regard, the "ethnic moment" that emerged in the Eastern bloc nations is to be conceived as not much different from similar phenomena of fragmentation (from subcultures to paramilitarism) in the Western nations. These micropolitical, separatist movements are simply the obverse of the overall logic of consumption. It has long been a marketing truism that advertising must seek as its *ideal* the direct communication with the particular consumer: *broad*casting is not as economical as *narrow*casting.[28] Thus the overall trend in marketing has been the identification of (or invention of) ever smaller subgroupings within the body politic. The result is that middle-class technocrats in Barcelona, for example, might have much stronger identifications with their counterparts in Milan or London than with other demographic groups in their own Spain.

As regionalist forces both large and small dissect the national space, what is rendered more and more evident is the *textuality* of the nation. Far from becoming outmoded, the nation is continually invoked in the discourses of popular culture, providing a kind of point of stability for the negotiation of complex social antagonisms inherent in capitalism. (Here, for example, one need only think of the way that American national myths serve to stabilize the potentially disruptive discourses around race and gender, discourses that are centrally inscribed in just about every American mass-cultural product today.) The nation is not to be conceived as some static entity, however, but rather—as Homi Bhabha argues—as the dynamic interaction between the occluded traditions of the past and the ways in which the present continually reperforms those traditions. The text is what performatively "vitalizes" the dead letter of the national idea.[29] Methodologically, this suggests that "the nation" is to be found by taking a kind of cross-section of the discursive constructions at any given period of time, whether the sources come from films, television, advertising, or elsewhere. For whatever the counterdiscourses that are seeking to gain legitimacy, the battle is invariably played out on the terrain of the national myths, not outside of them: this is precisely the way in which "nation" functions as the real, as a leftover or stumbling block.

Finally—and this brings us to our last point regarding conditions 1 and 2 above—while the nation can be "detected" and thus "mapped" by looking at the ways it is performed in texts and discourses, Lacanian theory holds that there is always something (at the level of the real) that subtends these discourses. Žižek is perfectly clear about this: "To emphasize in a 'deconstructionist' mode that Nation is not a biological or transhistorical fact but a contingent discursive construction, an overdetermined result of textual practices, is thus misleading: such an emphasis overlooks the remainder of some *real,* nondiscursive kernel of enjoyment which must be present for the Nation qua discursive entity-effect to achieve its ontological consistency."[30] While this notion of the nondiscursive real is central to Lacanian thinking (at least from 1960 onward), it is only recently that it has made its way into critical theory; and additionally, it challenges the poststructuralist position that everything can be reduced to one or another effect of discursive practices (what Žižek has called "discursive idealism").[31] Such discursive idealism does not account for the profound resistances that greet discursive challenges to national mythology (such as, to take a random, recent example, the discourses in the United States around gays in the military). These resistances lie at the level of jouissance, and of the fantasies that stage it. This is why these resistances are so notoriously difficult to overcome through discourse; for if the symptom is something that must be interpreted discursively, the fantasy is that which must be *traversed*. This is certainly not to say that critical theory cannot analyze phantasmatic material: but this analysis will be effective only to the extent that it allows for—or makes clearer—the visibility of a fantasy that evaporates as soon as we approach its disturbing core.

We could say that cultural studies, the second of our two methodological groupings above, enters the picture precisely at this juncture: that cultural specificity is just one way of approaching this "hard core" around which the ethnic community or nation organizes its jouissance. We must, however, be always aware of the caveat that we are not seeing "the thing itself" but rather the repeated circulation of symbols around it, repetition being that which announces the presence of the real. For if the lessons of Eastern Europe have taught us anything, it is the rapidity with which the object of the drive can change form.[32] That said, Marsha Kinder's study of Spanish cinema, *Blood Cinema,* is exemplary in the way it negotiates the issue of cultural specificity. Spanish cinema *does* present us with a unique representation of violence (and sacrifice); it *does* reinflect the Oedipal scene via the mother's phallus. As Spain moves from fascism through the *apertura* to democratic socialism, we see the way the nation reconstitutes itself discursively at the same time as it reperforms the same (unconscious) drama. This is not an essentialism of culture, but rather the view that—as Fredric Jameson and others have put it[33]—history is of the order of the real.

To conclude this methodological survey, it will be useful to look at a concept put forth by Dudley Andrew in his recently published, superb study of French cinema of the thirties—the notion of an *optique*. Andrew is concerned to avoid—as I am in this study—the twin dangers of, on the one hand, the reification of a canon and, on the other hand, a sociology where "the social touchstone it employs neuters whatever it is that films bring to culture, reducing them to evidence, the equivalent of votes in an election."[34] To do this, Andrew resuscitates Roland Barthes's original, structuralist conception of écriture, as the limited set of options available to a text at a given historical moment. The notion of an optique, then, leads us directly to the question of textual address; as such, it seems to me that it is not so very different from the notion of symbolic identification outlined above. In both cases, we are looking at the ways the text carves out a symbolic position that it asks the spectator to occupy. But structuralism also asserts that within any *combinatoire,* there must be one element that marks the very possibility of difference. Within the linguistic system, this element is the "phallic signifier";

within the system of visuality, it is "the gaze." It is in this sense that the gaze of the Other can be said to subtend the forms of textual address adopted by a given cinematic tradition.

The Existence of Italy

When Theodor Adorno and Max Horkheimer wrote, "Not Italy itself is given here, but the proof that it exists,"[35] they were of course making a point not about Italy but about the culture industry. And yet there is something not only sardonic but also absolutely "right" in their choice of Italy—something one can see if one tries to substitute "England," say, for Italy in the quote. For if Italy's roots extend back to antiquity, there remains still the sense that somehow we can't quite be certain that it "exists." Italy's regionalism is so intense that it often renders comic the actions of the national government; and if a region does concede to the nation, it can always reinflect the national in a way that sardonically suggests the superfluousness of the national entity.

In an age when—as discussed at length above—the nation is increasingly bypassed by macro- and micropolitical structures and discourses, it might seem that Italy would be central to the study of the nation in postmodernity. Eric Hobsbawm sees the era of the nation-state as lying between two "transnational epochs," that of the Middle Ages and that of postmodernity.[36] Italy's regionalism, in this light, can be seen as providing a kind of historical continuum to the three epochs, insofar as Italy's belated unification into a nation-state (1871) was always an incomplete phenomenon. This point is made clearly by Gramsci: because the Catholic Church was the dominant institution on the Italian peninsula, the regions of Italy retained the Church's local/international worldview long into the era of the nation-states.[37] For Gramsci, the unification was an unfinished business, a view that—as will be discussed at length in later chapters—is central to understanding postwar Italian cinema.

The issue for the cinema becomes, thus, the issue of constructing some sort of consensual idea of "nation" and "citizen" within a strongly heterogenous cultural field. In the fascist period, James Hay notes how Italian popular cinema divided itself generically into the "essentialist/ epochalist" binary opposition; the "Strapaese" films constructed the national around rural, agrarian myths of rootedness and tradition, while the "Stracittà" films constructed an urban national subject who, while cosmopolitan, nonetheless adopted culturally specific modes to express modernity.[38] That is, the spectatorial addresses of both genres were "overseen" by the gaze of fascism; so that it is *through* this gaze that myths of agrarian simplicity (for example) organized themselves around the constitution of the "Italian." The emergence of neorealism necessarily tore down the generic binarism, by giving us what was excluded from the images of the city—poverty, for one thing—and by deconstructing the idyll of the countryside (in, to take two prominent examples by Luchino Visconti, *Ossessione* (1943) and *La terra trema* (1950)—significantly, Vittorio Mussolini (son of the duce and associated with movie production at Cinecittà) reacted to *Ossessione* with the exclamation, "This is not Italy!").[39]

If in a country like Italy the images of both city and countryside are automatically weighed down by a primary regionalism, then the Italian cinema (as national) must of necessity reinscribe these images into a national discourse, into a narrative space that speaks "Italy." In this study, the cultural specificity of the Italian geography will be a central concern: both within the urban space and in the natural landscape. In both of these, temporality—and ultimately history as well—are concretized in spatial relations. When Freud made a casual analogy between Rome and the psychoanalytic model of the psychic entity,[40] he was talking about precisely this spatialization of "memory." Like "the mystic writing pad," Rome seems to retain all traces of its past, each one "written over" by succeeding ones, fragments that are subject to spatial "condensations" and "displacements." Ideologically, the national project seeks to *orchestrate* these fragments, mobilizing certain historical associations while repressing others.

We can see this more clearly if we consider the fascist urban planning that reorganized certain sections of old Rome—particularly, the area near the capitol and the Borgo approaching Saint Peter's. In both cases, blocks of buildings were razed to lay down wide avenues, one connecting the central Piazza Venezia with the Colosseum, the other creating a triumphal view of the opening to Saint Peter's Square. Both cases are subtended by the fascist gaze, and function to create new ideological relationships among the elements of the urban landscape. The first renovation—which is not quite as universally despised today as the second—connects within one sightline the Vittorio Emmanuele monument (to the unification of Italy) to the Colosseum at the other end, with the ruins of the ancient capitol spread between them. Clearly, this works to place the modern nation at the culmination of an imperial history, now redeemed by fascism. (As if to underscore this, a series of plaques run along the wall at the sidewalk of Via dei Fori imperiali, depicting in a series of maps the gradual expansion of the Roman Empire.) The second case is more complex. Before Mussolini's changes, the approach to the Vatican was through a maze of buildings along narrow streets; the Vatican was not visible from a distance, and one came upon it by surprise. Underlying this spatial logic was an essentially religious gaze, that of "lost-and-found," of wandering and redemption. The new avenue spectacularizes Saint Peter's, turning a private experience (e.g., that of the pilgrim) into a public one, an experience now orchestrated and designed by those in power rather than one resulting from an at least partly random historical juxtaposition.

What the above example highlights is the way that movement through space—and of course cinema as a practice is such movement through space—is never "innocent" but always imbricated in ideological discourse; but it also illustrates the way that the spatiality of Italy—"profilmic Italy," let's say—is *already* densely polysemic. Thus, the profilmic space is something that must in every film be renegotiated anew; and the dense layers of history that are inscribed in the Italian space give the space an "arresting" quality—stopping one in one's tracks, so to speak—so that time itself becomes the "stumbling block" to what we can call the "use value" of the image in the cinematic construction of the nation. This is of course a very broad generalization that will attain specificity only in the chapters that follow; here, it is simply the articulation of the starting point of this study.

To summarize, then: in looking at how Italian cinema constructs the nation, we must look at several interconnected things: how the image is detached from the purely regional in order to function in a national discourse; how cinema's traversal of space creates cognitive maps that function, not simply to organize an itinerary, as in Kevin Lynch's early elaboration of cognitive mapping, but to construct an ideological picture of the nation (as Mussolini's urban planning did). Within this interpretive grid, the issue of center and periphery takes on critical importance.[41] For if the nation can be seen conceptually as a kind of center, then in a country of strong regionalism, the center is more easily seen as the site of contestation and arbitrariness that it always is. In Italian cinema, the issue of center/periphery can be seen not only in the representations of the great cities, but in the north/south divide that has historically been *the* great cultural divide in Italy. It takes on importance in relation to the internal migrations of people in the postwar period. It manifests itself in relation to the circulation of foreign (and particularly American) images within Italy. And in the work of Visconti and (especially) Pasolini, the position of the homosexual works to reimagine the relation of center to periphery.

2 NEOREALISM AND THE STAIN

The notion that neorealism was a project haunted by some sort of excess that always surfaced to "stain" its purity is not original; Millicent Marcus begins her study of Italian cinema with this observation, which in turn is taken from a pun by Roberto Venturini: "Neorealism is realism with a '*neo*,'" *neo* being Italian for stain or blemish (usually on the skin).[1] The two quotes that serve as epigraphs for this chapter were selected to bring out the aesthetic dimensions of this paradox: on the one hand, the faith that the work of art can give us everything; on the other hand, the realization that in the process, something will always, inevitably be lost.

Yet it is important to realize just how much this uncovering of the "stain" in neorealism was a retroactive, critical construction. Initially, realism was seen as a way of countering the pervasive sense of unreality in the official cinema of fascism, an unreality achieved as much by the use of Hollywood enunciative strategies as by the phantasmatic iconography of luxury (epitomized by the "white telephone"). As we saw at the beginning of chapter 1, what Bazin saw as essential to neorealism was its status as reportage, which in turn was connected to the fact that the *meaning* of the postfascist nation was still in the process of being fixed. It is because of this that the products of the first flush of neorealism might best be considered "vanishing mediators," in the sense that Jameson has developed the term. For Jameson, the vanishing mediator is that which emerges in moments of historical transition, in the mo-

ment when the historical situation is radically "open," and which vanishes as soon as the new order establishes itself and necessarily then
erases any notion of contingency, i.e., that it could have turned out any
other way.[2] Thus, as the Italian Christian Democratic government so-
lidified its power from 1948 into the early fifties, neorealism too lost its
sense of radical openness (to be sure, a sense that was evident only in a
handful of neorealist films, those which, like *Paisà* [1947], we now consider the exemplars of neorealism); in this sense, neorealism "vanished"
and left in its wake its "stained" child, pink neorealism.

Audience studies, such as those of Vittorio Spinazzola, confirm this
view. If we look yearly at the top ten grossing Italian films in each of
the postwar years, we see that the seminal works of neorealism—*Roma,
città aperta* (*Open City*, 1945) and *Paisà* especially—were great successes
at the box office. But in successive years, only a handful of films that we
would call neorealist made the list: only three for 1947–48. After 1948,
neorealist films almost completely drop out of the top ten box office
receipts. Spinazzola reads this as the failure, within the neorealist project, of forging a new relation between cinema and public. He goes on
to argue that the cinema-going public finally became unified precisely
around the films of "pink neorealism." In 1954 and after, films such as
Pane, amore, e fantasia (*Bread, Love, and Fantasy*, 1953) and *L'oro di Napoli*
(*Gold of Naples*, 1954) took the trappings of neorealism—everyday life
among the poor, location shooting, and so on—and stripping them of
any political engagement, used them to make programmatic, bland
comedies.[3] By the early sixties, Italian comedy was to be charged with a
new seriousness, as will be discussed in the next chapter; however, the
emergence of a public around pink neorealism is consistent with the
triumph of a Christian Democratic government, one of whose major
spokesmen, Giulio Andreotti, railed against the "false images" that the
neorealist films were exporting to the world.[4]

Yet if neorealism was a heroic enterprise destined to vanish, there are
nonetheless signs that it had been "stained" from the very beginning. In
the largest sense, of course, it couldn't help but be stained; for as Bazin
pointed out, realism is always an *aesthetic*, even in a medium that seemed
to Bazin to have a natural affinity for recording "reality." Choices always
had to be made; structures always had to be imposed. It is when these
aesthetic choices moved toward the simplified moral positions of melodrama that the neorealist film most clearly showed itself as stained.
When, for example, at the very end of *Ladri di biciclette* (*Bicycle Thieves*,
1948), we move to a close shot of the son reaching up to grab his father's

hand, it is as if the entire aesthetic of distance toward the profilmic is thrown out in order to provide a facile (if ambiguous) closure.]

In fact, the very installation of *Roma, città aperta* as the inaugural film of the neorealist project itself partakes of a historical repression; namely, that Visconti's feature debut, *Ossessione*, was made in 1943 and must be considered the first decisive break from the official aesthetic of the fascist regime. Everyone knows about *Ossessione*, of course; it is just that Visconti's film is such a stumbling block to the writing of the history of neorealism that nobody seems to know quite what to do with it. If Visconti's output was always to be marked by a fascination with melodrama, then his first film—a noir melodrama based on James M. Cain's *The Postman Always Rings Twice*—announces neorealism's limits *avant la lettre*. The temporality of melodrama, its insistence that everything is "too late," runs completely counter to the immediacy demanded by the commitment to neorealism. To look at neorealism through *Ossessione* is to entertain the idea that this "vanishing mediator" had always, already been a lost object.

But this is an idea better looked at after a detailed study of the neorealist film at its purest: and for this, there is no better example than Rossellini's *Paisà*. Its very title means "compatriot," "fellow citizen," yet at the same time can retain an ambiguity regarding whether the compatriot belongs to the same nation, or to some more regional *paese*. As we shall see, *Paisà* resists narrative closure at every level, making it truly a remarkable document of the nation in the process of its becoming.]

Mapping the Nation

Benedict Andersen's notion of the nation as "imagined community" is one of those ideas that are so "elegant," so seemingly self-evident, that one might forget just how ground-breaking the notion has been in reconceptualizing the nation in an age of "globalization." For it seems obvious that within the nation, any particular citizen is likely to encounter only a tiny fraction of those identifying themselves as fellow nationals; yet it was Andersen who then asked the crucial question: what is it then that creates out of these fragmentary interconnections a group identification with the nation?[5] For media studies in particular, the asking of this question has been extraordinarily productive in helping us to theorize the ways in which national cinemas, and national media in general, function to create those "imagined communities."

In the case of Italy, for example, neorealism can be looked at as

just such an attempt to create an imagined community to replace the
(equally media-constructed) imagined community of the fascist period.
That this project—the neorealist project—seems so vital within the texts
of neorealism itself attests to the profound disarray that Italy found itself in at the end of the war, a disarray marked precisely by the collapse
of a coherent national narrative that could be taken as meaningful by
Italians. Thus, neorealism functions not only to imagine a new Italy for
Italians, but also a new Italy to be exported to the world: and in this
regard, we must look not simply at "representations" of postwar Italy
within the films but also, more importantly, at the enunciative strategies
of the films. Neorealism constructed narrative space in decisively different ways from the dominant model of classical Hollywood cinema (and
the *telefono bianco* films of fascism); the question becomes one of dis-
cerning the ways in which the construction of narrative space is imbricated in the construction of the nation, of the cognitive maps that will
define "Italy."

Looking at this interplay between narrative, realist enunciation, and
spatial mapping in relation to *Roma, città aperta* has the potential to lead
us out of the critical impasse over this key film. Certainly the trend in
the critical literature over the last twenty years or so has been an emphasis on the ways that *Roma, città aperta* is *not* the radical break it perhaps
appeared to be (and that would happen later for Rossellini, with *Paisà*).
Many thus talk about the film's melodrama, or about its classically edited sequences (for example, the scenes in the Nazi headquarters in Via
Tasso); Peter Brunette talks about the film's tight narrative construction[6] (as opposed to the "looseness" that, since Bazin, has been seen as
a signature trait of neorealism). However, this then presents us with a
conundrum: in its initial release (especially in France and the United
States) and for decades afterward, the critical response was precisely that
the film *was* presenting us with a new kind of filmmaking. The more
recent critics must then somehow explain away this earlier response as
some kind of misrecognition; the explanations can range from the effects of using "short ends" of film stock to the need in 1945 to mytholo-
gize the Allied victory. These explanations, though, are inadequate, not
least because they simply "invalidate" the experience of the film's early
receptions. I would argue that, before moving to contextual explanations for the film's "realism effect," we instead begin with the premise
that the signifying systems of the text itself must be reexamined, specifically to account for this disjuncture in the film's historical receptions.

Here, the narrative structure is crucial. While it may be true that the narrative of *Roma* has "tightness" insofar as the actions of the disparate groups of Italians are interconnected through an intricate network of causes and effects, some of the most striking scenes of the film are ones that seem to erupt out of nowhere, as if outside the linearity of a cause/effect chain. Think, for example, of scenes such as the ambush of the Germans by the partisans after Francesco's arrest: the sense of "reality" we get from the scene—the sense that we are witnessing what Bazin calls "reportage"—can be attributed precisely to the fact that it is not enchained to the narrative system so far set up, but rather erupts with the force of a "fact" (to invoke another idea from Bazin). The same goes for the famous scene of Pina's death as she runs after the Nazi truck taking Francesco away. Here, the impossible eyelines between Pina and Francesco—before she runs after the truck—momentarily disorient us in relation to the diegetic space of the building and courtyard, and this disorientation is what gives us the sense that the camera is able only imperfectly to capture an event that is unfolding independently of its presence. This, indeed, is the logic of "ellipsis" that is such a celebrated feature of Rossellini's style,[7] and is clearly evident as early as *Roma*.

How then to resolve this issue of the narrative's relative "looseness" or "tightness"? If the lives of the various Romans become entwined in an intricate net of causes and effects, this is precisely as a result of, and in reaction to, the Occupation; the Resistance being—by its very nature—reactive. We could then argue that the occupying Nazis are setting the terms for a "master narrative" (pun intended), and that the film's depiction of the many acts of resistance (both small and large) to the imposition of this "narrative" works as a kind of force of narrative dissolution within the film itself. The film's narrative, that is to say, is self-reflexive about the very process of narration. Here, Michel de Certeau's distinction between strategy and tactics becomes useful, strategy being the top-down deployment of discourses and practices of social control by a centralized power, and tactics being those "practices of everyday life" that work to carve out a space of resistance to the hegemonic forces. *Roma*'s entire narrative strategy is to juxtapose these two, and in so doing, it sets up a tension between a totalizing narrative structure and the constant attempts to subvert it.

Thus, we can see that the conundrum we started with—a tension between realism and melodrama, or between realist stylistic codes and the established codes of Hollywood—is not really the critical problem it seemed to be, since this tension in fact is what *constitutes* the film's aesthetic. Thus, if we look at the world of the Romans, the ensemble that is often talked about in terms of *coralità* (itself a critical term I think more appropriate to *La terra trema* than to *Roma*),[8] we find a man and woman planning a marriage, a looting of a bread shop by a hungry populace, a bedridden old man, a group of children playing war games, and so on. It is precisely the Nazi occupation that weaves these disparate elements into a narrative line: and were it not for that, the storyline would simply dissolve into a kind of documentary reportage of everyday life in a Roman palazzo. The film would then move toward that self-abolition that Bazin saw as the ultimate aim of the neorealist project, achieved, he thought, with *Ladri di biciclette:* "No more actors, no more story, no more sets . . . no more cinema."[9]

On the other hand, we have the scenes with the Nazis (and collaborators), particularly in the elegantly appointed quarters in the Via Tasso. It is in these scenes where the enunciative system of the film—the camera setups, the lighting, the decor, the sequence construction—most resembles that of the classical Hollywood melodrama. In fact, it would not be much of a stretch to argue that these scenes are in fact throwbacks to the aesthetics of the *telefono bianco* films of the fascist era, or even to argue that the telephone is itself a central narrative and mise-en-scène element of these scenes[10] (used particularly in the attempts to get Marina to betray the resistance). The Nazi headquarters, in fact, is the site where we see concentrated the tools for modern bureaucratic social control: from the communications system (the phones) to the large map of Rome that hangs on the wall.

Ultimately, then, the brilliance of *Roma, città aperta* lies in this tension between the "tyranny" of classical cinematic enunciation and the repeated attempts to subvert it. The film, in a sense, allegorizes the birth of the aesthetic of reality out of the bankrupcy of the fascist aesthetic. It is with *Paisà* that the new aesthetic seems to have achieved its full realization.

The film, consisting of six narrative "episodes" in the liberation of Italy, inscribes the map of Italy as its central organizing device: indeed, the map of Italy is the only constant in a collection of narratives whose characters and locations change from episode to episode. At the beginning, the entire map is colored a dull gray; and as the narrator describes the progress of the Allied forces through the country, the movement of liberation is shown by a wave of white that sweeps up from the south. Each episode of the film is introduced by the map, becoming whiter and whiter as we reach the final episode.

The first thing to note about the use of this map is that, even before

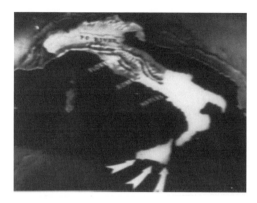

1
Use of the map
in *Paisà*

the liberation, "Italy" is seen as a discrete nation: the very topography of the map tends to naturalize the northern border at the Alps, while the framing unproblematically links Sicily and the Continent. Italy, then, already exists; but because the gray blends in with the rest of the Continent, there are suggestions of occupation, loss of identity.

Secondly, we note that the map is *doubly inscribed*. On the one hand, the flow of whiteness follows a trajectory determined by foreigners, by the Allies and in particular by America. (*Paisà* tends to minimize—and sometimes even caricature—the British involvement in the liberation while focusing strongly on the American. There are probably many reasons for this: Italy's strong ties to America from emigration; the "imaginary America" of mobility and freedom from history; and on the other side, the rather patronizing stereotypes of Italians held by the British on the "grand tour.") On the other hand, the movement of the liberation recreates (loosely) the historical movement of the Risorgimento, the unification of Italy. Thus, a problematic is set up: to what extent does the "new" or restored map of Italy represent the nation at its historical moment of formation; and to what extent does it suggest a contamination by the foreign? In a way, this double inscription reinforces traditional (American) notions of U.S. foreign policy: namely, that the United States intervenes only to "help" a nation throw off foreign domination and achieve its "natural" borders—and this is certainly one way to render the problematic less threatening. Still, what is being set up in the film is an issue that will become central to European media debates in the coming decade: here, the flowing whiteness engulfing the nation holds the threat of homogenization and loss of cultural identity by the influx of American images in postwar Europe.[11]

There is yet another dimension that Italian audiences would surely have added to the progressive mapping: namely, the notorious "delay" in liberating the North in 1944, announced publicly by General Alexander, head of the Allied troops there, after heavy losses sustained in October. This policy put the lives of many in the Italian Resistance in great danger, and in fact many lost their lives during the winter. Whether these results were intentional or not, it was clear that the British were particularly concerned with communist involvement in the Resistance, especially given their experiences in Greece and Yugoslavia.[12] Thus an ominous cast is put on to the way the flow of whiteness is stalled at the Po Valley; and within the film's narratives, it helps to explain the different stances taken toward the British and the Americans.

Within the six narratives themselves, Americans become central "actants." And they introduce within the images a circulation of foreign commodities: cigarettes, candy bars, "Pet Milk." This, then, becomes a metaphor for the potential of "capture" by the mass-produced object, a metaphor that is often invoked in later Italian films. In Paolo and Vittorio Taviani's *Notte di San Lorenzo* (*Night of the Shooting Stars*, 1982), for example, the Americans themselves are a structuring absence, visible through the "traces" they leave behind: rubbers, cigarettes.

Finally, we must note that the map itself never becomes fully "filled in." The final map, introducing the last section dealing with fighting in the Lake District, shows the liberation moving all the way up to the top borders of Italy, but leaves a gray hole in the Lake District, a hole that will never be filled in. (We might note parenthetically here that the Republic of Salò was located in this region.) Rossellini thus introduces a notion of "structural incompleteness" in the imagined map of the nation; for, while the gap is closed by the voice-over narrator ("Spring came, and the war was over"), the final image subverts this closure. The

2

Paisà's final map:
the Liberation
incomplete

camera looks down at the waves of the sea while, one by one, captured partisans are being thrown in by the Nazis to drown. The camera then lingers on the waves as the narrator speaks, and the film ends. Rossellini ends his film not on "solid" images but on the fluidity of the sea, of waters marked by the death of a certain kind of Italian. Unlike in the fascist film, here the nation is not "fixed" by what we might call "solid signifiers"—the flag, the parade, and so on—but instead is acknowledged to be inherently in flux, subject to contestation.

The maps, then, provide us with a set of issues that we can examine as they play themselves out in the narrative construction of the film (and here, we will look at only one episode, the one set in Florence). For if the maps set up a kind of confusion over Italian identity—over the extent to which the larger, "liberation" narrative is controlled by America or is a repetition of Italy's own unification—then the smaller, episodic narratives, in their enunciative strategies, construct a narrative space that is decisively different than that of classical Hollywood. It is in the construction of narrative space that the Italian cinema, in this period, would address the concerns of cultural capture, and would produce a national cinema marked distinctively "Italian."

The Florence episode is interesting for many reasons, the most important being that it shifts the process of mapping the nation onto the urban space. This is a critical move, insofar as the city provides us with cognitive maps of our world. Florence is par excellence the city that is already organized by narratives. There is a humorous sequence in this episode where two British soldiers sit on the grass in the Oltrarno and, armed with binoculars and a guide book, attempt to piece together a "map" of the city on the other side of the river by its monuments, occasionally asking a distraught Italian such things as, "Say, do you know who designed that bell tower?" But there is a much larger narrative than the guidebook that maps Florence: Dante's *Commedia*. In fact, as one walks through Florence, one can see (in real life, not in *Paisà*) inscribed on the stones of various buildings lines from Dante, as if the text provides a way in which to negotiate one's way through the city. Of course, the *Commedia* is *the* cognitive map, encompassing as it does an entire culture's view of the universe and our place in it. But Dante always anchors this larger map to the particulars of his native city, which, in Dante's time as well as in the time of *Paisà*, was riven by internal division.

In the Florence episode, the Oltrarno is in the hands of the Allies, while the "city proper" on the other side of the river is the site of intense fighting between Nazis (along with Italian fascists) and the partisans. Harriet, an American nurse who had once lived in Florence, finds out that a former lover is now known by the nom-de-guerre "Lupo" and is the head of the partisans fighting across the river. She hooks up with an Italian friend, Massimo, who has become separated from his family living in the occupied city. Together, they cross into the city, where they witness a skirmish between fascists and partisans, and a dying partisan "incidentally" reveals to Harriet that Lupo has died.

Here, the urban space has fallen apart. All of the familiar landmarks are there—the Uffizi, the Piazza della Signoria, the Duomo and Baptistery—but they are rendered "unreadable" by the shifting dynamics of power within the city. There is a sense that Italy itself has fallen into anarchy: that it is not so much a question of an external border being violated but rather the proliferation of all sorts of internal borders. Thus, it is the impediments to free movement within the city that stands in for—that "cognitively maps"—the fragmentation of the national narrative itself.

There is a remarkable scene that illustrates this process. In the heart of the city, an old man sits at the top of the palazzo where he lives, continually monitoring the sounds of the gunfire in the city.[13] From his knowledge of weaponry, he is able to judge whether the shots are from partisans or Nazis, and by "placing" the sounds, he can create up-to-the-minute maps that describe who is in control of what sections of the city. Here we can make a comparison to a key early text involving the mapping of the city, George Loane Tucker's *Traffic in Souls* (1915). In Tucker's film, the city's infrastructure, its network of communications, is what allows the crime ring to operate, but also what allows for the heroine's intervention in breaking it apart. The film thus spatializes (literally) the network of relations in the city in order to draw its map. In *Paisà*, the infrastructure is gone, destroyed by the technologies of war; in its place is human contact, word of mouth. And the old man must rely upon *sound* rather than the direct perception of space to map the city.[14] Interestingly, this leads to a fatal mistake: for he tells Harriet and Massimo that the Ognisanti is in the hands of the Italians and is thus safe, when in reality there are Italian fascists still active in the area.

In order to look more specifically at how the film constructs narrative space, it would be useful to look at the final sequence of the episode in detail. First, there is a clear narrative desire in place, split between Massimo and Harriet, as both continue their dangerous quest to unite with loved ones. But this narrative desire slowly becomes "unhinged" from our movement through space, as the space of the city begins to take on a kind of autonomy with the sudden eruption of a chaotic gunfight between partisans and fascists. At the sequence level, Massimo just disappears from the narrative space altogether, never to reemerge in the episode. This unhinging of space from narrative can also be seen in specific shots: in the second shot of the sequence, the cut to the doorway is completely unmotivated by the movements of Harriet and Massimo through the space. Shot 4 is more extreme: while syntactically in the position of the point-of-view shot—Harriet watching the battle from the doorway—the spatial orientation is confusing, we have no coordinates for understanding the battle lines, and the events transpiring on screen are unreadable. By the eighth shot of the sequence, narrative desire has been disseminated throughout the space, once again accomplished by a false point-of-view following a shot of Marco looking out the doorway. What initially appears to be a point-of-view becomes instead an entrée into the "other scene" of the scene: the confusing groupings of fighters slowly organize themselves as Marco enters the frame, so that we are finally able to see the fascist collaborators who were "repressed" from the earlier cognitive map.

Paisà, in the end, is a picture of the nation in the radical process of becoming. Central to its project is the representation and traversal of space—narrative, geographic, and symbolic. This is, ultimately, the logic of the film's construction as an omnibus of separate anecdotes. For the problem itself is how to construct the nation out of the fragmentary itineraries of everyday life, and the cognitive maps those itineraries produce.

Time, Melodrama, and Visconti

In contrast to the ways that Rossellini subverts temporal closure, Visconti in *Ossessione* constructs a melodramatic time, in which everything of importance is always, already "over." (In fact, the very title "obsession" suggests that time itself will be the film's central concern: a circular time based on repetition.) This is why, as I've already noted, *Ossessione* is always problematized in relation to neorealism. Yet if the neorealist project is itself a problematic enterprise, then it makes sense to look at *Ossessione* not as some incomplete "dress rehearsal" for the flowering of a coherent aesthetic movement, but rather as that which announced its limits in advance. For in 1954, just as pink neorealism was consolidating the cinema public, Visconti's *Senso* appeared and radically redefined—through its use of melodrama—the goals of neorealism. To be sure,

Senso's melodrama was the melodrama of the nineteenth-century novel and not that of the *giallo*. But precisely because of that, Visconti's strategy represented a move toward historical analysis.

Significantly, *Ossessione* is set entirely in the flat expanses of the Po Valley, in the very region that the map of *Paisà* left indeterminate. The spatial indeterminacy of the Po's foggy marshes—used in the sixth episode of *Paisà* to subvert any notion of an articulable national boundary—is also deployed by Visconti in the scene of the lovers' final tryst: Gino and Giovanna are engulfed by a space where the light diffused by fog obliterates the horizon. It is as if the materiality of the world has disappeared, allowing them briefly to indulge the fantasy that has driven their "obsession," the fantasy of an escape from temporality itself.

Overall, the film is built around repetitions that reinforce the film's obsession with time. (In fact, in the first sexual encounter between Gino and Giovanna, there is on the soundtrack the insistent ticking of a clock, while Giovanna—whose own shadow follows her around the room and who finally catches herself in the mirror—wonders aloud whether their love will last "forever.") The shot of the road from the moving car that opens the film—itself a signal of the fatality that governs the narrative— is repeated in the final sequence as the lovers run from the law. Gino's entrance in the back of a truck is repeated later, when he is forced to escape the police in Ferrara by jumping on the back of a truck. And the dramatic chiaroscuro of the love scene between Gino and Giovanna is recreated in later scenes of intimacy, in the hotel room with Spagnolo and in the room of the prostitute in Ferrara.

It is, in fact, this very structure of repetition which has to my mind resulted in a critical "line" about the film that partakes of a misrecognition. It is often said that the film's critique of fascism lay at least in part in its setting itself within the squalid world of the petty bourgeoisie, and so the film's setting is often described as being unremittingly sordid. Yet this account "forgets" the way that, *at first,* the film melodramatically invests its mise-en-scène with the same supercharged eroticism as the (Italian) dialogue. (From Gino's initial salvo to Giovanna—"Si mangia qui?"—to her provocative line a few scenes later—"È tornata la fame?"—the dialogue abounds in double entendres.) The opening sequences proceed with breathtaking assurance to create a landscape of desire: from Giovanna's bare leg swinging casually as she sits on the table, to Gino attempting to fix the "broken pump" while Giovanna's (offscreen) voice sings a love song, the voice implacably drawing the camera toward the door in the distance, whose open curtain beckons

Gino. This economy of displacement reaches a climax at the dinner that evening, as Bragana leaves the house with his rifle to kill the screeching cats that are driving Giovanna crazy. Gino and Giovanna move toward each other as the hot wind from a brewing summer storm sets the curtain billowing and the hanging lamp swaying, until finally Bragana's shots explode on the soundtrack. It is only *later,* after the murder, that this environment is systematically drained of its erotic charge and we can see it in all its sordidness.

In the character of "Spagnolo" lies the key to the film's articulation of temporality to history, since he is at once a "textual representative" of the Spanish Civil War and a homosexual. Mira Liehm notes how the production of *Ossessione* was marked by harassment from the fascist secret police, since all the key creative people belonged to the newly formed, antifascist "Cinema group."[15] Given this, it is natural to consider how the Spanish Civil War might provide a central point of reference for European resistance to fascism. But given that the Civil War ended in the triumph of Franco's fascism, any textual invocation of the event is necessarily going to be overdetermined by, on the one hand, nostalgia, and on the other hand, fatality. Thus, the figure of the Spaniard collapses into one the problematic dyad that neorealism was soon to face: history as the already written versus history as radically "open."

That the Spaniard is a vagabond, congenitally predisposed to wandering, never allowing himself to settle, ties him to one pole of the historiographic binary opposition, to a radical openness; at the same time, he earns money by selling cards which reveal to the buyer his or her fate. The Spaniard is at the center of the circulation of "pure signs," subject to any and all possible interpretations (which, incidentally, links back to his early speech in the hotel room to Gino, where he expounds a philosophy of money as pure liquidity). Here, of course, we are approaching the terrain of the "modernist" construction of the homosexual, as the figure inextricably tied to the radical polyvalence of signs and the interpretation without end that they engender.[16] This "modernist homosexuality" ultimately links homosexuality to the project of ontology generally, insofar as its interpretive project always has as its aim the unveiling of the hidden, the sudden, fleeting apprehension of "the thing itself."

But a very similar imperative is what drives "the melodramatic imagination," as Peter Brooks has noted. Melodrama stakes itself on a dialectic between the "seen" and the "unseen,"[17] so that an invisible world, a "domain of spiritual forces and imperatives,"[18] subtends the manifest world and charges it with meaning. This, of course, is exactly what we have seen happens in the very opening sequences of *Ossessione,* where the manifest world is "saved" from banality by the sense that there is something hidden underneath. Even something as immaterial as the wind, or the premonition of a summer storm, is turned into a sign.[19] Once again, we see how Visconti has already stumbled upon the "stain" that would haunt neorealism: namely, whether and how the rigorous recording of the manifest world can ever connect appearance to concept.

Angela Dalle Vacche has pointed out yet another connection between Brooks's argument and the neorealist project: namely, that melodrama's hidden domain is *mute,* thus forcing the audience to view carefully the exteriorities that lead us toward this hidden realm. Similarly, neorealist aesthetics entails a kind of muteness, where character is not given through dialogue and self-examination but rather through gesture, positioning in space, and architecture.[20] Dalle Vacche's point takes on added resonance when one considers something rarely mentioned in Italian cinema history: namely, that until recently, Italian films were almost invariably postdubbed (whether or not synchronous sound was recording at all during the filming). This separation of sound from image shows the extent to which the neorealist project staked itself on the primacy of vision; and thus, in the cinema of the sixties, it will be precisely the eruption of the uncanny sound that symptomatically enacts the limit point to this faith in the image.

But for Visconti in 1954, the solution lay in a kind of backward movement, toward the "melodramatic imagination" of the nineteenth-century novel. This, at least, is how the debates around his 1954 film *Senso* were framed in Italian cultural discourse. In *Senso,* Visconti abandons most all of the trappings of neorealism to construct a historical melodrama set in the years immediately before the Italian unification. Here, I will not be concerned with producing another reading of the film but rather with examining the ways in which the discourses about it illustrate the cultural divide that marked Italian cinema in the mid-fifties. This is the period—as we've already noted—when pink neorealism was consolidating its public, thus marking the death knell of neorealism as political praxis linked to the transformation of the nation. For many Italian intellectuals, *Senso* was yet another sign that the neorealist project had come to an end. For Guido Aristarco, the influential editor of *Cinema nuovo,* however, *Senso* marked the movement "from neorealism to realism,"[21] a development Aristarco considered an important advance. By realism, Aristarco meant the realism valorized by Georg

Lukács, whose work, first appearing in Italian translation in the early fifties, quickly became the orthodox Marxist cultural position.[22] Just as the nineteenth-century novel, however bourgeois, could be considered to be anchored to the world in such a way that the deeper structures of exploitation and historical movement were revealed, so too was *Senso* able to reveal the failure of the national bourgeoisie to lead the nation in the early days of the unification, precisely *through* its adoption of the formal strategies of the novelistic.

During the fifties, the less reductionist cultural theory of Antonio Gramsci didn't really take hold in official Marxist circles but was rather a counterdiscourse among younger Marxists; Gramsci's influence is seen, for example, in the early critical writing of Pasolini and others associated with the journal *Officina*. Still, when in 1953 Roberto Rossellini moved the questions of neorealism to entirely new ground with his film *Viaggio in Italia* (*Voyage to Italy*, 1953), it took André Bazin to find a way to defend it. For Lukácsian critics like Aristarco, Rossellini's film was hopelessly bogged down in bourgeois subjectivity. This is a debate that we will return to in detail in chapter 6.

Fellini's Voyage to the End of Neorealism

If the middle years of the decade of the fifties can be seen as a period of aesthetic retrenchment—with neorealism either diminished to a kind of populist celebration of local color, or adopted as a method for cinematic experimentation (with Rossellini and Antonioni; see chapter 6)— it was also the period in which Federico Fellini emerged as a fully developed auteur. And while Fellini's formative roots were solidly within the tradition of neorealism, his emergence by 1960 as an international auteur was based upon a rather systematic reshaping of the "neorealist film"—if we can assume that such an entity has at least a conceptual existence—into what by the late fifties became known as the "foreign art film." The shift in genre characterization is quite important, because it now made it possible to remove the specifically formal innovation (ellipsis, for example, or episodic narration) from the equally specific historical situation from which it found its imperative; thus the sense with Fellini's films of the fifties that they are transpiring as if dreams. Thus also the critical importance of *La dolce vita* (1960) in presenting us with a cognitive map of Rome unlike any in earlier films, Rome as an international capital of image production and the "society of the spectacle" then in emergence in the advanced capitalist nations.

The parameters that have already been set up in our discussion of neorealism can provide a key to understanding just how Fellini arrived at his picture of "Rome," which, ultimately, is the vital subject of most all of Fellini's work from the late fifties on. The earliest neorealist films can be seen, in retrospect, to engender a paradox: on the one hand, we see the attentive registration of the everyday, into which there sometimes erupts the "event"; on the other hand, any attempt to ascribe "meaning" to the world thus registered always ends up delivering us over to the "unseen" and thus potentially to the realm of the melodramatic. But in this early moment of neorealism, what makes the paradox so productive is the presence of a vital historical imperative—the imperative to discover "Italy," to construct new maps that incorporate social, cultural, and economic *difference* into the homogenous map of fascist ideology. The nation, in a sense, became a stand-in for the "unseen." But by the 1950s, history had ceased to be the radically open potential that it was in the immediate postwar period, and in this climate it was Fellini more than any other director who was able to capitalize on the neorealist legacy by articulating the unseen, not as a social project, but rather as a metaphysical one: to redeem the world of appearances through a poetic or oneiric rendering of that world.

This is precisely what André Bazin noted as the essential feature of Fellini's aesthetic in the 1957 film *Notti di Cabiria* (*Nights of Cabiria*), in a remarkable (if sometimes obscure) essay entitled "Voyage to the End of Neorealism."[23] Bazin had always understood that neorealism—like any realism—would of necessity need to evolve, if only because what seems to be "realistic" will undoubtedly, through repetition and the formation of conventions, at some point seem artificial or constructed. Thus his notion that Fellini has taken us to "the end of neorealism" is not meant to be a lament, but rather a celebration of the vitality of the realist impulse in Italian cinema. *Cabiria* is a loosely episodic string of set pieces around the figure of the prostitute Cabiria, with one overarching narrative repetition: the betrayal that led to Cabiria's initial suicide attempt is repeated with another man at the end of the film. But other than this, the narrative building blocks seem interchangeable: a working night at the Baths of Caracalla; a trip to the Via Veneto; a pickup by a famous movie star; a religious pilgrimmage. This, indeed, is the outstanding feature that allows Bazin to link the film to neorealism: as he puts it, the film suspends the "horizontal" dimension of narrative causality and instead instantiates a "vertical" dimension, a dimension of "the event" that "befalls" the character. So far, we are on familiar ground: on the one hand, the mundane world, and on the other, the unseen that subtends it.

We could then say that what happens at the level of the *image* in Fellini is that the two—seen and unseen, "appearance" and "reality"— become thoroughly mixed. Technically, no doubt, this is the result of Fellini's insistence on recreating Rome on the studio sets of Cinecittà; but the effect is oneiric, as if the characters are materializing from, and disappearing into, a great void. To return to Bazin's argument, in *Cabiria* Fellini moves from "a realism of appearances" to "the other side of things": Bazin, that is, puts the problem in terms of idealist philosophy's dualism of appearance (*Schein*) and thing-in-itself (*das Ding*). But what could this possibly mean, to arrive cinematically at "the other side of things"? Bazin can only provide us with a suggestive series of signifiers: "the supernatural," "magic," "poetry." If, as Bazin noted in a different essay, the cinema is "the asymptote of reality"—that is, a tangential line that will never quite meet its destination—then here it seems that Bazin is suggesting that a kind of exchange, or short circuit, is occuring between the two: the cinema here has *overshot* its impossible convergence with reality. Bazin remains profoundly humanist—and I'm not using the term pejoratively—because he believes that by so overshooting the mark, the cinema achieves the possibility of actually reordering our experience of the world: a redemptive project. But this most profound discovery by Bazin can be looked at through other philosophical or theoretical lenses: in particular, through Heidegger's notion of language (and poetic language) as the "house of Being"; or through Lacan's notion of the gaze as that which appears on the other side of things; or, through Lacan's appropriation of the concept of "das Ding" to refer to the formless "stuff" of the Real, most appositely for Fellini's next film, *La dolce vita*. Indeed, much of the remainder of this book will attempt to explore the possibilities suggested here, in light of the Italian cinema of the sixties and the historically specific imperatives that shaped it.

Bazin's last turn of the argument concerns *Cabiria*'s final shot, of Cabiria on the road with the reveling youth, looking back toward the camera. It is the tentativeness, the indefiniteness of that glance that Bazin zeroes in on, as he argues that what redeems it from cliché is the way that it finally "remove[s] us . . . from our role as spectator." It would seem that, in light of the above, what Bazin is getting at here is the necessary obverse of the realist camera overshooting its mark; namely, that such an exchange—from image to world to image, and so on—has

Fellini : Cabiria

as its correlative the transformation of the spectator into an engaged "being-in-the-world." But I think Bazin's argument here has an important lacuna: namely, the emergence on the road of the spectacle itself, which sweeps Cabiria up into it in much the same way as the film then asks us to give up our role as spectator. The self-reflexive turn of Cabiria toward the camera thus ratifies a well-known characteristic of Fellini's work as a whole: namely, the interchangeability of life and spectacle. Gilles Deleuze, to my mind, has done the most with this Fellinian trait. If the spectacle in Fellini is ever-expansive, to the point of being all-encompassing, then what happens is that the images of particular spaces are continually "divided" into entrances and exits, which are not simply theatrical—though theatrical "wings" indeed are central to the construction of space in Fellini's nightclubs, for example—but "geographic entrances, psychic ones, historical, archeological."[24] This is not so far in its view of the topography of Rome from that of Freud described in the previous chapter; and it achieves its most interesting realization in *La dolce vita.* Rome becomes filled with "holes" that lead forth into yet another spectacle: an image literalized by Fellini in the whorehouse sequence of the *Satyricon* (1969), where the "rooms" seem carved into the side of a rock and are presented to us in a lateral dolly shot that reveals a succession of tableaux or "specialties." This view—that Fellini's cinema is constituted by an image in endless, proliferating division—helps us understand why, in Fellini's films after the mid-sixties, the scenes contract to ever smaller lengths, to the point that many (American) critics see Fellini's later work as "undisciplined" or "self-indulgent."

La dolce vita *and the Postmodern City*

With Fellini's *La dolce vita* (1960), an entirely new relationship between space and time becomes articulated, against the background of the Eternal City. Seldom has a critic failed to mention the shock effect of the film's remarkable opening sequence, where a statue of Christ floats suspended from a helicopter over the city. Here, the temporal is short-circuited: the unfolding of archeological space that characterizes walking in the Italian city is replaced by the shock of the chiasma, a feedback loop created by sudden juxtaposition. (And thus the shock cut becomes one of the principle editing strategies by which the film constructs cinematic space: for example, the abrupt cut to the close-up of the screaming masked dancer in the nightclub.) By 1960, the economic miracle is in full swing in Italy (a fact that underlies the new power relationships dissected in the film). This leads to two issues related to space: first, How was the urban space itself refashioned by neocapitalism? and second, How was that refashioned space turned into cinematic space? Finally, what are the new parameters of the nation and the national subject within such a new space?

These are the questions that the rest of this book will explore; *La dolce vita* is an excellent place in which to set forth preliminary observations, simply because this film was certainly one of the most important Italian films in the period we are studying. In the first place, Fellini was certainly the most influential of the Italians in establishing internationally the domain of the "art film," insofar as he (along with Ingmar Bergman) set the parameters for themes, enunciation, and style for a huge international audience. But this film was also an immense popular success in Italy, cutting across all regional and class distinctions.[25] Vittorio Spinazzola uses the term "superspettacolo d'autore"—which might be translated as "auteurist blockbuster"—to describe an essentially new type of Italian film which for him encompassed not only Fellini's work in this period but also, for example, Visconti's adaptation of the epic bestseller *Il gattopardo* (*The Leopard*, 1963: based on the novel by Giuseppe Lampedusa).[26] The term itself is an odd hybrid, suggesting as it does on the one hand, the schlock-laden *supercolossi* of the fifties, and on the other, the "authored" films of the postwar period. In fact, both *La dolce vita* and *8½* (1963) embed within their texts the supercolossi as films within the films: the "biblical epic" that brings Anita Ekberg to Rome; the science-fiction film that Guido cannot finish (and thus which "turns into" the Fellini film we are watching).

What strikes one most about *La dolce vita* today is the way in which it is so dominated by the "information industry." Marcello is a novelist manqué, whose job as a hack writer is to circulate through the city with his paparazzi in tow, ceaselessly turning events into commodities. As P. Adams Sitney notes in his iconographic analysis, the film is dominated by what we could call the "false sign": the statue of Christ flying over the city, for example, which disjoins the icon from any referent.[27] Another word for this false sign is, of course, the *simulacrum*. In a way, everything in *La dolce vita* occurs on the surface, on the same plane of immanence. This is why the sequence of the "Madonna-spotting" is so central: at one point, the little girl gives her brother a sly wink to cue him to "see" the Madonna once again. But this detail in no way establishes their subjective experience in relation to their "vision": at this point, they and everyone else are caught up in a media frenzy, and it hardly matters whether at one point earlier they had actually believed in their vision. The signs themselves become self-generating. While Sitney's allegorical reading of the film ultimately "redeems" the false signs by noting the ways they point to the *Inferno*,[28] I am arguing a counterreading in which the *Inferno* is the film's own defense mechanism against the triumph of the simulacrum. That is to say, the allusions to the *Inferno,* like the mysterious appearance of the Beatrice figure at the end of the film, function as (ultimately failed) attempts to "ground" the representational frenzy.

La dolce vita is centrally concerned with postmodernity. Thus, its often noted paratactic structure—of sequences strung together with no "necessary" spatial or temporal connection—signals the way in which, within the space itself, connections between things are no longer readable. This characteristic of the Fellini world can be connected to the theories of postmodern space developed by such theorists as David Harvey, Fredric Jameson, and Edward Soja; neocapitalism brings with it, they argue, a transformation of space such that the relations of exploitation created are rendered invisible (or, more accurately, that the relations become visible only through such privileged "technologies of vision" as the cinema).[29] In *La dolce vita,* the new class structure becomes visible in the dichotomy between the central city and the periphery; but the film's paratactic structure blocks any way of putting the two in relation. The Via Veneto glitters with international money and glamour; but as soon as Marcello drives his Fiat outside the city walls, it's as if we've dropped off the face of the earth (so validating Deleuze's idea that Fellini's cinema is one of entrances and exits). Like moonscapes, the space becomes dominated by vast tracts of mud upon which occasionally rises up some monstrously ugly concrete-block building.

There is, however, one sequence in the film when an "older" spatial system is evoked, the scene in which Anita Ekberg discovers the Trevi fountain. Here, temporarily, the logic is one of being seized by the arresting quality of the space. As Ekberg wanders through the labyrinthine streets, the camera—though following her—often moves quite unexpectedly independently of her, following the logic of the space rather than the logic of the action. Or Ekberg will often stand at the intersection of three possible routes, and the image will leave her choice of movement completely open. This, as we noted earlier, was the logic of the approach to the Vatican through the Borgo, until Mussolini's modernization: movement through space leads to revelation. But in this sequence, the revelation is ultimately just another false sign, as Ekberg performs a mock baptism in the fountain after Marcello asks her, "Who are you?"

The collapse of depth brought forth by the simulacrum, by the unanchored equivalence of signs, has as its psychic consequence what Lacanian theory calls the "approach of the Thing." In *La dolce vita,* the textual embodiment of the Thing is the strange creature pulled out of the sea at the end of the film: it at once expresses both the radical loss of form, and the utter indifference of the life force to any question of particular being, and is known psychoanalytically as "the death drive."[30] Within the postmodern text, it is the very appearance of the Thing that precludes the possibility that the world itself is "inexhaustible." Of course, Fellini tempers this vision of the Thing by counterposing against it the appearance of the young girl, the Beatrice figure that I earlier called a "defense mechanism."[31] What is critical to this scene with the girl, however, is the *failure of the voice* (something that Sitney notes well, and connects both to the Matelda encounter in the *Purgatorio* and the tape recording at Steiner's party).[32] This failure is connected to the peculiar deformation of sound that occurs on the space of the beach, as if the air itself becomes a sponge sucking up sound waves and thus blurring the boundary between the internal (the breath, the voice) and the external (the "breathing" of the sea). As I will show, the disarticulation of voice and body becomes a central symptomatic mark of trauma, one that emerges most fully in the work of Antonioni, and which presages the fully postmodern deployment of sound that Michel Chion has characterized as "the quiet revolution."[33]

The possibility of the world's inexhaustibility was absolutely essential to the neorealist project. Thus, we can expect that the reinvention of neorealism at precisely this historical moment (1959–60), which is marked in Fellini by a profound exhaustion, will present us with quite a provocative set of problems.

part II

THE NATION, THE BODY, AND PASOLINI

In 1965, Pasolini coined the term *neo-italiano* to refer to the emergence of a new national language, one that threatened to displace once and for all the regional dialects that had, throughout Italian history, defined the parameters of reality for "national subjects" who had remained essentially regional in their primary affiliations.[1] At the time, few Italians were more aware than Pasolini of the ways in which language itself constructs subjectivity; thus, we can argue that Pasolini's neologism can be applied not only to the emergence of a new, hegemonic national language but also to an essentially new *subject* — precisely, the "Italian" — constructed out of the rapid modernization of the nation brought about by the economic boom of the late fifties and early sixties.

By the early sixties, there were in place in Italy all of the requisites for the flowering of an economic organization and a culture organized around consumption. Between 1950 and 1980, the Italian gross domestic product, per head, more than quadrupled. A dramatic shift in the constitution of the workforce took place: agricultural workers dropped from nearly a third of the entire workforce to only 10 percent, while the number of white collar workers doubled, to 24 percent of the workforce in 1983. The result of this was a massive shift in population from the countryside to the cities (and particularly Rome, Milan, and Turin). Naturally, economic reorganization on this large a scale left its mark on family structure, mores, and culture. In the thirty years after 1951, families with five or more members declined from 50 percent to 33 percent of the total number of families, while single-person households almost doubled. And finally, in the period from 1950 to 1970, there was an explosion in the ownership of two products that were definitive in shaping a society of consumption, mobility, and spectacle: the car and the television. In those two decades, car ownership jumped from eight cars per thousand Italians to two-hundred cars per thousand; and television ownership, negligible in 1950, reached 82 percent of households by 1971.[2]

A "new" nation, with a "new" subjectivity, speaking a "new" language—obviously social change on this vast a scale fully justifies the use of the word most commonly deployed to describe it: the "miracle." In fact, the word "miracle" condenses into a temporal *coup* a process that obviously occurs over time; it thus expresses at the level of lived experience—the lived experience of the Neapolitan artisan working from a *basso* in the dilapidated central city, or of the displaced day-laborer of the rice fields of the Po Valley—the quality of shock that such sudden change effects. But to the cultural theorist looking back upon the period from a distance of thirty-five years, what becomes most important is the process by which this change occurred. The economic miracle must be seen as a dynamic series of negotiations across a cultural field traversed by the forces of multinational capital, by the resistances or inertias of local practices—all played out against the background of a series of different "imaginary Italys." This implies the adoption of a Gramscian model of culture, especially as it has been elaborated by the practitioners of cultural studies of the Birmingham school. Specifically, then, we see in the years of the economic miracle a shift of power away from the traditional "structures in dominance"—that is, the essentially *regionalist* bourgeoisie and intellectual class—toward the "emergent structure" centered on the technocrats who are administering this miracle, and one of whose essential features is a new *mobility* across the national space. Thus, as we shall see, the road becomes not only a new reality in the physical landscape of Italy, but also becomes a central trope in the construction of a new Italy based on a culture of consumption.

A crucial feature of this social transformation is the extent to which it was directed from the North. To some extent this transformation also needs to be seen as having been "refracted" through Rome, through the capital city that remained the political center of the nation. I use the word "refracted" for a very specific reason: Rome can be characterized as an essentially liminal space within the nation, in the way that it is perched strategically between North and South, between antiquity and modernity, a fact central to the work of Fellini from *La dolce vita* onward through the films of the sixties. Rome is thus what is *"in* Italy *more than* Italy," to invoke the Lacanian formula: suffice to note how Rome remains throughout the period the center of image production within the nation, so that the Roman story stands in for the story of the nation itself.

But however mediated by Rome, the prosperous economic centers of the North provided the engine that, allied with multinational capital, was to transform the national economy and with it, the entire culture.

The South remains more or less what it was in Gramsci's day: a problem, the *problema del Mezzogiorno*. It is not simply that the South was not set up with the requisite capital and infrastructure to take off on its own; it was also the case—and this of course is a "problem" structurally related to the former–that the southern Italian adhered to an essentially different conception of the world than the northerner. He or she belonged to a quite different Symbolic Order. When Pasolini asked Oriana Fallaci about the sexual mores of the South in his documentary *Comizi d'amore* (*Love Meetings,* 1964), Fallaci replied, simply, and with a sardonic grin, "The South. That's another planet."

When the cinema attempted to address the problem in the first half of the sixties, the genre often used was the *commedia all'italiana.* Pietro Germi's *Sedotta e abbandonnata* (*Seduced and Abandoned,* 1964) is paradigmatic of what Gian Piero Brunetta calls a new complexity in the commedia all'italiana after 1960; Brunetta argues that the commedia was the best genre in which to examine new forms of "comportment" (*comportimento*) brought into being by the economic boom.[3] Thus, for exactly this reason, the South becomes the ideal site in which to explore the changing manners and mores of a new society; for the South, in its very "backwardness," its cultural distance from modernity, provides the widest possible distance requisite for the effect of comedy. In *Sedotta e abbandonata,* for example, what better way to explore the new sexual morality than to play it out within the feudal system of sexual exchange still operant in Sicily? The randy fiancé gets his bride-to-be pregnant simply by doing what every man in the masculinist culture of Sicily would do if given the chance; and then, by the implacable logic of that same culture, refuses to marry her because she is not a virgin. Now this is a logic that had played itself out for centuries in Sicily and without a shred of comedy about it: what turns it into a comedy now, in 1963, is precisely the knowing gaze of the Rome that creates it. In other words, Rome, in its position as outsider to the culture of Sicily, constructs the main character Agnese (Stefania Sandrelli) as its surrogate within the film, as the woman who steps outside of her own culture in order radically to negate it. In this way, the South becomes for the nation a site of displacement, the place upon which its own anxieties about the transformations wrought by modernization can be displaced.

All of this leads us to two preliminary premises to be made about the construction of the nation during this period. The first is that in many ways, the South needs to be conceived of as a postcolonial space which exists within the very nation. The second is that, in whatever attempts are made to construct a unified nation, the regional divisions that traverse the nation must be taken account of in advance. Taking these two conclusions together, we can see the extent to which the construction of Italy as a coherent national entity occurs *not* under the discourses of modernity in which the other great Western nations were constructed but rather within the tensions between that modernist, democratic impulse and an incipient postmodernity that would valorize (for the purposes of consumption, of course) the very dispersion that renders the idea of the nation already an antiquated one. This tension, I will argue, thoroughly animates both the artistic practice and the theoretical work of Pasolini. But more than that, it leaves its mark upon the entire cultural output of the period.

Paradoxes of Modernization

In the early sixties, Pasolini—along with other filmmakers such as Ermanno Olmi, Francesco Rosi, and Vittorio De Seta—were concerned with reinventing neorealism, so that the cinema would directly engage the new issues confronting the nation. As we saw in part 1, postwar neorealism was intimately connected to the process of nation building after fascism; thus there is a sense in which this *rétour* of the sixties, this return to a crucial historical/aesthetic conjuncture, reveals the extent to which the Italy of the economic miracle was once again a nation "under construction." So that however neorealism is reimagined, it will necessarily be forced to confront—in the form of a repetition— whatever paradoxes that threw the first wave of neorealism into contradiction.

This is best seen in the differing ways that De Seta and Rosi attempted neorealist approaches to the figure of the Italian bandit, in the films *Banditi ad Orgosolo* (*Bandits of Orgosolo,* 1961) and *Salvatore Giuliano* (1962) respectively. To begin with, the figure of the bandit is bound to take on particular resonance in cultures undergoing modernization. Historically, the bandit comes out of very specific conditions: he is a figure of peasant societies, and specifically, from the mobile, surplus population of those societies. Thus, while banditry is a phenomenon that has been constant throughout human history, the modern world has just about wiped it out, at least in the developed nations. As Eric Hobsbawm notes, economic development, the emergence of modern communications, and the encroachment of the national bureaucracies into the countryside, have removed the conditions necessary for banditry to exist.[4] Thus, the figure of the bandit is *doubly marked* by impossibility: at the level of legend and at the level of history. We can see, then, how interesting the bandit figure will appear to a society in the throes of the social dislocations connected with modernity. For the bandit at one and the same time speaks of a nostalgic ideal and the impossibility of its fulfillment; within the bandit we see not only the impossibility of our desire, but also the inevitability of history.

De Seta's *Banditi ad Orgosolo* takes on the "problem" of banditry in Sardinia. Sardinia in 1962 was probably the most "hopeless" of the regions of Italy: as Hobsbawm notes, the interior of Sardinia was one of the few places in Europe where banditry still existed in the 1960s.[5] Locked in an agrarian/feudal economy of shepherdry, with a dialect that some linguists consider a different language from Italian, it remained untouched by the economic miracle that was so radically transforming the country north of Rome, while at the same time it was pitched toward the dramatic changes that would inevitably come to it. (During the sixties, the coastal areas of Sardinia were developed for tourism, and by 1966, about 300,000 foreigners flocked annually to the island;[6] in this respect, Sardinia was following the Spanish model of development.) Thus, to the north, Sardinia could be seen at the same time as a "problem" and as a site upon which to play out its own anxieties toward modernization.

De Seta's approach to his material could be described as "more neorealist than neorealism." The film is shot on location, with nonprofessional actors drawn from the local population, and the film's plot is inscribed within a documentary-like record of everyday events. And unlike Rosi's *Salvatore Giuliano*, it takes for its central character not a legendary historical bandit, but an ordinary shepherd who is driven by circumstance to become a bandit. The narrative structure of the film is simple: we begin with a series of shots of the everyday life of the shepherds around Orgosolo, voiced in what Marsha Kinder has called the "iterative" (i.e., the cinematic equivalent of such a typically Proustian phrase as "We would often go to —").[7] As the main character and his brother (who is still a boy) tend their sheep, he notices that a group of bandits have hidden some stolen hogs in a nearby hut. When the police come and question the shepherd, they are ambushed by the bandits, and the shepherd is wrongly implicated in the crimes. He tries to run away, taking his sheep with him, since he hasn't paid the loan on the sheep. But the sheep are driven to exhaustion and die, thus forcing the shepherd to take a gun and himself become a bandit in order to save himself from the bank. The final shot has him driving a flock of stolen sheep across the plain, as the victim of the theft "hails" him a bandit.

Curiously, the overall narrative form of *Banditi* is an almost exact duplication of the form of *Ladri di biciclette* (*Bicycle Thieves,* 1948), Vittorio De Sica's canonical work of postwar neorealism. We can recall that *Ladri di biciclette* follows the impoverished Roman who, after himself being a victim of the theft of the bicycle upon which all his economic prospects lie, finally in desperation himself becomes a bicycle thief, only to be caught and "hailed" a thief by the Roman crowd. Why, we may ask, when faced with the new problems created by modernization, did De Seta choose to reduplicate an old form? Certainly, in *Banditi,* De Seta worked to purge his film of the traces of melodrama that "stain" the realism of *Bicycle Thieves:* this is the film's primary achievement, aesthetically. But the stain that is repressed in the enunciative stance of *Banditi returns* in the repetition of the cyclical form. Given that the figure of the bandit is inherently implicated in a nostalgia, we could argue that here, the nostalgia that is rigorously repressed from the narrative events is precisely what is emerging in the overall narrative form. What the cyclical structure does here is to *naturalize* the process of becoming a bandit: it is as if anyone could become a bandit if put in a certain set of circumstances. Now this may be true, of course; but the crucial point is that even at its formal level, *Banditi* works in a curious way to "contain" the bandit, to mark banditry as just another social problem that the forward march of progress needs to address. So that, just as *Sedotta e abbandonata* takes the problems of sexual mores and displaces them onto the South, in the same way *Banditi* avoids the issues surrounding modernization by displacing them upon the backward interior of Sardinia.

Ultimately, the paradox that emerges in *Banditi* is the ethnographic paradox: namely, the realization that the ethnographic project, whatever the motives of its practitioners, always ends up "contaminating" its object of study—always, that is, situates its object within the discourse of power that will ultimately vanquish it. To frame this whole issue in terms of the bandit's relation to modernity, what happens in *Banditi* is that the cinematic apparatus itself becomes implicated in the proceedings, on the side of "progress." For the characters and the situations are "real," and the cinematic apparatus becomes part of the very historical processes that will wipe out the bandit. In a sense, then, the film is not sophisticated enough to "lament,"[8] to lament what will be *lost* after all the gains of the economic miracle.

In *Salvatore Giuliano,* Francesco Rosi also turns to neorealist strategies in telling the story of the Sicilian bandit assassinated in 1950 — but, like Pasolini and unlike De Seta, Rosi is concerned with rethinking neorealism for a new generation. Rosi's strategy is to adopt the form of the "film inquest," a strategy articulated by writers like Cesare Zavattini in the early fifties, but rarely successfully employed until Rosi's film. In 1952, Zavattini argued that neorealism needed to move from an *attitude* toward the phenomenal world to an *analysis* of the world: [9] ultimately, this was an argument for moving neorealism in a more explicitly political direction, for making the film ask questions about the origins and nature of the "reality" it is recording. With Rosi's *Salvatore Giuliano,* this style of the "film inquest" was brilliantly deployed to unmask the criss-crossing social forces that found their intersection in the legendary Sicilian bandit.

The result is a film that in many ways inverts all the terms of the traditional bandit story. Rosi's film opens with the bandit already dead, his corpse sprawled in a courtyard while an army official dictates aloud the description of the murder scene. The film then flashes back to 1943 and the emergence of the Sicilian independence movement, opposed by the Americans, the large estates, and the mafia; shows the army's unsuccessful attempts to subdue Giuliano's band; and ultimately settles on the massacre of communists at a 1947 rally, and the subsequent trial to determine who was responsible. Throughout all this, the figure of the living Salvatore Giuliano is completely repressed from the text: Rosi never shows him except as corpse. By marginalizing in this way what is supposed to be the central figure in the story, Rosi purges the bandit legend of its inherent nostalgia, thus rendering the figure less the emblem of traditionalist values and more a kind of invisible "force field" around which swirl the social antagonisms of the country.

Gradually, we learn that the mafia and the carabinieri are colluding to defeat the radical independence movement (as well as the communists) and are using the bandits as pawns in this game. Ultimately, it will be this right-wing alliance that will engineer the assassination of Salvatore Giuliano. Once again, Rosi represses the bandit from the film until after he is dead; then, in a brilliant repetition of the opening overhead shot of the corpse, Rosi shows the conspirators planting the body in the courtyard. This of course radically undermines the opening of the film, where the soundtrack presents us with an "official" description and inventory of the crime scene that we now see has been completely constructed by the conspirators. And, in a coda set in 1960, Rosi repeats once more this overhead angle in the last shot of the film. First, in long shot, we see a crowd bustling in a piazza in a Sicilian town. We hear gunfire, see the crowd scattering, and notice a body falling in the distance. Then comes the cut to the overhead shot—with the position of the body duplicating that of Giuliano—as in the top and right of the screen we see ominous shadows fall into the frame as "onlookers" gather around the body.[10] This final shot brilliantly evokes the impenetrable conspiracies that lie behind the anonymous murder. But more than that: the impenetrability of the shot to a clear "reading" repeats, at the micro level, what the overall narrative construction accomplishes at the level of the entire film. The film inquest allows Rosi to deploy ellipses so strategically that the spectator comes to realize that a political imperative falls upon him or her: for to penetrate the mysterious conspiracies that the film can only partially uncover would itself become a transformative political act. This is the unique quality of the film that led Umberto Eco to hail the film as an exemplar of the "open work."

Rosi's principal formal device is a certain way of positioning the camera—usually in overhead shots, and always at a distance from the action—that functions to subordinate characters to their positions in the natural and social landscape. Panoramic camera shots carefully lay out the relationship among the town, the surrounding hills, and the road that winds through them; it is as if the landscape becomes a chess board upon which the various characters are placed. In other words, the specificity of character is replaced by the *position* the character occupies. In this way, the characters come to seem almost interchangeable, pawns caught in the movement of much larger historical forces. This is why the "position" of Salvatore Giuliano in this film is so ironic: not only because he is a corpse, but because his corpse itself is "produced" by larger, historical forces.

Rosi's film not only deconstructs the figure of the bandit but also anticipates some of the more recent work on the nation as discursive construction. For the film clearly shows how the triumphant emergence of "Italy" in the postwar period was based upon the silencing of the voices of others.[11] Thus, Rosi's film is by far the most radical of the two we have considered, in that it clearly links the economic miracle to the construction of a certain kind of Italy, one engineered in part by foreign capital, the mafia, and the Christian Democratic government in Rome.

The Urban Margins

Pasolini too was a central figure in the revival of neorealism in the early sixties, but his first two films, unlike the films discussed above, did not mobilize the underdeveloped south as a site for the critique of the economic miracle. Instead, he set *Accattone* and *Mamma Roma* (1962) in the *borgate* surrounding Rome. The mass internal migration to Rome of the impoverished surplus population of the countryside led to the springing up, in the peripheries surrounding the old city, of the slums and makeshift living spaces that came to be known as the "borgate." In a sense, the postwar urban development of the Italian city is thus the reverse of the American model, where working-class and lower-middle-class (white) households were encouraged to move away from the central city and into the planned housing of suburbia. Pasolini's strategy suggested that the uneven development characterizing the nation as a whole was repeated spatially in the new urban megalopolis.

The revival in the past decade of academic interest in Pasolini (in both his films and his theoretical writing) has produced several fine readings of *Accattone,* which, in English and easily available,[12] needn't be repeated here in great detail. One could generalize that what the new readings have in common is the need to understand just what it is about the film that made it so scandalous in 1961—for critics of both the Right and the Left—that Pasolini was taken to court on charges of the film's "immorality." From the film's first shot, we are plunged into the masculinist, subproletarian culture of the *borgata,* a culture that Pasolini at once criticizes (through various distancing strategies) and celebrates (through erotically charged camera work). The contradictory positions we are thus forced to take in relation to the pimp Accattone become part of what Pasolini thought of as an aesthetics of "contamination"— not only through the high-cultural references to Dante and Bach used to comment on the squalid lives but also, as P. Adams Sitney has astutely noted, through the adoption of the bourgeois form of the spiritual autobiography (shaped into an art-film genre by Carl Dreyer and Robert Bresson) to tell the pimp's story.[13] It is partly this strategy of contamination that led to charges of decadence and fatalism. But it is also this strategy which makes the film so vital today, as if Pasolini hit upon the connection between the breakdown of the high/low binary and the new modes of experience engendered by the changed social and cultural spaces of neocapitalism.

In keeping with the argument of this chapter, my reading of *Accattone* will focus on these issues of spatiality, and the "cognitive maps" of new cultural relations thus produced. To begin this analysis, I would like to focus on the most original of the new readings of the film, that of Maurizio Viano. For Viano's argument implicitly moves us toward an analysis of spatiality through his uncovering of a remarkable binary opposition produced by the film in relation to vision itself: on the one hand, a partial and obscured vision produced by a point-of-view shot taken from within an outdoor urinal, and on the other hand, the suggestion of a panoptic "gaze" through obsessive cutting to a decontextualized extreme close-up of a policeman's eyes. This, he argues, provides the key to understanding just how Pasolini is reinventing realism: for the "reality" produced by an omniscient, panoptic gaze is fundamentally different from the "reality" produced by the look of the outsider, the marginal. Though Viano doesn't say it, what these shots reveal is what Lacan referred to as the split between the eye and the gaze: the gaze is fundamentally an abstraction on the side of the Symbolic Law, while the look is always embodied, invested with desire, and thus "partial" in every sense of the word. Pasolini's realism can thus be said to be the result of a series of "encounters"—between variously partial, variously "deviant" views set against an overarching ideological gaze. This is what allows Pasolini's alterity as a homosexual to enter into a symbiosis with the marginalized characters of the borgata, in an example of the method of "free indirect discourse" that Pasolini was only to articulate formally several years later.[14]

What thus becomes clear is that *spatially,* the symbiosis enacted by Pasolini connects "marginality" (in all senses of the word) to a geographic periphery, so that the issue becomes how to narrate a history (the neocapitalist slums) that remains too recent to have been written. Pasolini's contamination of the high with the low, of the center with the periphery, of the text with the margin, is precisely what allows us the entry into history. In this sense, what Viano calls "the dual vision" in Pasolini is, I believe, better seen as Walter Benjamin's "dialectical image." For Benjamin, the dialectical image was, in a sense, heuristic, enabling one to become conscious of one's positioning in history. The objects comprising the world exist in relation to traces ("fossils," or "ruins") that contain the lost utopian impulses of earlier epochs; when a painting or a poem sets in motion a dialectic between object and the failed dreams of the past, we become conscious of our immersion in history, not simply as dead weight, but as a redemptive future project.[15]

Such an image arises when the film moves into the ancient city center. *Accattone* plays out its drama mostly within an entirely new space, that of the borgata. But the film is bookended by two trips to the old city center: once at the beginning, when Accattone dives off the bridge, and then at the end, when Accattone—now apprenticing as a thief—

steals a motorbike to escape from the police and in an offscreen accident meets his death. Interestingly, none of the recent criticism of the film bothers to identify the location of the early scene, beyond stating that Accattone jumps from a bridge "with angels." But the bridge is clearly the Ponte Sant'Angelo, the bridge—adorned with Bernini's sculptures of angels—that connects the lowlands of the old city with the ancient fortress of the Castel Sant'Angelo, which in the Middle Ages served as a prison. (The monument is indeed visible very briefly in a few shots.) The Castel Sant'Angelo is also the site—whence its name—where the Emperor Constantine reportedly saw the apparition of the angel that led him ultimately to decree Christianity the religion of the empire. Such an overdetermined site displayed so prominently in the film's opening sequences immediately constructs just such a dialectical image, collapsing as it does the utopian wish for a stable boundary (and, even, a "city of god") with the image of the prison that contains those who threaten the order "from within." Within one image is collapsed the entire "tension" of the film, its *spatial* polarization. It comes as no surprise then that the prison (now no longer located in the Castel Sant'Angelo, of course) will become a central iconographic element of the film, one that can combine freely with the images of the borgata.

Deleuze has identified this type of image (though, to be sure, not referenced in relationship to Benjamin's dialectical image, but rather as part of Deleuze's own taxonomy) as characteristic of what he calls "modern" cinema; his paradigmatic example—surprisingly close to the image in *Accattone*—is taken from Rossellini's *Europa '51* (1952). There, the upper-bourgeoise character played by Ingrid Bergman, upon encountering the tenements and factories of the working class, thinks, "They looked like convicts." And in one sudden stroke, a new thought—indeed, a new consciousness—is born. As Deleuze so compellingly puts it: "A different type of image can appear: a pure optical-sound image, the whole image without metaphor, brings out the thing in itself, literally, in its excess of horror or beauty, in its radical or unjustifiable character. . . . You do not have the image of a prison following one of a school. . . . On the contrary, it is necessary to discover the separate elements and relations that elude us at the heart of an unclear image: to show *how and in what sense* school is a prison, housing estates are examples of prostitution, bankers killers, photographs tricks—literally, without metaphor."[16]

Ingrid Bergman "sees, she has learnt to see."[17] This, for Deleuze, is how the "new" emerges: an image presents us with an indeterminacy ("an unclear image") that a sudden act of "naming" allows us for the first time to see. And what is especially important to stress—given the criticisms of ahistoricism leveled at high theory—is that, just as with Benjamin, the sudden revelation in the face of the image *is fundamentally historical.*

This then is at the heart of Pasolini's aesthetics of contamination: it is a way of teaching us to see, even those aspects of the new order that the old Left of Pasolini's day refused to acknowledge—not the metaphor, so easily turned into a cliché, that the borgate are a prison, but "how and in what sense" the new urban geography has created a prison.

An Italian Road Movie

Dino Risi's comedy, *Il sorpasso* (*The Easy Life,* 1964), doesn't present us with the kinds of aesthetic problematics that arose in the more "serious" films of the period, probably because of the traditional "populism" of the form of the commedia all'italiana of the fifties. However, it does exemplify that turn toward complexity that Gian Piero Brunetta sees as marking the Italian comedy of the boom years. "Il sorpasso" is the act of passing another automobile on the road, and the film organizes itself around the frenetic but aimless driving of the main character Bruno (Vittorio Gassman) and his more serious-minded "buddy," Roberto (Jean-Louis Trintignant). The film is a veritable catalogue of the emerging "lifestyle" of the new Italy; and while it situates itself almost exclusively in the terrain of the new, it is always against the backdrop of an old way of life that only occasionally surfaces with a shock. But perhaps the word "shock" is too dialectical in its "Benjaminian" implications to apply to the juxtapositions that suddenly occur in *Il sorpasso:* for the film tends to handle these irruptions symptomatically, through a reversion to stereotype and caricature (when, for example, a group of priests, standing around their broken-down car, discuss their predicament in Latin), thereby abandoning the comedy of *comportimento* (or behavioral analysis) which is the film's main strength.

The film begins with the character Bruno speeding in his car through Rome, trying to find a telephone just as everything is closing for the *ferragosto* vacation, the near universally celebrated vacation taken in the weeks around August 15. This opening—which culminates in a storefront grate closing just as Bruno tries to reach for a phone—aptly condenses both the old and the new. For, in a society still tied to the old tradition of long midday breaks, the problem of finding something open at a particular time is quite common; but the fact that for Bruno it is a *problem* already marks the film with a double sense of time and marks Bruno as "out of sync" with the rhythms of the city. Yet the irony here is that it is ferragosto, and the entire city (and later, the nation) is closing all at once, so that everyone can be part of the enforced conformity of the new leisure society.

Bruno and Roberto meet by chance, as Roberto is looking out his window when Bruno stops for the telephone. Roberto is a student of law, living alone in a rather dreary, modern apartment in the periphery of Rome, an urban space thrown up quickly in the fifties to accommodate the tremendous influx of population from the country. Bruno comes up to make the phone call, and significantly, the woman he is trying to reach isn't home, which not only reinforces the series of missed encounters that opens the film, but also marks Bruno's frenetic activity as essentially futile. Then, when Bruno goes to the bathroom to wash up, he ends up breaking (off screen) the vase that Roberto was about to warn him to be careful of. This break becomes the first in a series of ruptures to the hitherto smoothly functioning—if "repressed"—world of Roberto.

Roberto, studying for his upcoming exams, seems immune to the vacation mania that has taken hold of the nation; as such, he stands for the older *homo economicus* of renunciation, savings, and investment. This represents a significant inversion of terms in the duo Roberto/Bruno, for Bruno is the elder, and what he teaches his young *compagno* is all about the obsolescence of the old ways that still govern Roberto's life. Significant too is the fact that Roberto is played by a foreigner, while in the role of Bruno we have an actor central to Italian cinema as an institution. Bruno in many ways exhibits the traits of a certain Italian (and more specifically Roman) "type," who lives by the art of *arrangiarsi,* a kind of improvisational way of getting by through a combination of bravado, seductiveness, and "smarts." By making this typical southern Italian figure into the prototype of the new Italian, the film (perhaps unconsciously) suggests that it is the very adaptability of the Italian, the "chameleon-like" quality that is so often to foreign travelers a central trait of the Italian stereotype, that allows the discourses of consumption to so easily remold the Italian character. For in many ways, adaptability and improvisation are the very traits that are required to be activated in such postmodern spaces as, say, the shopping mall. In any case, this inversion of semic combinations—the youth with the foreign and the sublimated, the older with both traditional Italy and obsessive mobility—is something we will return to shortly.

After the scene in Roberto's apartment, Bruno convinces Roberto to abandon his studies for a while and join him in a *giro*—a "spin," we could say—in the car. Needless to say, they can't find an open bar or trattoria, and so the giro widens as they drive into the countryside. In fact, as the film progresses, the movement encompasses ever more kilometers,[18] until by the end of the film we are in Viareggio, on the Riviera, where finally we are presented with the social totality that is "Italy"—a society clad in bathing suits and diverting itself with dancing the twist. And throughout the ride, the film has presented us with the images and sounds of a mobile, consumerist Italy. One of the film's principal visual motifs is the broken machine: first, a broken cigarette vending machine; then, the door handle of the toilet at the cheaply constructed rest stop; and ultimately, the wreckage of the automobile itself. This is an Italy not of permanence but of disposability, and the film's soundtrack is dominated by the incessant beat of equally disposable pop tunes, the most prominent of which is Domenico Modugno's "Dimmi quando," the lyrics of which—with its obsessive repetition of the "when, when, when" in the indirect question "Tell me when you'll want me"—is the perfect anthem to the perpetual present of the consumer.

In terms of what we might call, after Jameson, the film's allegorizing function, most crucial are the two set-pieces that involve family visits, first to Roberto's aunt and uncle, then to Bruno's ex-wife and daughter. The aunt and uncle, solidly bourgeois, live in an old villa in the countryside, a villa where Roberto often spent time as a child. Here, the portrait painted is strictly "Italian gothic," complete with "eccentric" (that is, homosexual) butler, the unmarried daughter who will linger at home until she turns into an old maid, and the local peasant who resembles the "Maciste" of the Italian cinema of the teens and twenties. While Bruno later indicates to Roberto his contempt for the whole group, as a guest he deploys all his formidable charm to insinuate himself into the family, to the point where Roberto not only becomes jealous, but begins to doubt his understanding of his own past. For Bruno—in asides to Roberto—continually reads the "gothic subtext" to the family narrative: the butler, he explains, is called "Occhiofino" because he is a "finocchio," a "fag"; the uncanny resemblance between Roberto's fatuous cousin and the somber peasant, he notes, is sure proof that Roberto's aunt needed "wilder" sex than her bourgeois husband could provide. In these scenes, Bruno is anticipating the role that later Terence Stamp would play in Pasolini's much more deadly ironic *Teorema* (1968): in one scene, he wins the heart of the spinster by undoing her hair and showing her what she'd look like as a "Roman girl." Bruno's ultimate triumph is the acquisition of the uncle's grandfather clock: he cons the uncle out of the patrimony that rightly belongs to Roberto, so that he can wrest it from family ties and put it into circulation. In fact, Bruno makes at least part of his living by recycling the antiques of a dying social class.

In contrast to Roberto's family, Bruno's is thoroughly modern: atomized, alienated, mobile, and pleasure-seeking. Bruno's decision to make a surprise late-night visit to his ex-wife is at least partly motivated by a series of failed erotic encounters; it is as if these relatively unimportant failures remind him of the one failure that is important, that of his marriage. Now, at this point in Italian history, divorce has not yet become legal; it is, however, a major focal point of public discourse (as we shall see) and as such is a kind of barometer of just how successfully modernization has been accomplished. In any case, Bruno and Roberto are thoroughly drunk when they look up Gianna at one in the morning; nevertheless, Gianna, who hasn't seen Bruno in well over a year, takes the two men in as if this were an expected occurrence. Gianna, that is to say, is so completely contemptuous of Bruno's "masculinism" that she puts up with him as if with a wayward child. Thus, in a film that is otherwise thoroughly masculinist in its enunciation, there emerges in the subtext of this scene that crisis in the sexual relation that is concomitant to modernization, and that in the American cinema had found earlier expression in the noir and melodrama of the fifties.

Thus it is no surprise that Bruno, almost as a defense mechanism, suddenly adopts a patriarch's concern over the whereabouts of his fifteen-year-old daughter at one in the morning; nor does it come as a surprise when she walks in with a "boyfriend"—Bibi—who is years older than Bruno. For in popular culture generally, one of the ways in which the "crisis in masculinity" that accompanies modernization finds expression is through a pathological Oedipalization of the daughter's sexual choices: in the American cinema of the fifties once again, we can cite *Written on the Wind* (1956), *Imitation of Life* (1959), and *Rebel without a Cause* (1955) as particularly prominent examples of this. In the American scenario, the generalized collapse of the Law renders all the men in the films incapable of living up to the phallic mandate; but within the melodramatic economy, this failure is turned back upon the woman, whose "voracious" qualities then work to gender the entire economy of consumption as "feminine." In *Il sorpasso,* we can see a simi-

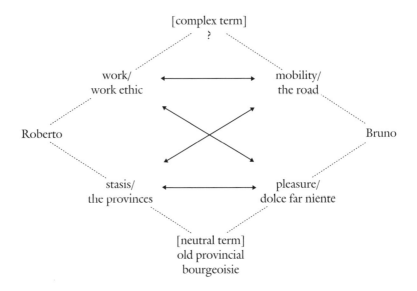

lar dynamic with Bruno's wife and daughter, where their pursuit of material security renders them—in the context of the men unable to provide it—unfathomable.

In *The Political Unconscious,* Fredric Jameson demonstrates how the semiotic rectangle can be used to uncover the ways in which a given text attempts to "solve" the textual antinomies that reflect real, historical contradictions.[19] In the case of *Il sorpasso,* we could say that the principal contrary that the text produces is that between work (and the work ethic embodied in Roberto) and mobility (or the road), which would produce the results in the diagram on this page. What the semiotic square makes apparent is that the social tension around which the film constructs itself (or which, in Jameson's terms, the film allegorizes) is the movement of hegemony from the old provincial bourgeoisie to a new class; and that it is precisely in the attempt to visualize this new hegemonic class that the film "stumbles." What is unimaginable in *Il sorpasso*—what indeed is the principal stumbling block for the cultural imagination as a whole—is the subject that embodies both mobility and the (northern European or "Protestant") work ethic; in short, the new class of technocrats who were transforming both economy and culture throughout the 1950s. As soon as Roberto is uprooted from his sheltered world, the film can imagine his trajectory ending only in his sudden and arbitrary death in a car accident.

As the semiotic square of the previous chapter makes apparent, *Il sorpasso* makes visible for us a kind of "void in the Symbolic" that confronted Italy in 1964—precisely, the subjectivity at once mobile and "employed." While today it is relatively easy for us to characterize this subjectivity as that of the "postmodern," in the Italy of 1964 this subjectivity remained to be articulated. Thus it was around this opening that all types of discourses—in advertising, journalism, and politics as well as popular culture—competed in an attempt to pin down the meaning of this new Italian and thus deploy it for ideological ends.[1] Here, the phrase "to pin down" is a deliberate deployment of the Lacanian notion of the *point de capiton* as that quilting point which serves to gather up a series of signifiers and fix their meanings; the understanding that this process is invariably ideological has been one of the central contributions of Slavoj Žižek to the reinvigoration of psychoanalysis in media studies today. An even more crucial contribution of Žižek to ideological analysis is his elaboration of the Lacanian order of the Real as that which lies outside of symbolization. For a symbolic order must have an "outside" if we are ever to account for change (and thus history itself). In the case of the semiotic square constructed from *Il sorpasso*, for example, what is made evident is that *something new*—that is, not yet articulable within the culture—has been produced, and it is this "trauma of the new" that must be named.

But it is crucial to realize that, in this redefinition of the national subject, we are dealing not simply with discourse, but with discourse in relation to space and to spatial practices. For neocapitalism confronts us with two interrelated phenomena: one, the transformation of space (insofar as we hold to Henri Lefebvre's notion that a shift in the mode of production must invariably be accompanied by the production of a new space),[2] and two, the transformation of subjectivity in relation to the space. The *nation* is thus one particular entity that is mobilized in order to mediate these two processes. The problem is thus how "inner space" is connected to "outer space."[3] This chapter will devote itself primarily to how this connection was attempted by the hegemonic forces at work in Italy in the early sixties, particularly in the weekly *L'Espresso.* Chapter 5 will look at the ways in which the hegemonic forces impacted themselves at the level of the locality, at the level of everyday life and the body.

Porosity and the Postmodern

Before looking at *L'Espresso,* however, it will be useful to lay out a more detailed conceptual scheme for dealing with the transformation of the national space. To start with, we can note briefly that much has been written about the relationship between *flânerie* and the early cinema; taking Walter Benjamin as a starting point, the argument is that the early cinema was a kind of culmination of a certain experience of the city that emerged in the middle of the nineteenth century in response to the transformed spaces wrought by the development of capitalism. Giuliana Bruno does an admirable job of summarizing the vast literature in this area, and her work has the added advantage (from our viewpoint) of inflecting it through the lens of Naples in the early twentieth century.[4] It should be noted here that feminism has been a primary impetus in the development of this work: the emergence of the *grand magasin*— where women could both earn and spend money—allowed women increased access to the space of the city (which access was then greatly expanded by the cinema). This development, then, is one of liberation, either from an enforced domesticity or from the alterity of being seen as a "streetwalker." There is, however, a way in which flânerie retains its alterity: we need only imagine the *flâneur* (now male) to be a homosexual, and his passage through the urban space to be *cruising.* What would result is a generalized "queering" of the urban space, insofar as the transgression cannot be immediately read, but rather must be somehow decoded.

In any case, the transformation once again of the urban space in the postwar period requires that the older Benjaminian conception of flânerie be adapted to the space of—in Margaret Morse's words—the freeway, the mall, and television. In this new space, the Benjaminian "shock" is replaced by the "everyday distraction," producing a kind of hyperspace in which the phantasmatic of the object layers itself across the entire spatial field.[5] This is what Lefebvre has termed "global space," which, he argues, actually emerges as a *possibility* within modernism itself—with the wresting of the (painted, for example) object from space, with the disappearance of the (architectural) façade—where a spatial void is created that only later would be filled by "commercial images, signs, and objects."[6]

But the question that becomes most insistent at this point is, How does such a spatial system establish itself within an Italian urban space dense with traces of the past? One would expect this process to be inflected with highly culturally specific forms. In the United States, the explosive postwar growth of the Sunbelt cities provided neocapitalism with a vast, "already leveled" space with which to work. The greater spatial inertia of the Italian city would tend initially to produce a great divide between center and periphery. But this must be seen as only a starting point: in some way, the center must gradually come to be "peripheralized," even as it retains its medieval, Renaissance, or baroque form, in order to accomplish the transformation requisite of neocapitalism.

Here it is particularly useful to develop a concept originally articulated by Walter Benjamin: the "porosity" of the urban space. It is a concept deployed in his analysis of the space of Naples, but it is equally useful in considering the various other spaces that comprise the imaginary maps that come to stand in for "Italy." For Benjamin, Naples was an urban space that was unique in the way that various boundaries are blurred between binary oppositions essential to the functioning of capital: in particular, boundaries between public and private, work and leisure, the individual and the social. Thus the city's "porosity": it is as if two essentially different worlds are layered upon one another, so that it is always possible to "see through" the present in a particular "scenario" and into an essentially precapitalist world.[7] We might take for an example the famous Neapolitan *truffa* (or swindle), which remains alive even today. You are walking through the old quarter of *Spacca Napoli* with a companion who is clearly a tourist, and a friendly young man approaches to express his concern for the safety of the lady's jewelry. Don't you know how dangerous this neighborhood is? Haven't you heard the way they rip jewelry right off women's necks? You thank him for his concern, but he becomes more insistent that the woman should really remove her jewelry before taking one more step into the neighborhood. By this point, you have hopefully understood the situation and have whisked your friend and yourself away from the seemingly friendly stranger, and thus have avoided the truffa in which you literally collaborate in the theft of your jewelry.[8]

What Benjamin sees in the truffa is the way that it marks within the urban space the uneven development characteristic of a certain moment of capitalism. Precapitalist modes of behavior and social codes not only become suddenly visible, but provide us with a kind of spatial and temporal "gap" from which we can better view the functioning of capitalism itself. Thus, from the truffa described above, we can see the way in which an act becomes reified as an exemplar of "local color," played out specifically across the figure of the tourist. For Benjamin, of course, the swindle is simply one of an entire host of urban details in which the porosity of Naples is manifested; ultimately—in the unfinished Arcades Project—Benjamin's goal was to develop a system of reading the urban space so as to render visible the social forces that have made it into what it is now.

In looking at Benjamin's work on porosity and space, Victor Burgin has uncovered an important ambiguity: namely, the observation that alongside the possibility of spatial porosity or "the fusion of spaces," Benjamin at some level wants to draw a line, to assert the possibility of an independence or an "integrity" of those spaces—in short, to hold on to a *boundary*. As Burgin puts it (in a reading of the dedication of *One Way Street* to Asja Lacis), "An ambivalence inhabits this textual fragment: as if two different spaces—one sealed, the other permeable—compete to occupy the same moment in time."[9] Only the "sealed space" could guarantee that the public and the private would remain separate and uncontaminated. Porosity, then, becomes that which enables us to forge a link between the precapitalist spaces of the Italian city and the postmodern space generally, insofar as it is precisely this contamination of the public and private that characterizes postmodern space.

Because Benjamin is uncovering a type of "spatial polysemy," his work is particularly useful in looking at how Italian advertising functioned in the 1960s. Of course, polysemy is central to understanding advertising in general; advertising works by mobilizing the sliding of signification, insofar as it can then reconstruct meanings to its own ends. But advertising constructed its own heterogenous space, one that mobilized the older Italian space while attempting to supersede it. We move from one heterogenous space—where the precapitalist seeps through the pores of the capitalist city—to another heterogenous space—namely, the postmodern space constructed (as we will see) by turning historically situated space into *signs* within an economy of pure difference.

This is why Benjamin's choice of Naples seems so prescient to us today, for the porosity Benjamin saw in the Naples of the 1920s is so much akin to the (now more generalized) porosity of the urban space in postmodernity. Thus, by the 1990s, the doubly inscribed space of the "impossible cities" of the South—Naples and Palermo specifically—becomes the means whereby politically committed filmmakers like Francesco Rosi can uncover the workings of global capital within the "ruins" of the central city. In *Dimenticare Palermo* (*The Palermo Connection*, 1990), for example—a film to be explored in detail in the last chapter—the Sicilian American's quest for "roots" and for "authenticity" is both catered to and undermined: all of the folkloristic details that reach back through centuries of history are recoded, so as to become signs of an international drug economy that is simply the shadow of the global economy itself.

"Authenticity," of course, has historically been a central signified for Italy-as-signifier when seen through the eyes of the foreigner, whether it be the British on grand tour in the novels of E. M. Forster or the American spinster on holiday in a slew of Hollywood films made at Cinecittà in the fifties. In fact, Lefebvre has noted how the Mediterranean space has become marked as a space of leisure, to be distinguished from the industrialized spaces to the north.[10] Within this space permeated with traces that run back to the archaic and the mythological, one can have the sense of an "escape" from complete subordination to the logic of work: one can experience, that is to say, a kind of "waste" or "nonproductive expenditure" that itself is mirrored in the chaotic spatial bricolage that is Rome today. Of course, in reality this "authentic" experience is already planned, often even micromanaged by the tourist industry. Still, what is being activated is the *seductive* quality of the Italian space, predicated on the fact that in the transparent society of postmodernity, there is something that still remains *hidden*.[11]

For critical theory today, what is ultimately at stake in the issues surrounding space and porosity has been lucidly brought out by Fredric Jameson in his reading of Manfredo Tafuri's *Architecture and Utopia*. What one senses when reading Tafuri is that with neocapitalism we have finally arrived at a state in which the Totality has reached closure, the green revolution having eliminated nature just as the saturated media environment has contaminated the public/private divide.[12] The implications are that for the individual subject, there is no longer any space of escape, any space outside the totality, whether one looks inwardly (and finds a phantasmagoria of objects) or outwardly (and finds that the *tropiques* are indeed *tristes*). In a way, this argument mirrors the one put forth regarding the nation in the first chapter of this work, where the possibility of "the concept" has given way to the immediacy of experience.

Quite astutely, Jameson connects the fairly recent popularity of Antonio Gramsci to this impasse. For Gramsci sets forth a *spatial* model for change that obviates (but only partially) the need for an "outside": the enclave or the subculture is a new space which emerges *within* the totality. But while the Gramscian position seemingly provides us with the Archimedean point needed for social transformation, by now we are all familiar with the problems that lie in wait for the overly optimistic: namely, that the institutions of power will quickly soak up any alterity, homogenize it, and allow it to circulate harmlessly in electronic space as a sign of "progressivism" or daring. Thus, it would seem that studies of resistance and the practice of everyday life would do well to complement themselves with a kind of "critical" cognitive mapping. That is to say, we must look within the representations of space itself—whether in cinema or in advertising—to uncover (through the symptoms, through the aporias) not only the strategies of power but also the incipient spaces of the truly new.

Reconstructing Italian Space

By 1964, *L'Espresso* was certainly one of the important instruments in the creation of a national audience in Italy. Traditionally, Italy has been a nation of low newspaper readership, probably because of the late arrival of mass literacy in the country, as well as the lack of a "British model" popular press. However, the fifties saw the emergence of the nationally distributed news magazines, and total readership of these magazines went from 12.5 million to 21 million in 1972.[13]

Still, we cannot see *L'Espresso* as simply the instrument of the new bourgeois elite of the northern industrial/communications center; within the magazine, there is in fact a tension between the older literary and professional elites that were traditionally regional but whose centers would be Rome and Florence, and the new elite of the North. Thus, for example, the magazine is fascinated with up-to-the-minute fads from

New York and Paris while it holds on to the tradition of the "public intellectual"; rather than supplanting the old elites with new, narrowly defined "experts" to contextualize the social changes in the nation, it continued to insist that it was precisely these older, "liberally educated" elites whose mandate it was to contextualize those social changes.

Thus it came about that Pasolini became—within the pages of the magazine—the center of a national debate on language and its relation to the changing economic "base" in the nation. The debate started after Pasolini delivered a public lecture called "New Linguistic Questions."[14] This lecture, reported on in *L'Espresso* (17 January 1965), was followed up on 7 February by an article of response by Pasolini, and in the following week's issue by an overall summary of the debate that was engendered by both lecture and the journalism surrounding it. Pasolini argues in his article that now, for the first time, the possibility for a single Italian language exists: a "communicative" as opposed to an "expressive" or poetic language. First, we can note the way in which Pasolini's binary opposition mirrors the very tension we can see in the editorial content of the magazine, where an old and a new elite are rubbing against each other. Pasolini argues that linguistic unification is possible only because of the emergence of this new, "instrumental" or technocratic elite. The old bourgeoisie, while dominant, was not hegemonic; this is in sharp contrast to the emergent new bourgeoisie centered in the northern industrial/communications center, which was strongly hegemonic, giving the newer, more standardized language the potential of diffusing itself throughout the population.[15]

It was in the South where this diffusion "hit" the old Symbolic orders with the most violence; and it was because the hegemony of the northern elites had the quality of being imposed upon the South that the South can be looked upon as a postcolonial space. The problem of the South, of course, was not new: Gramsci had written the seminal essay on the subject decades earlier. In the fifties, the government set up the Cassa per il Mezzogiorno to develop the South. But quickly, these development projects were seen as problematic, for rather than fostering indigenous economic development, they became rather like "colonial outposts" of the northern economy. The South was simply not equipped infrastructurally to integrate the developments. The projects funded—electrical plants, factories—were dubbed "cathedrals in the desert." Essentially, they created isolated enclaves of technocracy and bourgeois consciousness, while leaving most of the region unchanged;

and often, these projects fell into disuse.[16] But at the level of culture, these developments ruptured irrevocably the old Symbolic orders of the South.

Pasolini's "New Linguistic Questions" prompted public discussion by seemingly all the writers and intellectuals of the country, including Alberto Moravia, Umberto Eco, and a host of lesser lights; and much of the discussion was reported in *L'Espresso*. From our vantage point today, we can see more clearly how the magazine's very reporting on this issue reflected, symptomatically, the split among the intellectuals: between those whose ideas were grounded in "theory" (whether Marxist or Crocean Hegelianism) and those, seemingly more "modern," whose ideas were grounded in a pragmatic and scientific empiricism. For the magazine criticizes Pasolini's argument by recategorizing Pasolini's essentially Gramscian argument as "sociology," and then goes on to say, "but sociology is an exact science or it is nothing: to use it, it is necessary that the scientific premises be credible."[17] In other words, ultimately, the magazine comes down on the side of an instrumental (as opposed to "heretical," the characterization Pasolini gave to his own "empiricism") empiricism, in keeping with its hegemonic function of constructing a new subjectivity for a more "modern" (i.e., Americanized) Italy.

This new, "scientific" approach to questions of everyday life—sex, hygiene, lifestyle, and leisure—becomes the centerpiece of *L'Espresso*: quite literally, in that the center of the magazine is often reserved for the discussion of issues ranging from divorce (not to be made widely accessible until 1970), homosexuality (and sexuality in general), all the way down to the high incidence of penile problems among young army conscripts, which problems are ascribed—of course—to inadequate education.[18] What we see, then, is an overdetermination in the very *format* of the newsweekly: that is, if we ask the question why—and for whom—the newsweekly comes to augment or even supplant the daily newspaper, the format of *L'Espresso* makes clear that the answer lies in the issue of *contextualization*. On the one hand, this contextualization applies to the implied reader, who is a "truly" national subject, even one who is finally too busy to get bogged down by the leisurely format of the newspaper. On the other hand, what is traditionally called news (i.e., the "hard news") becomes the opening pages of text leading up to the really "sexy" story in the middle of the issue.

Finally, to take this logic of contextualization to its conclusion, we can say that the advertisements, which are of course scattered throughout the magazine, function rather like "islands of enjoyment" floating within the sea of text; they are the textual "outposts" that take the lifestyle and leisure issues at the center of the issue and disseminate them throughout the magazine. In the period from 1961 to 1965, the advertising centers on the construction of leisure. The most prominent ads are for oil companies, automobiles, and auto products—ads that directly address the consumer. There are also a considerable number of ads for synthetic fabrics created by the new chemical companies; these ads are less motivated by the creation of sales—after all, few of the readers would buy products directly from the chemical companies—as they are by the creation of a new sense of history among the readers, a sense of history pointed forward to a new age of progress. These ads are also of interest in the way that they illustrate how postwar Italy is deliberately constructing an identity as a fashion and design capital. These particular signifiers of Italy were a large part of what the Italian cinema circa 1960 was exporting; and as we shall see in the next chapter, Antonioni deliberately "plays" with these signifiers.[19]

The sense of a new age at hand that advertising—particularly that of the chemical companies noted above—is playing upon is directly connected to the suddenness of Italy's economic miracle. Italy has changed radically in little more than a decade, while the Italian subject has remained locked in discourses and political configurations that emerged out of the Second World War. A page of advertising in *L'Espresso* of 19 January 1964 is remarkable in the ways that—by a totally contingent juxtaposition of two advertisements—it uncovers this historical rupture. On the top half of the page is an ad from the chemical group SNIA, touting a new synthetic fabric "with all the advantages." The headline of the ad is "É arrivato" (loosely, "It's here!"); the ad depicts a stylishly dressed woman confidently striding toward the reader, as if she is about to walk right off the page. On the bottom half of the page, *L'Espresso* is seeking new subscribers by offering a three-record set of songs from the European resistance. Spread across the ad is a ragged band of partisans, rifles slung across their shoulders, and the Italian flag waving off in the corner. On the one hand, history is seen as a march toward the future, where the most logical attitude for the Italian to take is a turning back on the past. On the other hand, we see the ways in which that past—still a potent force in a country where the Communist Party has between one-fourth and one-third of the electorate—is becoming

3
L'Espresso
19 January 1964

4
Paisà's
image of the
partisans

commodified and turned into nostalgia. And while we must be careful not to draw the wrong conclusions from a (perhaps) totally fortuitous juxtaposition, we can nevertheless note the irony in the "sexuation" the ads present: there is one "Woman," walking toward us with no baggage and no regrets, while below her, a rag-tag group of men are scattered in the distant Italian landscape, almost as if they were ridiculous "worker bees" setting the stage for the triumphant emergence of the queen.[20]

It is significant, too, that the chemical company ad is *drawn;* it is not a photograph. One of Fredric Jameson's most interesting observations about the materiality of video (as a quintessentially postmodern medium) is that its formal precursor is best seen, not as the narrative forms of fiction, but rather the material forms of animation. As he puts it, "Animation constituted the first great school to teach the reading of material signifiers (rather than the narrative apprenticeship of objects of representation . . .)."[21] Now, this observation is highly useful when looking at the historical conjuncture we are dealing with; for in terms of the construction of the postwar nation, it was precisely the neorealist cinema that staked everything on the question of representation, and on the concomitant "apprenticeship" of the national audience. Indeed, in the sixties it is these two questions—of representation, and of pedagogy—that faced serious filmmakers, and this precisely in their attempt to create a discourse of *resistance* to the growing cultural homogenization wrought by the hegemonizing forces of the economic miracle.

Ultimately, then, the logic of the point de capiton is the logic of social antagonism and contestation within the ideological field, as the various camps try to "pin down," or conversely to subvert, what it means to be a citizen of this new nation. And here is where de Certeau's distinction between strategy and tactics becomes useful. For insofar as the discourses of advertising and of the new national language are so palpably material in their effects—because the changes in the object-world of Italy are so seemingly unstoppable—these discourses can be seen as strategic moves by the hegemonizing classes. Thus the only appropriate response from the filmmaker is to adopt a set of tactics that will draw the lines of battle at the level of the particular, the local, and the everyday.[22] And it is *this* aspect of the earlier neorealist tradition that the new filmmakers of the sixties find usable, even as they realize the extent to which the first wave of neorealism was recuperated by the national project of the Christian Democrats.

Advertising, then, brings us to the junction of hegemony and everyday life. The British cultural historians Michael Bommes and Patrick Wright put it particularly well when they note that hegemonizing discourse functions by "deploying/restaging everyday life in particular coded sites, images, events."[23] Advertising, cinema, and television all are engaged in articulating spatial relations through which the nation, and the national narrative, is experienced. In a sense, then, we can say that the nation, Italy, is being "remapped" in this period, particularly through advertising in magazines like *L'Espresso*.

As we've already noted, the advertising in *L'Espresso* during this period is dominated by travel and movement, and it attempts to inscribe mobility within the traditional images of the nation. To begin with, we can look at a kind of "public service" ad done by the government touting the completion of the L'Autostrada del sole. This "highway of the sun" was of great symbolic importance to the new Italy, as it not only

5
L'Espresso
25 October 1964

linked the North to the South in a kind of transportational "backbone," but also was the visible sign of government's progressive alliance with the new economy. The ad is beautiful: the highway is an empty ribbon running across the verdant hills of (what looks like) Tuscany and skirts a walled medieval city perched on a hilltop. The opposition between bounded and unbounded space is buffered by the composition as a whole, which makes the highway look as natural as the landscape it traverses. Just as the medieval city is a work of man in perfect harmony with the hill it is built on, so too—the ad seems to argue—is the highway in perfect harmony with the landscape.

Hertz Rent a Car ran a series of ads that were based on the regions of Italy. The headlines were "In Sardegna," "In Veneto," and so on. Each of the ads features a smartly dressed woman with a car key standing in front of the rental car, while in the background are hand-drawn images "characteristic" of each region. In Sardinia, we see a lonesome shepherd riding a mule through the mountainous terrain, in a jarring juxtaposition to the woman and the car. In this series of ads, we can begin by noting the formal similarity to the chemical company ad discussed earlier: that is, its use both of cartoon and of Woman as central figure. Here, the medium of the cartoon (and its "material significa-tion," as Jameson puts it) illustrates perfectly the processes of conden-sation that advertising deploys generally: the ads condense a number of key signifiers of each region (e.g., cliffs, beach, shepherd, animal, and so on) in which their only relationships are to each other, to the "master signifier" ("Sardegna"), and to Hertz Rent-a-Car. This process detaches the region from its historical context (and thus to the "narrative appren-ticeship" required of, say, the film *Banditi ad Orgosolo*) and turns each detail into just another element of the touristic or the folkloristic. And it is precisely the one incongruity within the cartoon—namely, the car—that is central to performing this feat of decontextualization. The ads thus construct a new, postmodern Italian space where the regions—seen through the mediation of the automobile—become purely differ-ential elements of a signifying system.[24]

Gulf Oil Company employed a similar technique of "touring" fa-mous national spaces, but with the sophistication and pizzazz of art photography. The series used the headline "Corre sfrecciante . . . Gulf carburante" ["Full speed ahead . . . by burning Gulf"], and an almost full-page picture of a time-lapsed car speeding through one or another landmark public space, such as the Piazza della Signoria in Florence. Here again, the advertising is attempting to reinscribe the space of Italy

Corre sfrecciante... Gulf carburante

Gulf Super NO-NOX dà più potenza
alla vostra automobile, perché man-
tiene pulito il vostro motore.

Gulf

Gulf è petrolio in Italia e nel mondo.

6
L'Espresso
24 May 1964

with new signifiers; in particular, it attempts to resolve the contradiction between the speed of the automobile and the cramped and labyrinthine urban spaces of Italy. Here, what comes to mind is the futurist
ideal of *Velo-città,* their attempt, in the action painting, to inscribe
within the Italian city the idea of modernity and "speed." The ads, with
their time-lapse photography, seem consciously to allude to the futurist
action paintings, and we can recall that futurism was the aesthetic most
aligned with the construction of the nation during the fascist period. As
James Hay perceptively notes, futurism was determined to create "hy-
pertechnological tropes" in order to produce "new ways of perceiving
temporal and spatial relations in Italian cities,"[25] where, of course, the
dominant organizational principles come from the high Middle Ages
and Renaissance.

The series done by Shell Oil is the most interesting and complex of
the automobile-related ads. Each ad in the series features a child constructing a narrative of travel with the family. Often, there is a large
picture of a happy or pensive child, with a little story underneath. The
case of "Luisa" is different, however; her advertisement is constructed
of six photographs, which, together with her commentary underneath

Io sono Luisa

... Io e papà siamo grandi amici. Papà mi ha insegnato a sciare e a nuotare. Ogni domenica organizziamo una gita. Quest'anno abbiamo deciso di visitare dei posti lontani. Fare il programma è un compito nostro. La mamma è d'accordo con quel che si decide noi. L'ultima volta abbiamo scelto il paese di Giulietta e Romeo. Siamo sempre contenti di partire. "Cambiamo un po' d'aria" dice papà.

Poco prima di Brescia abbiamo fatto uno spuntino in un ristorante tutto di vetro. Si vedevano passare le macchine a tutta velocità sull'autostrada.

Verona è proprio una bella città. Papà mi ha parlato a vedere Piazza delle Erbe. Papà conosce bene Verona. C'è stato anche due anni per lavoro.

Papà ha fatto benzina: si ferma sempre alla Shell. L'uomo della Shell ha controllato l'olio e papà si è messo a parlare con lui.

Siamo ripartiti. Papà era molto contento. l'uomo della Shell ci era accinto della cinghia del ventilatore allentata e l'avevo rimessa a posto.

Da Verona eravamo andati a Montecchio. È il paese della storia di Giulietta e Romeo. Ci sono ancora i castelli.

Era già tardi quando siamo tornati. Abbiamo voluto vedere il panorama di tramonto. In macchina io mi sono addormentata accanto a papà che guidava.

Su tutte le strade · Shell è con voi · Shell viaggia con voi each one, constructs a narrative. Luisa tells the story of how she and her daddy (who are "great friends") take little trips every Sunday. The six pictures creating the narrative are, first, a stop at a restaurant along the autostrada ("all of glass"); then Piazza delle Erbe in Verona ("a really beautiful city"); then two photos detailing the pit stop at a Shell station, where a helpful attendant notices the fan belt is loose; then Montecchio and the castle of Romeo and Juliet ("There are still castles!"); and finally, the autostrada by night, as the father-daughter couple return home.

On the most obvious level, we see how the ad naturalizes leisure travel by inscribing the unfamiliar or novel scenes within the age-old landscape of Italy. At another level, the ad mobilizes the Oedipal scenario, as the young girl runs off with Dad every Sunday (where's Mamma?), dreaming of castles and Romeo and Juliet, and snuggling up to Dad on the road home. Thus, we see the process whereby the ad attempts to "colonize the unconscious," by allowing leisure travel and Shell Oil to negotiate the sexual desire that runs through the family.

Insofar as all these ads are working upon the urban spaces of Italy, they bring to mind the discussion in chapter 3 of Benjamin and the porosity of Naples. Certainly, these ads do present us with the shock of historical disjuncture, of the juxtaposition of two modes of economic organization within the same space. The ads, however, work within a completely discursive economy, purged of the historical "Real" that underpins the Benjaminian experience of Naples. This is the reason we can describe the nation-space created by these ads as postmodern: each potential referent is turned into a pure sign, in the manner described by Jean Baudrillard,[26] and each relates to the other as pure difference, whose meaning becomes fixed through the mediation of the commodity. This is the hidden logic underlying Pasolini's key notion of "homogenization," the dark side of the economic miracle. A 1966 advertisement for AGIP aptly illustrates this: the map of Italy now completely uniform, each region is indicated by an identical rectangle indicating the number of gas stations, rest stops, and hotels available.

*Even the last place in which
reality resided, that is, the
body . . . has disappeared.*

—PIER PAOLO PASOLINI

A National Inquest on Sex

In 1964, Pasolini made the documentary *Comizi d'amore* (*Love Meetings*)
while scouting locations for *The Gospel According to St. Matthew* (1964).
It is through this film that we can draw together the various notions of
spatiality, textuality, and the body that lie at the heart of the economic
modernization. For the film is not only a record of how the discourses
and practices of modernization traverse the physical body itself; it also
shows us the tension between a nationalizing, hegemonizing discourse
and the practice of everyday life. Sex, then, has become an "issue"—
which is not surprising, since this period is one in which sex has become
an issue in just about all of the advanced capitalist nations. What Foucault would call the "regulation of bodies" has become the agenda of
the nation; the social goal is to arrive at some sort of consensus regarding a wide range of practices. The documentary reveals a profound lack
of consensus in Italy, but even more important, it shows how that lack
of consensus is *mapped* into the nation by regions.

In calling the film "a national inquest on sex," Pasolini (most likely
consciously) alludes to Zavattini's ideal of the "film inquest," which as
we've seen was already deployed by Rosi in *Salvatore Giuliano* to create
a powerful critique of the nation-building process itself. Nevertheless,
for the viewer today, the question that comes up is the same one that

haunted the neorealist project generally: to what extent does an act of resistance unconsciously partake in the very logic of the thing being resisted? Or, to put it in Michel de Certeau's terms, to what extent is the film a tactical resistance to the hegemonizing discourses, and to what extent does it actually reflect the very strategy of those discourses? Certainly, the very act of putting on the table the issue of sex, the very act of "speaking sex," is—Michel Foucault teaches us—precisely the social project of modernity. In this sense, the film is certainly complicit in this project; and this repeated double bind that Pasolini found himself in is certainly a major explanation for his later artistic movement to the premodern and the Third World.[1]

But there is a sense in which *Comizi d'amore is* profoundly subversive, and interestingly, it achieves this subversive quality through a means very similar to that found in *Salvatore Giuliano*. In both films, the spectator is forced to realize the *constructedness* of the Symbolic Order, is forced to see how the Symbolic Order is an arbitrary covering-over of some traumatic Real—of the body, of sexuation, of history. This is evident from Pasolini's very clever opening strategy for the film, where Sicilian children are being asked how babies are born. Of course, this is the question that represents in general the child's first attempt at a self-conscious examination of sexuality, and so children's narratives here are inevitably filled with gaps and contradictions that need somehow to be resolved. In the documentary, we see how the signifiers of the birth narrative—Mama's stomach, the stork, God—begin to slide under the pressure of Pasolini's "logic."

Pasolini's privileging of the narratives of the Sicilian children reveals a larger strategy in the documentary: that is, as we move through the interviews with adults, we begin to see the same kind of sliding of signification when the received discourses on sexuality meet their stumbling blocks.[2] Generally, the film employs two distinct enunciative strategies: one, a series of interviews by Pasolini with various ordinary Italians in everyday situations, in which these Italians speak surprisingly frankly about whatever is on their minds; and two, a series of interruptions to these interviews, where Pasolini sits with a group of rather prominent intellectuals (including journalist Oriana Fallaci and psychoanalyst Cesare Musatti) to discuss broader issues of sexuality and social change. On the surface, this strategy of interruption seems to reflect a "retrograde," televisual procedure of contextualization, where no "body" is allowed to speak for him/herself, without mediation from both media-anointed "experts" and the studio hosts who deliver everything up to the viewer. However, here the discourse of the intellectuals is not the contextual frame through which all the rest is viewed but rather illustrates in living form the ways in which the various voices of the film "rub against one another." It illustrates, that is, *the very problem of the constitution of the object of study.*

In this sense, the presence throughout the film of Pasolini's *body* becomes the critical self-reflexive move of the documentary.[3] For in documentary practice generally, the key ideological move is toward the disembodied voice, which becomes the vehicle for knowledge, for the universal. It is the presence of the body—as Joan Copjec rightly notes—that introduces the disruption of the particular into the attempted totalization.[4] Bill Nichols has noted how crucial is the body to documentary, in that the invocation of the body becomes a kind of "guarantee" of the *referent* (as opposed to the signified). He goes on to argue that the body becomes a kind of "stand-in" for "experience as yet uncategorized within the economy of a logic or system."[5] Or, to put it in psychoanalytic terms, the body stands as guarantor of the Real, even as it itself is traversed by the discourses of the Symbolic. This is a particularly fruitful way to look at Pasolini's documentary: it is *all* bodies. But they are narrating bodies, incessantly called upon to find ways of making sense of the new forces shaping their lives.

Nation and Narration

Thus, within *Comizi d'amore,* it is at the very juncture of the body and the discourses it produces that we see the friction between everyday life and the hegemonizing discourses attempting to produce "the new Italian." A key scene in this regard comes at EUR (Esposizione Universale Roma), the planned development north of Rome built by the fascist government for an international exposition that never took place—where Pasolini interviews a group of soldiers on the question of "Don Juan versus good husband." Here, the documentary cannily reveals the essence of the problem in the film's very enunciation. First of all, the army is seen as the traditional site by which the national subject can be wrested from his local ties and turned into an "Italian." But when Pasolini begins to question the group of soldiers, he distinguishes them by addressing them with nicknames for their regional origins. Thus, he looks at one man and says "Tu, abbruzzesino," for another, "Tu, romano," and a third he calls Venetian. In each case, the camera searches through the crowd of faces, finding and then framing the soldier addressed. Here, the body—physiognomy—functions as the ultimate sig-nifier of identity, and it is rooted in a region, a "bloodline."

This distinction between the palpable body of physiognomy versus the abstract body of the democratic state is crucial in understanding how the North/South divide is not simply one of economics but one of consciousness. For here, what is being articulated is a radical tension between an essentially "democratic" notion of the body and its relation to social space, and a corresponding feudal notion. As Žižek notes, it is the feudal consciousness that rests legitimacy in the physical body. The accomplishment of the bourgeois revolution is to separate the Law from the body, so that, for example, the Law acts *as if* everyone were the same.[6] A similar argument is put forth by Foucault in his *History of Sexuality*. Looking at what he calls the junction of the body and the population, he notes a transition from an earlier form of society cen-tered on blood as the central organizing symbol, to the new order in which sexuality takes its place. This, he argues, is why the new order is organized around *life,* its management, its potentials, as opposed to the feudal order which is organized around the notion of death.[7]

Certainly, what allowed these two forms of consciousness to con-tinue to exist was the relative failure, as of 1964, of the new hegemon-izing language to take root within the South. In a humorous scene set in a crowded piazza in Naples, a man explains to Pasolini why the new "Legge Merlin"—a law that closed down the state-run houses of pros-titution, and which we'll deal with in substance later—is a disaster for the city. Pasolini then asks him if he likes the idea of the state being a "pimp":

PASOLINI: You'd like the state to be a pimp [*magnaccia,* vulgar] then?

NAPOLITANO: Yes, if it was more *magnani.* . . .

PASOLINI: I didn't say *magnani,* I said *magnaccia*—a man who lives off women.

NAPOLITANO: No, here we call it *ricotaro.*

PASOLINI: So, you'd like the state to be a *ricotaro?*

NAPOLITANO: No, *ricotaro* is a man. . . .

Here, it might seem as though this were a simple case of an alternate dialect word. But note how, once we move into Neapolitan, it becomes difficult to associate the word relating to a man to the abstract concept of the state.

In a centrally inscribed section of the film, Pasolini implicitly rejects the possibility of ever finding "the Real Italy" by placing a question mark after this intertitle, which marks the section. It is in this central section that Pasolini inserts the interview that presents us with the seamless, "ideal" narrative of national identification. The man interviewed is a Tuscan father with a young son in tow, and the question is whether divorce should be legalized. The Tuscan argues that it should not, because the family is the foundation upon which the moral and civil education of the child rests, and any disruptions of the family will manifest themselves in a weakening of the nation. This, of course, is the characteristic argument of the Right—we see it in the United States today as well—and it was the kind of discourse mobilized by fascism. In this way, Pasolini hints at the continuity between the prewar fascist regime and the postwar Christian Democratic one.

Significantly, Pasolini's ironic search for "the Real Italy" takes him to the beach during the national holidays. This, as we've seen, is exactly how Dino Risi attempts to envision the social totality toward the end of *Il sorpasso*.

Regulating the Body

With the Legge Merlin, we come to the place where the junction between hegemonic discourse and the body produces the most visible rupture. The Legge Merlin closed all the state-run brothels in Italy, including the famous *case chiuse* (alliterative regional slang for Neapolitan houses of prostitution) of Naples. Clearly, this law was a product of the "enlightened" and modernizing discourses that were disseminated, for example, by *L'Espresso*. As Foucault notes, there are three areas that needed to be defined/regulated in the movement from prebourgeois to bourgeois culture: childhood, women, and the family (and by extension, nonprocreative sexualities).[8] In the documentary, a Neapolitan man links the new law with an increase in homosexuality among the young; in fact, what we are seeing is the *emergence* or the "invention" of homosexuality within a Symbolic Order that had hitherto held to more "antique" notions of desire. It is precisely in the discussion of homosexuality that Pasolini is able to bring into focus most clearly the ways that modern discourses were received at the local level, where tradition and resistance asserted themselves in fascinating and improbable ways. In fact, homosexuality in this film can be seen as the strand that interconnects all the other modernizing discourses about the body—from hygiene to prostitution to women's rights. Thus, homosexuality becomes in the film the most interesting site of contestation.

L'Espresso in the early sixties ran several articles attempting to "understand" homosexuality. The national magazine calls homosexuality "certainly one of the arguments of the day," and constructs homosexuality in several ways. First, there is speculation that it is a product of leisure society and the post–economic miracle of Italy. This argument is given relatively little weight. Second, there are discussions of the biological/ psychodynamic issue, which understandably is not resolved. Third, much focus is placed on the issue of therapy, and here (remarkably) the discussion is quite "advanced." The magazine privileges an existential therapist whose therapy is centered on "being in the world," where the idea is to find a way for the patient to live his sexuality in a "nondestructive" (i.e., following the heterosexist models of bourgeois marriage) way. Finally, the article concludes with a doctor's quote that, in the end, Proust understood everything. Here we see the way in which the magazine accommodates the old bourgeois elite in a discourse that reflects mainly the ideas of the new elite.[9]

So far, there is little to surprise us: for as Foucault notes, the bourgeois project is to construct homosexuality as "a personage, a past, a case history, and a childhood."[10] But when we move to the documentary evidence of attitudes in the south of Italy, we begin to see that homosexuality—insofar as it "exists" at all—exists in a radically different way from that constructed by *L'Espresso*. Pasolini interviews a group of young men in a piazza in Catanzaro. Among the group of six or seven men, attitudes toward "inverts" range from pity to disgust. Finally, one of the boys says, "Even though I go with them, it disgusts me." And then his friend says, "I go with them too."

This is quite a remarkable moment in the documentary. Obviously, among these boys there is a concept of "other" being employed, but how this other is defined is completely unclear. The boys are openly frank, among their friends, about their own participation in homosexual acts; what, then, is an "invert"? Perhaps—and this is speculation, for it is not brought out in the documentary—they are operating on a model of active/passive in defining the other: that is to say, the important thing in defining masculinity is the act of insertion, and not the gender of the person receiving. But in any case, the symbolic system they operate in allows for the practice of homosexuality without a concomitant need for definition or medicalization; and the interesting thing about an active/passive binary opposition is the way in which—in the privacy of a sex act—who is to know if one decides to "cross the line"?

In the South, there is a performative view of "sex," as opposed to the essentializing view of the emergent bourgeoisie (and of "modernity" in general). In the scene in Naples mentioned earlier, in which the Neapolitan is arguing against the Legge Merlin because he sees the law as encouraging sexual relations between young men, he says that before, the young men could find sexual outlet for three-hundred lire, whereas now, with prostitution moved to the streets, the cost has risen to three-thousand lire. He then turns to a young man next to him and says, "Tell him about the urinals." The boy then explains that young men spend all day at the urinals, whereupon the older man interrupts and explains that they later spend their "earnings" on the prostitute. Finally, the man pins the problem on the widespread unemployment in Naples.

As the new discourse on sexuality becomes concrete in the form of a law that impinges upon daily life, we can discern specific class and regional effects. The Neapolitan, engaging as he is, leaves us with more questions than answers. Is he implying that those sexual encounters did not go on before the Legge Merlin? Considering the way that young women were traditionally jealously guarded in southern families, sex among young men was rather inevitable and tolerated. Is it possible that the boys could have spent their "earnings" on something other than the prostitutes, having already been sexually satisfied? In any case, homosexuality is here not even mentioned, and the model of sexuality that is put forth is performative. The economic problem—which indeed is real for the young Neapolitan—is, in the discourse of sexuality, the smokescreen behind which the issue of pleasure can be left undecided.

To summarize the various discourses constructed around Italy's economic transformation, we can construct once again a semiotic square, this time around the notion of space, as in the diagram on the next page. The mediatory terms on the left and right present the social contradiction as it showed itself in its most tangible form: Italy, traditionally a "nation" of strongly insulated regions speaking their own dialects, is confronted with a new sense of space brought about by the superhighway ("limited access," of course) engineered by a new technocratic elite speaking a standardized national language (evident in written form in the weekly *L'Espresso*).

The complex and neutral terms (top and bottom) present us with the

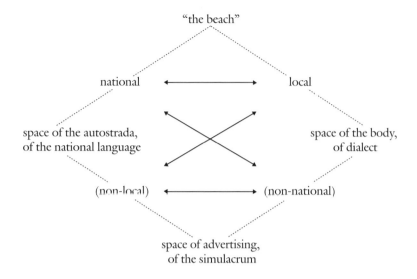

ways in which popular discourses attempted to mediate the contradiction through spatial strategies, but what is highly interesting is the ways in which both these terms contaminate each other. That is to say, the space constructed by advertising was largely nonlocal and nonnational, governed, as we have seen, principally by the forces of transnational capital in the process of consolidating its "third stage." Yet in order to do that, it needed to deploy local places in such a way as to reassure the mobile, consuming subject that s/he was still "Italian." To do this, it deployed the simulacrum, creating out of national places a system of pure signs.

The beach appears in both *Il sorpasso* and *Comizi d'amore,* and in both films, it is the place in which the new social totality is imagined: as a mobile, undifferentiated mass diverting itself in a national ritual of vacation.[11] As a cinematic trope, however, the beach brings with it the image of an "edge," of the place where the nation ends: thus it functions as a kind of limit point, the paradoxical, unsignifying space that allows all the other spaces to form the signifying system. This is why, in both films, there is a sense when we go to the beach on holiday that we are confronting a literally meaningless spectacle; and both films derive their ironic humor from this very idea.

Finally, when Pasolini goes to the beach, it is—as he says in the intertitle—in search of the "real Italy." And what he privileges when he gets there is the narrative of the Tuscan father holding his young son, delivering to Pasolini's camera the traditionalist notion that the state is simply an extension of the family. This discourse is, of course, the fundamental tenet of the fascist, "corporatist" idea of the nation, which Italy had embraced only a few decades before. What Pasolini uncovers, then, is the ghost that haunts any attempted mediation between the national and the local, and which the advertising of the period subtly reinvokes: the ghost of fascism.

Teorema *and the Melodramatic*

By the mid-sixties Pasolini moved beyond the "new neorealist" strategies deployed in his first films (which we see even in *Gospel According to St. Matthew,* with its *verité* stylistic marks clashing with the sacred/mythic character of the text). In the politically explosive climate of 1968, Pasolini made *Teorema* ("Theorem," 1968), a film unique in his oeuvre in that it takes for its subject an upper-bourgeois Milanese family, a terrain more associated with the films of Antonioni and one that Pasolini never explored cinematically outside of this one film.[12] There is yet something else that connects this film to Antonioni's work, and that is the fact that the melodrama is the form that underpins the narrative. We already saw in chapter 2 that the melodramatic is one of the ways to characterize the stain that haunted the neorealist project. Thus, it is not surprising that melodrama would emerge once more in the sixties, as neorealism once again became central to the national cinema. This time, however, the melodramatic is deployed in a more self-conscious and self-critical way.

In *Teorema* this is accomplished by setting up a visual binary opposition that forms a kind of outside to the family melodrama that is the main narrative: these are the recurring shots of the industrialist's factory, shot in washed-out monochrome and (at the film's opening) in a documentary style, and the recurring shots of the volcanic desert (the sulphurous slopes of Mount Etna). This opposition suggests that the purely documentary image is in itself incapable of arriving at truth—and significantly, the images being produced at the beginning of the film are being produced for television, and are thus conceived as being constitutively incapable of moving beyond the "surface" of the news event.[13] Against this stands the image of the purely inorganic, of a space "beyond representation" that emerges as each member of the bourgeois family confronts the *real* of his or her own situation.

The question the film poses is the very pressing (for 1968) question of the embourgeoisement of the working class (and thus the emergence of a consumer culture). What launches this question is a *passage à l'acte*, the industrialist giving his factory to the workers. As it turns out, this paradoxical act has been generated by the family melodrama that is revealed later, a melodrama in which a mysterious visitor enters the bourgeois family and — after having sexual (or perhaps more accurately, "sexualized") encounters with each member (father, mother, son, daughter, maid)—leaves, causing each member of the family to move to some radical limit point: the father, haunted by age and exhaustion, hands his factory over to the workers; the mother, pushed to an icy frigidity by a confining domesticity, begins to cruise the streets in search of anonymous sexual encounters; the son, ill at ease with both his body and his desire, throws himself into the production of action paintings; the daughter, oedipally fixated on her father, falls into repetition compulsion and finally catatonia; the maid, displaced from the preindustrial mode of experience which nevertheless still shapes her consciousness, returns to her village and becomes a saint. Pasolini conceives of this narrative development as a "theorem," the conclusions (the encounters with the Real) deducible from the givens of the family situation.

Mathematically, the theorem is "timeless": it is strictly speaking simultaneous with the premises that always already contain it. The only "time" one encounters in the theorem is the time it takes to demonstrate it, but insofar as the demonstration succeeds, it erases its own temporality. It is the implacable fatality of the theorem that links Pasolini's work to the melodrama, where an unseen set of relations has "already" determined the outcome despite the surface chaos of sudden and arbitrary turns of plot. As Thomas Elsaesser has observed, the family melodramas of the American cinema of the forties and fifties present us with a closed system of relations that come to stand in for "the characteristic attempt of the bourgeois household to make time stand still, immobilize life, and fix forever domestic property relations as the model of social life." [14] He goes on to note how none of the characters is ever up to the tasks that life demands of them in American melodrama. As we've seen, things are different in Pasolini's version of melodrama, where each of the characters moves to a radical passage à l'acte: Pasolini takes the immobilization of the bourgeois family and pushes it to a limit point, the real timelessness of the geologic. Thus, we can conclude that the American melodrama—by severely limiting the scope of action the characters can undertake—ultimately (and symptomatically) fails to articulate a connection between lived experience and conceptual understanding, and that Pasolini takes as his very project the attempt to make this articulation. This, as we saw in chapter 2 in relation to the cinema of Visconti, is the very logic that has connected neorealism to melodrama from the very beginning.

How Pasolini effects this shift is best seen by comparing his visual strategy with that of American melodrama—and indeed, it would be hard to imagine a more dramatic contrast. American melodrama works through a deliriously expressionist mise-en-scène and a highly plastic sense of space. Pasolini's cinematic space—as has been so often noted—is not "dynamic" in the American sense, emphasizing the pictorial frontality of early Renaissance painting. For Pasolini, melodrama's exteriorization of internal conflict is achieved not through excess (or *ululimm*) but through a kind of paring down (or *subtraction*), so that the individual images achieve a singular clarity. But when put together, the images become highly ambiguous, as if somehow the meaning is being carried in the very interstices of the images. We could take just about any sequence for an example: the sequence near the end when the father is in the train station is typical. The father stands in the station holding an open newspaper before him, when he spots a *ragazzo* sitting at a bench along the wall. He stares at the boy; the boy looks back. In response to the father's continued glances, the boy casually moves his legs further apart, revealing more of his crotch. Finally the boy looks at the father, then gets up and walks down the stairway to the men's room. At this point, the father begins "ritually" taking off his clothes; naked he walks through the train station and out of the scene. We can see here how the images fail to "compute," fail to come together in traditional narrative terms. The sequence remains mysterious: Did the boy remind the father of his encounter with the nameless "angel" played by Terence Stamp? Were the boy's gestures deliberate or casual? Did the father at some level desire a homosexual encounter, or did he conceive it to be a dead end? These are the kinds of questions that are generated by each sequence of the film, to the point where any possible meaning is pushed outside the realm of representation itself, which is why Pasolini cuts recurrently to the image of the desert as a kind of "ground zero" of representation.

The notion that there can occur, between shots, an "interval" or "interstice" is one developed by Gilles Deleuze, specifically in relation to what he calls the "modern" cinema emergent in the postwar period,[15] and this prevalence of the interstice is what gives the film its openness toward some not-yet-articulable concept. To understand this, we might go back to the image structure of the classical system; for Deleuze, the

8a–d
Teorema:
the "outside"
between the
images

image structures of the classical cinema are organized—"mechanistically" one might say, in keeping with the cinema's early identity as a machine for the reproduction of motion—around the sensory-motor schema connected to perception and response. This is what binds character, action, and world in the classical cinema, such that the open, the indeterminate, never emerges as an issue; the classical cinema gives us a closed totality. With the modern cinema, we see a breakdown of the sensory-motor schema (or of the relation between perception and response, between cause and effect); concomitant to this, images can now present us with mysterious, unexplainable "gaps," as in the station sequence above.[16] Preliminarily, then, we could say that Deleuze has here ratified our earlier observations on the differences between the classical Hollywood melodrama and Pasolini's: the Hollywood melodrama is still holding to the sensory-motor schema when it is manifestly clear that the very faith in "agency" is what has fallen into crisis and can be redeemed only by some radically new kind of concept. It is this emergence of the new that Pasolini's film is attempting to track.

But if this is so, then the entire concept of the "theorem" as some-

9a–b
Teorema: the father watching the son sleeping with the visitor

thing already contained in the premises needs to be revised. Of course, this last fact is mathematically speaking true; but we *come to know* something to be a theorem only because underneath it lurks what Deleuze calls a "problem." The problem points toward the open, toward the not yet known; it moves us toward the free play of the faculties that Kant noted in relation to the reflective judgment that the work of art (or the sublime encounter) forces upon us.[17] *Teorema,* then, is quite different from Pasolini's other "theorematic" film, *Salò* (1975); the latter, like the Sadean text upon which it is based, presents us with a strictly closed system, a semiotic "prison house" whose various conclusions are given in advance. This is why *Salò* is so relentlessly grim and difficult, while *Teorema* realizes that the semiotic system can be closed only through inclusion of the paradoxical (and phallic) element that doesn't signify. The difference between the closed and the open system is, we will see, going to be a central metaphor in Antonioni's *L'eclisse,* specifically in relation to the stock market.

The train station sequence is important not only in its illustration of a key aesthetic strategy in the film, but also because it reveals how vitally important it was for Pasolini to conceive of homosexuality as primarily an *alterity,* not an identity. This is important not only in order to avoid producing a "vulgar" reading of the film, in which a simple historicism connects the Reichian currents of sexual liberation rife in the late-sixties to the "theme" of the film. In fact—something that Maurizio Viano notes quite well in his analysis of the film—*Teorema* is centered more on the "crisis of the sign" than the crisis of the bourgeois family (though of course the project is to somehow show the inevitable interconnection between the two). For this reason, the camera's lingering on the genitals of the Terence Stamp character throughout the first third of the film is not constructed as a simple representation of sexual desire but as the very center of the crisis underlying all the characters' lives. In this sense, the character of Terence Stamp—who arrives and departs like the an-nunciating angel—is an apparition, is indeed *the phallus* itself. This gives us a way to understand the remarkable charge contained in the shot of Stamp's clothes strewn across the room: especially the unzipped pants that evoke both absence and presence. It is the encounter with "the ab-sent cause" that drives all the characters into positions of radical alterity and that renders any connection to the social impossible.

If in 1964 (in *Comizi*), Pasolini still held to the possibility of the neo-realist idea of the "film inquest," by 1968 it was clear to Pasolini that neo-realism led inexorably to the point of its own failure, at the level of the *ground* upon which the representational system is set. In part this is con-nected to the emergence of the televisual apparatus: for, as we've seen, *Teorema* begins with a "television inquest," which is oxymoronic insofar as television works to construct a completely self-referential system.

Now we have uncovered the most profound connection between *Teorema* and the work of Antonioni in the sixties: both take as their subject matter the problematic of neorealism as it played itself out at a particular historical moment, the moment of the emergence of neo-capitalism in Italy. Significantly, this manifests itself in both directors as an inarticulable limit point, an expression of the "postmodern sublime." Pasolini, of course, was more "brutal" in presenting this point of textual indeterminacy, because of the way he was able to present the body at its most "corporeal." Significantly, *Teorema* ends with the father screaming in the desert: as we shall see in the following chapters, the scream is central also to Antonioni's work, even though Antonioni surrounds it with so much ambiguity that it might not even have been heard.

part III

ANTONIONI AND THE

POSTMODERN SUBLIME

I found myself in that whiteness, in that nothingness, which took shape around a black point.

—MICHELANGELO ANTONIONI

The epigraph is taken from one of Antonioni's "fictions," those very short narratives that he wrote regularly throughout his career and that he considered to be potential "launching points" (*spunti*) for film projects.[1] Some of these have been collected in the book *Quel bowling sul Tevere;* and from reading even a few of the stories, one sees the concern with the enigmatic, the ephemeral, the paradoxical, that carries over into his filmmaking. Antonioni's remark is particularly telling, though: what we see here is precisely a zeroing in upon a stain in the visual field, the awareness of which literally dissolves the object world around it. In this particular story, significantly, the black point is actually a corpse floating in the Tiber; so this stain in the image is connected to a limit point—death, in this case—and thus a dialectic is set up whereby as soon as we focus on the stain, the very "reality" of the visual field fades from us, turns into "nothingness." In Lacanian terms, *meaning* (in this case, the very *form* of the world of objects) is gained only by leaving behind a residue of *being* (of a posited undifferentiated wholeness, before language). This residue takes the form of the stain, the uncanny object "floating" in the visual field, which serves to subjectify our views of the world, to allow us to appropriate it as "ours." In a sense, then, it marks par excellence the narrative moment as such, as sense "congeals" around some point of incomprehension. This procedure of rupturing or decentering the visual field with a stain is central to Antonioni's film work, and it will be the task of this chapter to understand this procedure.

Ultimately, though, Antonioni's work is part of the cultural production coming out of the cinematic legacy of neorealism and the postwar economic transformation of the nation. The fact that Antonioni's work might be crucially connected to the latter phenomenon—Italy's economic miracle—is something rarely dealt with in the critical literature, in large part no doubt because of Antonioni's seeming obsession with the purely formal.[2] But no less than Pasolini, Antonioni concerns himself with the problematic that led neorealism to its impasse in the fifties; he too addresses himself to that which had "stained" the early neorealist project. And the relationship between Antonioni's stained images and the "stain" that blemished neorealism is, it will become clear, not simply a rhetorical one.

Antonioni's relationship to neorealism was long-standing—going back to his work as coscreenwriter for the "protoneorealist" *Un pilota ritorna* ("A Pilot Returns," 1943), and his early documentaries on the people of the Po Valley and the streetsweepers of Rome. But given the cultural politics of postwar Italy, this relationship to neorealism was always strained, criticized from every quarter. Especially among those intellectuals of the Left, neorealism was seen as taking its impetus—not simply from the struggle against fascism, but after fascism's collapse, with the struggle for political and economic transformation in the turbulent years before the triumph of the Christian Democrats in 1948. After that decisive turning point, the Left—now organized in the PCI under Palmiro Togliatti—was frozen out of the national governing coalitions, yet at the same time played a decisive role both in national culture and in local political life.[3] Generally speaking, Italian Marxists in the fifties adopted a rather reductive view of the work of art, almost as if the work of art must wear its *impegno,* its political engagement, as a badge. In this climate, Antonioni's documentary of the people of the Po Valley broke all the rules: we do not see the social and economic interconnections that serve to place the peasants within a historically determined political context. Instead—and alarmingly, for many Italian critics—Antonioni's camera regularly abandons his characters to focus on the ephemeral formal beauties of the River Po and the mists it generates. And indeed, without a deeper consideration of what exactly Antonioni was trying to accomplish, it is easy to see how such meanderings might seem retrograde, even decadent.[4]

Interestingly, many of the criticisms leveled against Antonioni's work of the fifties resemble those leveled against Rossellini's work of the same period, which took a dramatically new turn in his collaborations with Ingrid Bergman. In fact, the terrible critical reception met by *Viaggio in*

Italia (*Voyage to Italy*, 1954) led André Bazin to write an open letter to Guido Aristarco, editor of *Cinema nuovo*, in defense of the film. Because Rossellini's new direction had important ramifications for the realist theories underpinning neorealism, and because his work has important connections to that of Antonioni, it will be instructive to look first at *Viaggio in Italia* and the discourses surrounding it.

Even a casual viewing (if such is possible) of *Viaggio* shows it to presage many of the concerns that would fully emerge in Antonioni's films of the early sixties (especially in the famous "trilogy" and in *Red Desert*). In *Viaggio* we see an attenuation of narrative movement in favor of a more randomly organized series of "observations" of the characters; in addition, we see the centrality of Woman's subjectivity and the impossibility of the sexual relation as major concerns; and finally, in *Viaggio* (as in the other Bergman collaborations), the world is seen through the eyes of the stranger, the cultural outsider. All of these would become equally central to the films of Antonioni (especially from *L'avventura* ("The Affair," 1960) onward). But the Rossellini/Bergman films always culminate in the epiphanic moment[5] that—however ambiguous— serves ultimately as an anchoring point; it is precisely this moment that is rigorously excluded from Antonioni's work.

Viaggio in Italia works by the slow accretion of metaphors; it is as if the object the camera is looking at is always pointing toward something deeper, as if Rossellini (and neorealism itself) is finally opening itself to the question of the status of the photographed object . As the film follows Katherine (Ingrid Bergman) in her wanderings through the environs of Naples, the narrative is always brought to a sudden arrest at precisely the moment when a metaphor is created: when Katherine confronts the dead stares of the antique sculptures of the Museo Nazionale, for example; or when a tour guide ironically shows her how the Saracens would have chained up "a beautiful woman like you"; or when at the Campi Flegrei she witnesses "the mystery of ionization," the smoke induced at one spring suddenly being reproduced at all the surrounding springs. These are all metaphors of interconnectedness—although neither she nor the audience understands them immediately as such—and suggest at once both the transitoriness of human life and a chain of being that persists beyond the merely individual.[6] This is, of course, precisely what is throwing Katherine into crisis, and precisely what will lead her out of crisis. In a sense, *Viaggio* is structured like a psychoanalysis: the narrative is repeatedly arrested by confrontations with purely contingent "scraps of the Real," points at which meaning is occluded and the image becomes mysterious. Retroactively, these scraps acquire meaning through the process of metaphor, but only after a traumatic encounter with the Real.[7] In *Viaggio* this encounter stretches from the unearthing of the plaster casts of the man and woman buried by the eruption of Vesuvius in a death embrace, to the moment when the Neapolitan crowd suddenly carries Katherine away from Alex, her husband, played by George Sanders. In this regard, it is significant to note, in the last sequence of the film (in its extant versions), that "mistakes" of continuity and framing are quite visible. It seems that Rossellini had no coverage with which to get Katherine and Alex back together without a jump cut;[8] and the shadow of the moving camera and crane falls across the crowd after the couple's reconciliation. It is as if the very form of the film is itself exhibiting a breakdown; as if Rossellini, faced with constructing a resolution to this crucial final confrontation with the Real, found himself unable to suitably manipulate cinematic language so as to contain it. Or more precisely: the camera trains its eye upon an "event" transpiring in the world and finds that it can record only its "before" and "after," but not the event itself (in this case, the "miracle"—but is it the lame man walking with crutches held jubilantly above his head? or the sudden turnabout in Katherine and Alex's decision to divorce? or, indeed, some sociocultural transformation that would itself later be dubbed "the (economic) miracle" in popular Italian discourse?). Not only does the event fall between some interstice in the images, but the cinematic apparatus itself contaminates the view of the world, as if to suggest that neorealist practice had arrived at a fundamental limit, that of the imbrication of the eye (and the "I") in the presentation of any visual field. It is thus doubly significant that the film's final crisis begins with the unearthing of the plaster casts of the couple buried by the eruption of Vesuvius: for like the photographic image itself, the plaster casts are indexical signs, the "death masks," as Bazin would put it, of a once living reality.

Now, clearly Rossellini is *not* practicing here the neorealism of *Open City* or *Ladri di biciclette;* and for Marxist critics who saw neorealism as intimately tied not only to nation building but also to social transformation, Rossellini's "metaphysical turn" here seemed nothing less than retrograde. (And this is giving the critics of the Left the benefit of assuming they recognized Rossellini's work for what it was, for there were many who collapsed the complexities of the film into the simplified psychologism of a character study.) But what was crucially important in Rossellini's film was the way in which it addressed the problem of sub-

11a–b
Viaggio in Italia:
the miraculous
reconciliation

ject and object: in *Viaggio,* he takes a culturalist position regarding the object—"Italy"—and a position of more-or-less complete "openness" with respect to the subject—the marriage of Katherine and Alex.[9] And neither subject nor object is fixed: rather, each throws the other into question.

The question of the subject/object relation is—as we saw in chapter 2—one of the ways of articulating the stain that haunted neorealism as it moved into the fifties. Clearly Bazin, in his defense of Rossellini, understood the dimensions of the problem, and so characterized neorealism not by a nominal program—whether nation building or social transformation—but by a methodology. Neorealism, he argued, was preeminently a "way of seeing," which thus precluded—or at least held in suspense—what one would eventually discover about the nature of the object looked at.[10] Bazin's position was thus aesthetic, insofar as it held that the work of art somehow always held a *surplus,* which theory or ideology could only apprise "after the fact," as it were.[11] Bazin's realist theory thus embodied a rather paradoxical position: philosophically,

12a–b
Viaggio in Italia:
the indexical sign
and Bazin's "death
mask"

his thinking was far more advanced than that of "vulgar" Marxists who adopted a programmatic view of the work of art; while it *seemed* to assume that through a "pure" phenomenology of looking, the object could be wrested from its ideological embeddedness (in a kind of "eidetic reduction" accessible through the long take).

It is here that the cinemas of both Pasolini and Antonioni make important advances, and they do this by attempting to work through the paradox at the heart of realist theory, not by abandoning the theory as retrograde. Pasolini's solution was to focus on the cultural embeddedness of both object and subject. In fact, he articulated this position theoretically in his important essay "The Cinema of Poetry." The impetus for the essay was the then emerging semiotic models of cinematic language. For Pasolini, what was missed in the attempt to understand the cinematic image as fundamentally coded was the fact that the cinematic image, unlike the linguistic utterance, by necessity must be forged through a process of *poesis,* a creative act in which the "sign" is constructed through the material of the world but charged with what Pasolini called the oneiric—traces of memory and dream. Thus, for Pasolini, one needn't see "the code" as the only possible site for ideology to come into the text. For both the object world and the memory traces of the subject are always, already traversed by ideology. As for the relationship of this object to the perceiving subject, Pasolini (significantly) uses Antonioni's *Red Desert* (1964) as an example of one possible way of articulating the relationship. Pasolini argues that Antonioni constructs his film through "free indirect discourse," a mode in which the writer (or director) rhetorically assumes the subject position of the character within the diegesis. This is the way in which perceived object and perceiving subject enter into a dialectical relation. Pasolini's only critique of the method was that of the choice of the subjectivity through which to view the world: by choosing "exquisite flowers of the bourgeoisie," Antonioni was then (covertly) free to invest the object world with the ecstatic intensities of poetry.[12] Pasolini was committed instead to selecting as subject the urban subproletarian produced by the economic miracle; one could say that this selection was the fundamental political gesture of Pasolini's work.

It is this free indirect discourse developed by Antonioni in the sixties (mostly with Monica Vitti) that links Antonioni with the experiments of Rossellini in the Bergman films. One of the crucial differences is that while Bergman was literally an "outsider" to Italy, Antonioni's women protagonists were outsiders through alienation and neurosis. By thus situating the woman as a product of the culture she observes, Antonioni asserts an interdependence between perceiving subject and the object of perception. In this way, his approach to the problem confronting the neorealist tradition is like that of Pasolini; but Antonioni takes this interdependence in exactly the opposite direction. Instead of focusing on cultural embeddedness, Antonioni moves toward the seeming detachment of both object and subject from their contexts. For Antonioni, the neorealist problem was best addressed by a "purely" philosophical analysis of the conditions for vision itself.[13] It is as if the problematic of perception—first uncovered by the *political* dimensions of the neorealist project—were taken by Antonioni into the "purely" "superstructural" discourse of epistemology. This is why it was particularly Marxist critics who could not see the value, the potential fruitfulness, of Antonioni's experiments.

Thus, "the object Antonioni" is to be taken in two senses. On the one hand, Antonioni addresses directly the very constitution of the object world the camera registers. And thus—through this very interrogation—Antonioni addresses the issue of the object of the cinematic enterprise itself. It is in this sense that Antonioni's work builds upon and expands realist theory: for Antonioni, the object of the cinema is inextricably bound to the constitution of the object world in relation to the perceiving subject.[14]

The Gaze and the Other

In 1964—the year of the release of *Red Desert,* Antonioni's last great experiment in the free indirect discourse of the Woman-as-subject—Lacan first began to outline a theory of the gaze, in his eleventh seminar, *The Four Fundamental Concepts of Psychoanalysis.* The year 1964 was a watershed year for the dissemination of Lacanian theory throughout the Parisian intellectual elite: Lacan, prohibited from training analysts at Hôpital Saint-Anne because of his excommunication from the International Psychoanalytic Association, was offered a space to lecture at the Ecole Normale Superieur. Abandoning the planned seminar on the Names of the Father, Lacan—realizing his audience represented now a much wider cross-section of disciplines—lectured instead on the "fundamentals." In the middle of this seminar, there emerges—almost as an anomaly—a section comprised of four lectures, grouped under the heading "Of the Gaze as *Objet petit a.*" Lacan himself admits that these lectures were an unanticipated development emerging from some comments he made regarding Maurice Merleau-Ponty's *Le Visible et l'invisible;* in any case, they set forth a theory of the scopic drive whose implications for film theory have yet to be fully mined.

The scopic drive represents one of the (at that time) four fundamental drives of psychoanalytic experience, the other three being the invocatory, the oral, and the anal. One might expect that the analysis of the scopic and invocatory drives would be of great possible relevance to a medium that itself relies on the manipulation of image and sound. In fact, in the final lecture of this seminar, Lacan himself admits of this possibility: "Perhaps the features that appear in our time so strikingly in the form of what are more or less correctly called the *mass media,* perhaps our very relation to the science that ever increasingly invades our field, perhaps all this is illuminated by the reference to those two objects, whose place I have indicated to you in a fundamental tetrad, namely, the voice—partly planetarized, even stratospherized, by our machinery—and the gaze, whose ever-encroaching character is no less suggestive."[15]

Two things are of interest here: one, that the media theory "implicit" in the quote is one in which image and sound would be conceived as two interdependent but separate planes that intersect in various ways through the "machineries"—which we could say comprise not only the technological but the narrative as well—of reproduction; two, that psychoanalysis clearly views representation as thoroughly embedded within an object world connected to a history (i.e., to the material traces left by human actions). Clearly, the "planetarized" voice (and today, the planetarized spectacle) situate both voice and gaze within the field of the Other, within a Symbolic order that preexists subjectivity. And whereas the apparatus theory of the late seventies deployed Lacan only to end up *reducing* the object of study (not simply to the cinema *only,* but to the ideologically charged classical Hollywood cinema), psychoanalysis at least potentially opens up to the consideration of a multiplicity of possible sound/image relations (as their "plane of intersection" is continually modified by technology).

Lacan's theory of the gaze is complicated by the fact that the eye's relationship to the object is, at least on the surface, unlike the relationship between the other liminal zones and their "lost objects." With the oral, anal, and even invocatory drives, we can clearly connect them to specific objects that have fallen away: the breast, the feces, the *sound*. When we think about the scopic, what is its "lost object"? A dimension of self-reflexivity comes into play in the domain of the scopic which is unlike that of the other drives; which leads Lacan to conclude that the gaze is always on the side of the Other, it marks the point where the subject is "looked at" by the Other.

Lacan always insisted that a distinction should be made between "instinct" and "drive," and he would argue that even though Freud may have never formalized the distinction, Freud did not mean the concepts to be interchangeable.[16] In Lacanian theory, while both instinct and drive are governed by the pleasure principle, it is only instinct—that is, the impulsion governed purely by the *needs* of the organism—that produces the "homeostasis" that Freud posited as the ultimate regulatory principle in the organism. Drive, in contrast, is a kind of deformation of the instincts insofar as the instincts enter sexuality—that is, when *want* or *lack* is layered over need. (What the infant needs is nourishment; what the infant lacks is the breast.) It is at this point where confusion often besets the student of Lacan: for isn't lack the signal of *desire*? This confusion is resolved when we realize there are two lacks: the lack belonging to drive, whose dimension is that of the body; and the lack belonging to desire, whose dimension is that of the signifier (or language).[17]

At this point, the question to be asked is, What theoretical function is performed by the concept of drive? Why did Lacan find it necessary to move beyond the signifier, and the desire generated by language? The answer must surely be this: if psychoanalysis is to have any theory of the pre-Oedipal, then it must make this move toward the concept of drive. In the domain of the drive, there is no "subject," but only part-objects, once connected to the body but now irretrievably fallen away. While traditional object-relations theory sees breast, feces, and urine as part-objects, Lacan expands the list to include both voice and gaze (which then correspond to the invocatory and scopic drives, respectively). This is quite a brilliant move: now, the signifier is seen originally as part-object, as pure sound "lost" from the body and invested with jouissance. This is why the master signifier is always nonsensical: it is literally a montage of phonemes.[18] The notion of the gaze-as-object is perhaps one of the most paradoxical and misunderstood of Lacan's ideas. For if the gaze is an object that has "fallen away" from the body, then this can only be experienced as the field of vision *gazing at us*.[19]

Thus, when Lacan constructs a diagram to illustrate the relation of subject to gaze, what we get is a superimposition of two triangles that are mirror images of each other. One of the triangles illustrates the "traditional," Cartesian view of the subject's relation to the visual field: the subject is conceived of as the center, the convergence point, of all of the lines of light that construct the perspective. The other triangle in a sense illustrates the precondition for the "centered" view of vision: for, Lacan remarks, vision cannot be *only* a matter of the geometrical, because the blind are perfectly capable of "seeing" (i.e., conceptually) the idea of geometrical perspective. The aspect of vision left out of the geometrical is precisely the fact that light moves in *all* directions, not just one. It is in this sense that the light, the gaze, must be seen as the precondition for vision: paradoxically, the object gazes at us.

Ultimately, then, the convergence of the lines of light at the geometral point produces a *picture* for the subject; while the gaze—a point within the visual field—spreads out toward the subject, *intersecting the picture* in such a way as to produce in it a "stain." What is at stake here is Lacan's subversion of the notion of a purely "objective" visual field; in the Lacanian scheme, the subject becomes "centered" only insofar as the picture is stained by the eruption within it of the gaze of the Other. Further, Lacanian theory argues that this stain is—as a mark of the Real, of that which has eluded the formation of the object world through the Signifier—not perceptible as such; rather, it functions as a kind of limit point of vision, the point that necessarily makes every view of the world subjective. My visual world achieves consistency only under the gaze of the Other that eludes me.

Žižek shows us how the gaze must be conceived in two radically opposing aspects. That is to say, on the one hand, the gaze is the very precondition for any sort of "reality effect" to take hold; the effect of reality is obtained when the stain, rather than being perceived as such, instead functions as the frame that gives our visual fields consistency. However, there is always the possibility that the stain will become noticed; this is the point when the subject fades, where "reality" gives way to the unconscious within the visual field. This is precisely why the stain is always of the Real; like the symptom, the stain marks an obstacle to, or a limit point of, representation. Now the Real—in the form of the drives, let's say—always manifests itself at the boundary between inside and outside; for example, in the erogenous zones in the case of oral, anal, or invocatory drives.[20] What makes the gaze so paradoxical—to return to the initial point made in our discussion of the drives—is that the inside/outside distinction, insofar as it is the eye that is in question, must be "thrown outside the body." Or, as Lacan himself articulated the paradox: "I am photographed."[21]

While the Lacanian theory of the gaze might seem at first to be too counterintuitive to be of much use, it has—not surprisingly when one thinks about it—significant points of contact with other theories of perception that have been put forward in this century: particularly with those of Henri Bergson, as read by Deleuze. Both Lacan and Bergson insist that—logically prior to perception by a "subject"—light must be conceived as a kind of generalized "radiance" that emerges from all points. In Bergson/Deleuze, subjectivity emerges through a *screening* process, the subject being conceived *as* the set of images that instate a kind of temporal gap between action and reaction, leaving "unperceived" (or unsubjectivized) the infinity of virtually possible images that are "useless" to the potential action of a subject.[22] While there are important differences between the two (Lacan being concerned ultimately with unconscious processes), both posit a kind of generalized gaze that preexists (logically) the subject, and both argue that the subject's perception is not simply "transparent" to the object world but results from a type of screening process. What is important from our point of view in all this is the fact that both Bergson and Lacan are engaged in a *cri-*

tique of a "pure" phenomenology of vision, with its unproblematized notion of intentionality. And insofar as both realist theory and neorealist practice are informed by a kind of phenomenological view of perception, these critiques thus take on great significance when dealing with the issue of the *failure* at a certain level of neorealism and its theoretical underpinnings. Antonioni, then, can be seen as engaged in essentially the same critique, and the question becomes how these various *discourses* (some cinematic) can engage one another.

In Bazin, realist theory offers us a foundational myth, "the myth of total cinema." Its mythic dimension lies in the fact that total cinema would be nothing less than life itself: that is, the dream of the perfectly transparent, unmediated access to the world. And so the cinema is essentially "fallen," ever consigned to approaching (asymptotically, through *style*) that which it can never achieve. This is a Platonic notion, of model and copy; and this notion Bazin must hold to, precisely in order to affirm the logic of the phenomenological reduction, or rather its *wager,* that some sort of transparent relation between subject and object can eventually come about through intentionality.

One of Pasolini's most interesting critiques of the Bazinian position is set forth in his essay "Observations on the Sequence Shot."[23] The essay's occasion is the Zapruder (super-8) footage of the Kennedy assassination. This piece of film—shot as it was from the point of view of the crowd—ought to be an ideal specimen to illustrate the "ontological" status of the photographic image as fingerprint of reality. Instead, of course, it ends up telling us nothing; the film is cited as proof of any and all of the many narratives constructed to explain the assassination. Pasolini then asks us to imagine a scenario in which the event (the assassination) were filmed from all possible points of view. But the resulting "total cinema"—far from opening out on to a transparent, luminous reality as in the Bazinian myth—instead presents us with an infinity of virtual points of view, none of which can be decisive in telling us the truth of the event. We are confronted with a totality that cannot be grasped. And we move from the Platonic regime of model/copy to that of the simulacrum: no longer privileged by its indexical relationship to "reality," the piece of film (the sequence shot) is marked not simply by its limits, but by its essential *pretense* as well.

We could say that here, Pasolini constructs his critique in ways not dissimilar to that of the psychoanalytic model of the gaze. First, Pasolini argues for a radical expansion of the regime of images—images unbound to any particular subjectivity—as a logical starting point for analyzing the cinema as "mimesis."[24] Vision is located first of all on the side of the Other—it is significant here that when Pasolini ascribes (conjecturally) some agency to the production of all of these "ur-films," he invokes the FBI, that is, the Other as agency of the Law. And what event is the all-seeing Other "covering" here, if not the murder of the primal father?

Pasolini then proceeds to argue that it is precisely *montage* that can bring meaning to the totality of possible images. But once again, Pasolini's language and his metaphors are startling: montage is to the individual film what death is to the individual life. At the more obvious level, we can interpret this analogy to mean that the narrativization of an event through editing retroactively fixes its meaning, much as the Lacanian point de capiton fixes the meaning of any particular signifying chain. But on another level, we can look at the analogy from "this side" of death, that is, from the point before any final meaning is fixed. In this way, the dimension of contingency is introduced into the picture: for if the individual life's meaning can be fixed only at death, it is because life is lived in the dimension of freedom and not simply within determinate causal chains.[25] A paradox is thus produced around the notion of montage. Insofar as it organizes the views of the Other, it produces "dead meaning." Yet looked at in the process of its unfolding, montage holds out the promise of creating new meaning. Recalling the earlier discussion of Rossellini, we could say that *Viaggio in Italia* illustrates this paradox avant la lettre. With *Viaggio,* Rossellini relies almost exclusively on the shot-reverse shot to construct many of the key sequences, a use of montage that in itself seems to contradict the very basis of neorealist aesthetics. What keeps it within that neorealist tradition is the way in which Rossellini gives equal weight to both terms of the "field"/"reverse field," rather than hinging the world viewed to the "apetite" of a subjective eye. As we've seen, Rossellini then uses this montage to build metaphors in a process of slow accretion of detail; and in a sense, the inability of the framing and editing to "catch" the ending "event" of the film in itself testifies to the dimension of freedom that Rossellini takes as his very subject.

Antonioni's work of the sixties can thus be seen in the context of two larger intellectual currents: one, an interrogation of the phenomenological model of perception (within both psychoanalysis and philosophy generally; but also in relation to an invention—the cinema—that itself affected the dimensions of the question in this century); and two, the rethinking of a specifically national cinematic tradition in light of pressing historical circumstances. This chapter and the next one look at three films of the period: *L'eclisse* ("The Eclipse," 1962), *Red Desert* (1964), and *Blow-up* (1967). The rest of this chapter is a reading of the first and last of these films in relation to vision and the gaze, while chapter 7 focuses more exclusively on *Red Desert,* with the goal of situating Antonioni's aesthetic more fully within the historical context of the economic miracle.

Blow-up *and the Gaze*

It might seem an anomaly to begin our study of Antonioni's work of the sixties with the relatively late *Blow-up,* a film that in addition marks several breaks in Antonioni's work: he moves away from the woman protagonist central to his preceding four films, and he moves for the first time outside of Italy. But *Blow-up* takes as its very subject matter the relationship of the photographed image to the world it registers, and so in this sense it is an ideal starting point for an examination of the way in which the gaze operates in Antonioni's work.

Interestingly, part of the "popular-critical" discourses surrounding the release of the film in 1968 (at least in the United States) was that the film presented us with a portrait of the "swinging mod scene" in London; in other words, the film was seen as making claims to a certain kind of social truth value. Indeed, this latter was what allowed some critics to protest that Antonioni's picture of the mod scene—the "pot parties," the rock scene, and so on—was unconvincing. But as usual with Antonioni, the historical distance we have now allows us to see that Antonioni's interest was not in naturalistic truth but in structural truth: his project was to investigate the newly emergent culture of image production and explore its connection to what was quickly becoming a new international style, namely, "pop." By 1967, this style had taken on myriad forms, ranging from Andy Warhol and Carnaby Street fashion to the aesthetics of Richard Lester's Beatles films and the vogue for "playboy-spy" films and television series (whether James Bond or *The Avengers*). Ultimately, *Blow-up*'s brilliance comes out of its uniquely hybrid position: where the "Italian question" of the indexicality of the image—having been taken to its limit by the Italian cinematic tradition—now is brought to bear on a new, commodified image, and the resulting subjectivities that emerge from such an image culture.

Throughout the film, Antonioni presents us with two different, conflicting yet mutually contaminated "regimes of the image"—the "documentary" and the "manipulated" (or formalist; represented, for example, by the images produced for purposes of fashion and advertising). And these two regimes are connected—as intimated above in the reference to the phenomenon of "pop"—to the profound changes in social and economic organization that marked global capitalism in its postwar reorganization. In *Blow-up,* this shift from an economy of production to an economy of consumption is marked clearly in the juxtaposition of images that immediately open the film (after the important credit sequence). First we see a group of mimes aimlessly cruising London, and embodying a spirit of careless play and a renunciation of the work ethic. Then there is an abrupt cut to a shot of tired and dirty workers leaving a factory, in what is clearly an invocation of the Lumière *actualité* that—like his other short documents of everyday Parisian life at the turn of the century—indicates the realist impulse at the heart of the cinema's invention. The abruptness of the cut is made more jarring by the formal similarities between the shots: compositionally, both are boxed in by the geometries of the architecture; tonally, both employ the same limited, almost monochromatic palette of bluish-gray hues. The social question thus posed by this opening is, how are we to articulate the connection between these two radically different visions of life within the same social order? Is such a connection possible?

Blow-up's central narrative line, however, runs between these two series of images, between the fashion photographs that the photographer Thomas (David Hemmings) orchestrates and the documentary images that he furtively steals, camera hidden in a brown paper bag. Waiting for the proprietor of an antique store to return, the photographer takes his camera to the neighboring park and begins snapping photos; for the first time, we see him giving up his aesthetic control and giving himself

13
Blow-up and
Lumière's *Workers
Leaving the Factory*

over to a spontaneity that could conceivably turn the camera into a transparent window between him and the world. When he snaps photos of an older man and a woman—Jane (Vanessa Redgrave)—apparently engaged in a romantic tryst in the park, the woman, noticing him, becomes quite agitated and asks him for the roll of film. She later turns up at his apartment/studio, offering herself in exchange for the photos by removing her blouse and exposing her breasts. The sequence is elliptical: we are not certain whether or not they have sex. But the photographer gives her a different roll of film, and, his interest now heightened, he begins to develop the roll after she leaves. As he looks at the prints, he notices in one a shocked look in the woman's eyes. But what is she seeing? The most logical answer is that she has noticed *him,* the photographer spying on the tryst, but he places the glance toward the fence that runs through the background. Then, in another photo, he notices a strange glint of light from behind the fence, which when blown up begins to take on the contours of a gun. Because of the graininess of the blown-up image, however, what appears as the phallic object is at the same time somewhat "detumescent," and we are faced with an anamorphic distortion within the image.

This scene is usually talked about in terms of the technical paradox that lies at the heart of it: that is, the built-in "uncertainty principle" that renders the blow-ups more and more unreadable. But there is yet another self-reflexive dimension to the scene, namely, the photographer's attempt to *construct a narrative space.* Not only that: he is attempting to construct a classical ("Hollywood") narrative space in which his own enunciative position is effaced—that is to say, it cannot possibly be *him* the woman is looking at. In what is surely a wry joke on Antonioni's part, the photographer uses the 90-degree angle formed by two walls to construct an eyeline match between the woman's glance and the "gun" behind the fence. The entire scene of developing the blow-ups climaxes with the construction of a cinematic sequence—the entire screen gives itself over to the photographs, edited so as to construct the story (and the narrative space) of a man's murder in the park.

The psychoanalytic theory of the gaze adds yet another interpretive level to the entire scene. For we note that it is initially the stain, the iridescent flash of light along the fence, that drives the photographer to construct a coherence around what would otherwise be a random series of shots. This is in perfect accord with Lacan's notion that the stain is the placeholder of the subject's unconscious desire; and that it is precisely this unconscious desire that organizes all the visual fields in such a way as to subjectivize them. In this case the desire is clearly Oedipal: it begins with the primal scene of the photographer spying on the amorous couple, moves through the seductive relationship with the woman (whose sexual dimension is given only through the breast), and culminates in the "murder of the father." And if it might be objected that the emergence of the Oedipal here is somewhat of a contrivance, we will see in the next chapter that, on the contrary, it is of central importance to the film's engagement with history. But that aside, the Oedipal dimension to the scene is reinforced also by our earlier discussion of the way the gaze functions to textualize the visual field. That is, what the stain does here is to introduce the crucial *third term* into the subject/object relation, the term required for any Symbolic (i.e., intercommunicative) order to establish itself.

In fact, one of the curious series of details that runs as a motif through the film is that of the partial (or "lost") object: in particular, the propeller found at the antique store, the hand-held placard a demonstrator puts into the back seat of the photographer's convertible, and the broken guitar neck tossed into the crowd at a rock club. What is interesting in the case of the last two objects is the fact that they acquire their "meaning" (or really, their "density," or "exchange value") only within a very particularized, subcultural Symbolic system. Lacanian theory holds that the circulation of meaning depends upon just such a phantasmatic piece of the Real; and when that piece is wrested out of its context, the sublime object becomes the "gift of shit." [26] Within the rock club, the piece of the guitar is fought over by everyone; once outside the club, it becomes literally a piece of garbage on the street. Something similar happens with the placard: within the context of the demonstration, the placard is invested with a certain "energy" (and despite the insipidity of the signifiers written thereon—some placards saying simply "No! No! No!" and the one placed in his car bearing the inscription "Go Away!"); but the placard blows out of the car and onto the street where it is run over by traffic. Both of these part-objects speak of the fragmentation of the social fabric into postmodern subcultures whose relationships to one another can only be antagonistic. The propeller presents us with a new twist on the object: for the propeller has no context in which it really functions—that's why it's in an antique shop. The propeller, rather, marks a piece of history that—within the context of a new or transformed object world—has been irrevocably lost, which can be approached only through an aestheticized nostalgia. Interestingly, then, it is the very delivery of the propeller to the artist's atelier that interrupts the liaison between the woman and the photographer. Presumably, the body of the plane from which the propeller was taken has long since "died," but the useless, severed propeller—shiny and fetishized—still has the power to prevent the incestuous relationship.

The film's final sequence presents us with the final ironic twist on the object as guarantor of the Symbolic order, for in this sequence the object is nonexistent. The mimes seen at the film's opening have reappeared, and the photographer watches as two of them go into a tennis court and mime a game of tennis. One of the players lobs the nonexistent ball over the fence and into the lawn; the mime then "asks" the photographer to get it. The photographer walks to a spot on the lawn, picks up an imaginary ball, and tosses it off-screen, back onto the tennis court. He stands against the lawn in an overhead long shot; from off-screen, we now hear the *sound* of the nonexistent tennis ball in play on the court. The photographer then fades out of the image, leaving only the "background" of the lawn.

It might seem that this final sequence allegorizes the function of the object in producing the social consensus, precisely by making the object invisible.[27] Yet the film complicates the issue, not only through the addition of sound, but with the fading of the subject himself. For it is quite reasonable to argue that the mimes—insofar as they place themselves outside of speech—occupy a psychotic position in relation to the Symbolic order. Here, it is useful to observe that the opening and closing shots of the film are virtually mirror images: both present us with an undifferentiated background, and in the opening shot, the film's title pops on in block letters, *within which* we can see images of a possible "real world." The credit sequence, then, announces that the figure emerges from the ground precisely through the agency of the signifier. It is this, the signifier, that is foreclosed from the final sequence. The agency of the "reality effect" is displaced from image to sound, but this is not enough to ground either the image or the subject.

In fact, as Marsha Kinder has noted, the entire structure of *Blow-up* is constructed around this process of doubling or mirroring,[28] so that the effect is to fold the entire film in upon itself. The result is a kind of structural palindrome, which, insofar as it undermines our bearings, functions as the narrative complement to Antonioni's visual obsession with abstract expressionism—its complement, but not its equivalent, for in the great works of abstract expressionism, the problematization of the figure/ground relation (at least for high modernist commentators on the movement like Clement Greenberg) moves us toward a visual sublime, a kind of opticality (or "light") that precedes form itself, while in *Blow-up,* this modernist (or "dynamical") sublime will give way to a sublime that must be characterized as postmodern (or "mathematical"), one that overwhelms by numbers, sequencing, simulation. In *Blow-up,* significantly, the painter friend of Thomas is at work on an expressionist canvas; it lies horizontally on the floor of the painter's apartment and is a composition consisting of what appear to be droplets of paint allowed to fall on the canvas. The friend (Bill) indicates to Thomas that each of his paintings is a leap into the unknown, that only later does he find something in the painting to—as he puts it—"hang on to," and likens the whole process to a detective story. Bill then says regarding the painting on the floor that he doesn't yet know what that one is all about, and refuses to sell it when Thomas asks to buy it. Later in the film, Thomas walks across the courtyard to Bill's apartment and ends up watching through an open doorway Bill and his girlfriend making love, which is followed by an enigmatic cut to a pan across the painting on the floor. The girlfriend then comes to Thomas's studio to find out what he wanted, and when Thomas shows her the blow-up of the presumed corpse of the man murdered in the park, the woman notes that it looks like one of Bill's paintings.

Two things are worth noting about these (rather mysterious) "bits" in the film, the first being the way in which the principle of doubling or mirroring occurs with the most minute (or offhand) details of the film. For the painter Bill, the detective story is a metaphor for a modernist conception of art as a process of (self-) analysis; correlatively, Thomas's photographs throw him into what becomes a literal detective story, but only after the photographs have been blown up to the point where they resemble the canvas of the drip painting. And once again, just as in the park, Thomas finds himself arrested by a primal scene: in the later scene, the painter's girlfriend looks up from underneath Bill's "thrusting body" and releases a hand gesture and a facial expression that are strictly un-readable. Is she shocked at the intruding gaze? (It seems unlikely, given the casualness and rapidity with which she shows up at Thomas's place in the next scene.) Or is she experiencing something intolerable in her relationship with Bill? (This possibility is hinted at when she proffers and then retracts an attempted confidence to Thomas, the subject of which is never articulated.) In any case, her unreadable shock must be seen as correlative to that of the Vanessa Redgrave character in the park, a repetition that should have announced to Thomas the folly of his "ob-

14a–b
Blow-up: the
repetition of the
woman's look

servation," but which cannot, precisely because it is inscribed within a
larger repetition of the Oedipal scenario Thomas is locked into.

But more important is the way in which this procedure of doubling
renders problematic any notion of origin or authenticity: so that when
the photographic apparatus comes closest to what Fredric Jameson astutely identifies as the Heideggerian "clearing"—namely, the park[29]—
its claim to truth literally falls to "bits," as the blow-ups reveal more and
more of their digitality. This is why the London mod scene—and the
phenomenon of "pop" more generally—is central to the film's historicity, that is, to the very way the film embodies an historical moment.
For, speaking in the most general terms, the pop aesthetic—from Andy
Warhol to James Bond—is very much about the object's relationship to
its packaging, which now takes on the valences of what in philosophical
discourse would have been termed "Schein." But of course now, the
object's "Schein" or appearance can no longer be conceived as one or
another local manifestation of some more primal essence, but instead as

being in some fundamental way empty, ready to be charged with a purely phantasmatic significance. This is clearly what lies behind one of the staple tropes of the sixties spy genre, the presentation of a panoply of everyday commodities that are "actually" lethal weapons—like the chapeau in *From Russia with Love,* which is actually a decapitating boomerang. (From this, one could argue that the formula of the James Bond film is quite simple: a number of such commodities are presented and explained to Bond and the audience, and the narrative proceeds to "use them up," ending when the last [and most sophisticated] has been deployed.) The commodity thus derives meaning insofar as it becomes part of a combinatoire governed by fashion driven phantasy: the question posed to the object (or the image of the object) is no longer "What is it?" but rather "What does it go with?" This is the logic underlying Baudrillard's argument that, in the age of the simulacrum, the subject must be conceived as a kind of trajectory over the surface of a commodity-map:[30] something subsequently validated by new information technologies, where the subject is positioned by the itineraries of his or her "surfing." Ultimately, then, it is this historical shift—with all its implications both for the "World" and for the subject living in the world—that Antonioni manages to register in *Blow-up.*

The Gaze and the Limit

Blow-up, then, deploys the gaze in order to stage its allegory of the triumph of the simulacrum: the image can no longer function as guarantor of the referent, but rather hides within itself a lethal jouissance that always threatens the subject with disappearance. But if *Blow-up* presents us with Antonioni's most developed critique of the indexical, his two preceding films—*L'eclisse* and *Red Desert*—reveal the way the gaze-as-object begins to occupy the central place in his work.

L'eclisse begins near dawn in an apartment in EUR outside Rome, as Vittoria (Monica Vitti) breaks off a love affair at the end of an apparent "dark night of the soul," the lovers having been locked together in the apartment all night. Vittoria eventually begins an affair with another man, Piero, a young stock trader on the Rome stock exchange. Near the end of the film, they decide to meet later in the day at an intersection in the EUR district, a place where they had dallied earlier in the film. The film ends with the camera arriving at the designated meeting place, only to record that the two lovers do not arrive. This evacuation of the char-

15a–b
L'eclisse: the drapes
and the stain

acters from the narrative is accompanied by several allusions to the sublime: the possibility of nuclear annihilation, and the possibility of a literal (solar) eclipse.

Antonioni can be said to push to the limit the "arresting" quality of the Italian urban space—but with the result that the seductive quality of the space is shown to be a "framing effect." In the large body of critical work on Antonioni, the most often noted marks of his authorship are, first, the primacy of framing; second, *temps mort,* the presence of the space both before and after the action of the scene; third, repeated views of an object.[31] All of these techniques take to an extreme what we've already noted to be a central feature of neorealism: namely, the detachment of space from a strict enchainment to narrative (and its desire). But given our discussion of the gaze, it can be argued that all the above stylistic strategies can be subsumed under a larger strategy, to destabilize the entire visual field through the introduction within the field of the stain that makes visible the point of the gaze. This is most clearly seen in the twelfth shot of the opening sequence: Vittoria, on the sofa, turns around to the closed drapes behind her and, using her hand to separate the drapes, peeks out briefly. She then lets go of the drape and turns back to the room, but the drape fails to close entirely. For several shots following that one (and until Vittoria opens the drapes completely), the visual field is "marred" by the stain of the oddly shaped spot where the drapery has failed to close.

The apartment presents us with a riot of frames: doors, windows, mirrors, framed pictures. In the third shot of the opening sequence, Vittoria holds up an empty picture frame on the coffee table and rearranges objects within the frame she is looking through. The oddness of this shot lies in the way it self-consciously exhibits the strategy of free-indirect discourse, through a process that Angela Dalle Vacche calls "ventriloquism"[32]—that is to say, Antonioni has Vittoria mimic his framing strategy, but only partially, in that she is unable to conceive of moving the frame itself. Besides the framing, this opening sequence abounds as well in deceptive point-of-view shots: a character looks, and then we cut to a shot that seems to be the point-of-view, only to be forced to revise our reading when the character enters the frame. In this way, Antonioni foregrounds the fact that the camera's gaze is the gaze of the Other; Antonioni detaches the gaze from its (misrecognized) source in the subject, and locates it back on the side of the object.[33] The characters thus seem imprisoned by a gaze whose question they (and we) do not understand. In this regard, we might look at the extraordinary use of windows in the sequence. Through most of the sequence, the drapes on the two main windows are closed; however, a gap, an opening, is introduced into each set of drapes. At the window behind Riccardo, we note that there is a strip of light at the point where the drapes don't quite meet. At the other window (as noted above), Vittoria moves aside a panel in order to peek out, and when she moves away, the drapery doesn't fall back into place, but leaves instead a "hole" in the field. These strange "holes" in the space could be said to embody

16
L'eclisse: unveiling
the tower

the point at which the Other gazes upon the scene. When Vittoria opens the drapes behind Riccardo, the screen becomes the frame for a view of a strange, mushroom-cloud-shaped water tower. The positioning of the back of Vittoria's head at the lower right of the composition does not attach the "picture" to her point of view; rather, it illustrates the way the subject is *extracted* from the picture, is constituted by a gaze of the Other.

This inability to understand the question of the Other is, I think, directly related to the emergence of the view of the city as a set of arbitrary, contingent connections (as exemplified in the image of the intersection at EUR). The telephone, a recurring motif in the film, testifies to the new conception of space as a grid of networks; Piero is a stockbroker who is totally dependent upon being "plugged in" to an abstract network that no one seems to understand. At one point, when Vittoria hints that Piero spent an evening with a prostitute, she uses the slang word *squilla,* which is derived from *squillo,* the ring of the telephone. Piero jokes that *he* is the squilla, and a few scenes later, we see Piero in his study, as one by one the phones begin to ring, calling him back to work.

In *L'eclisse,* we see articulated for the first time in Antonioni's work the center/periphery problem: the film's action is divided between EUR and the city center. Significantly, though, EUR is the primary space of the film. Unlike most of the peripheral areas of the city, EUR is not populated by the underclass; it is a chic address to have. But EUR is (and this is repeated often enough to have become a cliché) a dehumanizing space: the city mimics imperial forms from the gaze of fascism, so that the harmony and proportion are completely self-referential, and position the spectator of the space as a member of the anonymous fascist crowd. In *L'eclisse,* we get views of the monumental center of EUR only from a distance; the action is set in the residential buildings that fan out from the center. And, of course, the key space is the famous traffic intersection with the zebra-striped crossing. Here, public space is seen as purely contingent—an arbitrary "connection" between two roads, which takes on more and more resonance as we move through the film, as all connections come to seem arbitrary. When *L'eclisse* moves into the old city, Antonioni's framing strategies stay the same: in this way, the autonomy of the space—which in earlier neorealist films was still linked to some myth of community, of the public sphere—now subverts that myth. The framing of EUR "contaminates" the central city, severing the space from its "seductive" depth. Space, then, is seen as an interaction between *subject* and surroundings, so that the dislocation of the subject makes it impossible for the space to provide the integrated subject positions of the past.

The above, sketchily preliminary observations about *L'eclisse* can be summarized in two overarching observations: one, that the film posits a gaze that exists on the "far side" of the visual field presented; and two, that this eruption of the gaze is in some way related to the disruptions of stable subject positions within the world of the film. The question then arises, how might these observations move us toward a new understanding of Antonioni's work in this period? Hal Foster has noted (in an article about contemporary art and its relationship to the gaze) that "in contemporary art and theory, let alone in contemporary fiction and film, there is a general shift in conceptions of the real: from the real understood as an effect of representation to the real understood as an event of trauma."[34] It is precisely this move toward the unrepresentable—whether conceived as traumatic, or sublime, or both—that allows the gaze to erupt into the field of visuality. Foster begins his essay by performing "yet another resumé" of Lacan's seminars on the gaze; arguing yet again that the gaze must be conceived as located in the world, and the subject as the effect of a screening process. What Foster brings to the discussion that is new—and immediately relevant to the issue of Antonioni—is the question of representation, and by extension, of realism. For Foster interprets the screen as being constituted by the codes and conventions of representation (or "the cultural reserve"):[35] those formations which indeed serve to protect us from the threat of an intrusive, threatening gaze, preserving for us the "reality effect" of the visual field. Finally, Foster observes that in postmodern visual art of the eighties and nineties—Cindy Sherman, Andres Serrano, and others—the cultural reserve that allows us to "screen out" the threatening gaze no longer holds, and the visual artists in a sense "tear at the screen," moving either toward a transfixing sublime or—more often—the frightening formlessness of the Thing itself.

Why this should be the case is something critical theory is only beginning to understand; but for this very reason, it attests to the importance of a figure like Antonioni, whose work of the sixties presages this development. As I have argued earlier in the chapter, what led Antonioni to "the gaze"—that is, to the limits of representability—was his interrogation of the phenomenological underpinnings of neorealist aesthetic practice. In *L'eclisse,* this is fundamentally experienced as a sublime event: from the film's very title, suggesting as it does not only the sublime of nature but also the unthinkable catastrophe of technology, all the way to the film's climactic sequences, in which we are brought to the site of a radical disappearance. But intimations of the sublime run through the entire film: most centrally, in the conversation between Vittoria and Piero after the disastrous stock market crash. Vittoria asks, "Where does the money go when the market crashes?"—and in one quick utterance, Antonioni has created an analogon to the economic miracle itself: that is, the paradoxical "event" that is only visible through its traumatic effects.[36] While Piero—perfectly naturally, of course—can do nothing but shrug his shoulders in response to such a "naive" question, one could say that there is in fact a way to address it: the question is paradoxical only because it assumes the stock market is a "closed system," when in fact it is an open system. But then we could say that Antonioni has constructed with this utterance not just an analogon to the economic miracle, but to his own cinematic practice as well: where narrative closure is resolutely denied, in favor of an "openness" that attempts to register the emergence of some new thing, new emotion, new mode of being.[37]

Throughout *L'eclisse,* Antonioni constructs images in which there is a kind of give and take between the natural world and the built world: when, for example, Vittoria runs out into the night to look for the runaway dog in the deserted spaces of the urban periphery, and the street lamps suggest a canopy of stars, or the strange metal poles suggest a line of trees. But it would be an oversimplification to take these images as "metaphors"; rather, as Deleuze would put it, they open up to an indeterminacy which initiates a process of thinking.[38] It is precisely for this reason that Antonioni could describe his work as "experiments," in which place, perception, and affect engage in a kind of free play,[39] where what is at stake is nothing less than the discovery of some entirely new subjectivity, one more in sync with the transformed world. "Eros is sick," Antonioni said in a much-quoted statement; but his project is much more positive than the description of alienation or malaise.

The recognition of the positive, experimental qualities of Antonioni's work is one of the great strengths of a recent new reading of Antonioni by Kevin Moore.[40] Moore especially singles out *L'eclisse* from the trilogy, arguing that Vittoria's willingness to take risks, to try on new modes of being, makes her rather unique among Antonioni's characters in this period. As evidence of this, Moore notes Vittoria's unwillingness—in the film's opening moments—to settle for a conventional, convenient love relationship, even though she has no words to articulate

17a–b
L'eclisse: dialectical interchange between nature and World

what might be missing, what needs to be discovered; just as she throws herself into a casual relationship with Piero—a man who, as I noted earlier in the discussion of the telephones and the allusions to call girls, has clearly escaped from the rigid masculinity of the past—as a way to arrive at some new accomodation between the affective life and the historical world. There are other scenes in which this character trait of Vittoria is evident: most especially, the scene in her neighbor Marta's apartment, where, surrounded by African photographs and artifacts, Vittoria blackens her face and "goes African" when a recording of tribal drumming is put on the stereo. With a mise-en-scène abounding in indexical signs of "Africa," the sequence can be understood as a continuation of Antonioni's critique of the ontological grounding of such signs: once wrested from the life-world in which they are embedded, these artifacts and photographic views cannot be reassembled in any meaningful way. They exist only as the "loot" of an acquisitive, colonialist gaze.

But Vittoria's performance reveals that she is engaged in a kind of mimicry, an attempt to escape the terrors of the gaze by refashioning the self in such a way that image and ground become indistinct. She cannot succeed at this point, because the space of the apartment is not a world but a museum. But this absorption of figure into ground—accomplished in *Blow-up* so suddenly through a single camera trick at the end—is also where *L'eclisse* is heading: for after having laid out an entire zone in the periphery of Rome (a construction site, significantly) as the privileged site for Vittoria and Piero's novel relationship ("We're halfway there," she says as they cross the zebra stripes), the film ends with the "disappearance" of both characters. The camera returns to the site where the lovers had planned to meet, only to record a series of views—some of them repetitions from the earlier sequence—charged with strange affect.

Here we have a culminating instance of the sublime that the film has evoked in various ways since its beginning; we have as well a detachment of the gaze from any possible subjective point of view, becoming finally a kind of pure surveillance that the mysteriously cracked drapes of the first scene already hinted at. But we cannot—as Kevin Moore does—enchain our interpretation of these purely formal developments strictly to the characters. Because Moore is invested in making the claim that Antonioni's method is fundamentally empiricist, he argues—quite cleverly, to be sure—that Vittoria ("Victory") has finally achieved an accord with the new world, such that she has literally transcended it, left it (and us) behind. But turning the film into an allegory of self-actualization misses precisely the fact that what is going on on the "other side of the image" is central to the film's project from the very beginning, and not simply when Vittoria has disappeared into it. If, however, we look at the optimistic interpretation of the ending as a fantasy—as one plausible interpretation generated by a highly ambiguous text—then we can arrive at the following, rather startling conclusion: that the film's final sequences enacts the same dynamic of disclosure and veiling as does Heidegger's "approach to Being." If Vittoria is finally "victorious" in escaping the confines of any preestablished frames of reference—as her manipulation of objects in a frame in the film's opening scene suggests is her desire—then she succeeds at the cost of her disappearance, a disappearance about which we know nothing and can in no way characterize in the evolutionary terms of empiricism.[41]

One of Lacan's sources for his seminar on the gaze, Roger Caillois, argued that when the relation of space to organism took on the dynamic of mimicry, this relation suggested a kind of death drive, an irruption into the world of the Real very much akin to the experience of the schizophrenic: "To these dispossessed souls, space seems to be a devouring force. Space pursues them, encircles them, digests them. . . .

[H]e invents spaces of which he is 'the convulsive possession.'"[42] Vittoria is arguably one of these souls, having been "devoured by the gaze,"[43] the same gaze that erupts within the spaces Antonioni films, investing his images with the "schizoid" intensities so often associated with postmodernity. This aesthetic, first fully elaborated in *L'eclisse*, will play a dominant role in his next film, *Red Desert*.

*When everything has been
said, when the main scene
seems over, there is what
comes afterwards.*

—MICHELANGELO
ANTONIONI

*To think the disaster . . . is
to have no longer any future
in which to think it.*

—MAURICE BLANCHOT

 THE SUBLIME AND THE DISASTER

In "Tentato suicidio," Antonioni's episode in the omnibus film *Amore
in città* (*Love in the City,* 1953), there is a remarkable moment of temporal
dislocation.[1] The woman we are following, now alone in her apartment,
gets a razor blade, lies on the bed, and prepares—we presume—to slit
her wrists. When the camera cuts to a close-up of the forearms and
hands, she turns the underside of her wrist to the camera to reveal the
scar of a suicide attempt that had already occurred. In one shot, we
move from the immediacy of an anticipated future event to the "scar"
of the already past. In the face of the suicide attempt—of the act that
transpires at the level of the Real—time "turns in on itself," so that the
event and its remembering have exactly the same status: the only material thing we have is the scar, itself a concealment of the inside of
the body.

Antonioni's temporal disruptions—which ultimately must be seen as
disruptions of narrative, causality, and the linearity of history—are central to all his work, though these disruptions take different forms from
Il grido ("The Outcry," 1957) to *The Passenger* (1975). In the latter film,
we come closest to the type of dislocation we saw in "Tentato suicidio":
when David Locke (Jack Nicholson) is in the hotel room after the gun-
runner has died, a shot suddenly shows the two of them having a con-

versation on the balcony outside the room. Then, a simple camera movement reveals that Nicholson is listening to a tape recording of the conversation that took place the day before. In *L'avventura,* the disappearance of Anna (early in the film) creates in a more subtle way a similar temporal disruption: for the subsequent narrative falls under the shadow of an indeterminacy that renders the "before" and the "after" problematic. *Il grido* is constructed as a near-perfect narrative circle: at the beginning of the film, Aldo descends the phallic tower to begin his vague wanderings through the squalid countryside of the Po Valley, only to end up returning (almost somnambulistically) to the place where he started, climbing back up the tower. The only "forward movement" in the film is Aldo's ambiguous fall/jump from the tower, which provokes Irma's "cry" or scream, which the title promised us. And both the fall and the cry represent limit states, points of indeterminacy.

Interestingly, the temporal disruptions of *Il grido* and *The Passenger* are both specifically linked to a phenomenon of sound and voice: the tape recorder, the scream. Sound, in fact, has a critical function in Antonioni's cinema, one that has been largely neglected in the study of his work. As an example, we can take the final sequences of *Il grido.* When Aldo finally returns to his town after his wanderings, the soundtrack gives us two other types of "outcry" before Irma's final scream: one, the cry of a baby, seen through the window as Aldo passes Irma's house; and two, the various cries of the townspeople who are engaged in a resistance to the (national) plan to raze part of the town to build an airport. The voices here present us with a radical ambiguity: on the one hand, voice marks the point at which historicity emerges in the text (in this case, the economic miracle as seen only by a disastrous and incomprehensible local effect: the airport); on the other hand, the very diffuseness of the cries (which are mostly off-screen) renders them almost as unfathomable as the infant's cry. To put it another way, the film's very title sets up the anticipation, not only of an outcry, but one that functions as a point de capiton, something that will enable us to pin down meaning. Irma's scream *is* that cry, and yet it puts under erasure any possibility of articulating the relationship between (narrative) action and the diegetic world of the film.

Given the previous chapter's discussion of the decentering function of the gaze in Antonioni's work, the question that presents itself at this point concerns the connection between the stains that mark the images with a certain limit and the temporal disruptions that threaten the narrative with indeterminacy. Second, insofar as these limit points are accompanied by "voice events," the problem becomes one of articulating a relationship between gaze and voice. This "double limit"—at the point of image and at the point of narrative—is, I will argue, the place where we discern in Antonioni's work the very historicity of the discourses of neorealism, of the cinematic tradition Antonioni was self-consciously extending.

Red Desert

Red Desert (1964) is often seen as the culmination of the great tetralogy of alienation that began with *L'avventura;* it is, nonetheless, Antonioni's first film in color, and as such occupies a transitional place between *L'eclisse* of 1963 and *Blow-up* of 1967. Thus *Red Desert* can be seen as a turning point in Antonioni's work, both a summation of past work and a movement forward toward something new. The previous chapter's discussion of the gaze was deliberately constructed around this pivot or hole; for it is the very visibility of the economic miracle in *Red Desert's* mise-en-scène—as well as its utter incomprehensibility—that links Antonioni's *formal* experimentation (with the structures of the gaze within the tradition that is neorealism) with the text's encounter with history.

Red Desert continues the style of free indirect discourse we see in *L'eclisse;* in fact, *Red Desert* is the film by Antonioni that Pasolini expressly refers to in the article in which he describes this style.[2] Monica Vitti plays Giuliana, a woman married to the head of a factory outside Ravenna; we gradually learn through the film's opening movement that Giuliana is recovering from what her husband calls an accident, but which we learn is more likely a suicide attempt. To call her neurotic is not to do justice to the state of crisis that she is in throughout the film; more accurately she could be called borderline, a term that conveys more accurately the sense of the extremity or the limit with which the film engages. In any case, it is the use of free indirect discourse that allows us to move immediately to the formal questions the film raises, with the assurance that in this film, character has become a pretext (or at least a vehicle) for the director to advance his own vision of the world.

What *Red Desert* also continues from *L'eclisse* is the prevalence within the image of the uncanny stain, now achieved by way of color. Giuliana moves through a world from which color has been drained—in fact, Antonioni went so far as to paint a dull gray the produce in a fruit vendor's stand and the foliage in the landscapes. Yet within these highly desaturated images, there is often a point of intense color, usually primary color, fixed to some odd or "irrelevant" piece of machinery or architectural detail: a pipe, an electrical box, a barrel.[3] Thus, for example, Giuliana will wander through a dingy blue-gray section of the industrial plant and lurking in the background above the characters' heads will be an intense, primary-red fixture or detail.

In an important new reading of *Red Desert,* Angela Dalle Vacche discusses the similarities in color strategies of Antonioni and the painters of the *art informel* movement, particularly Wols and Alberto Burri. As she notes, these painters have "a baroque penchant for open-ended, unthreaded, irregular forms charged with expressionist color whose intensity disrupts all shapes, exasperates all meanings."[4] In Burri's early work, this highly saturated limit point—for example, the red stain on the burlap or sackcloth ground—is directly evocative of bodily trauma, of the inside spilling out. On a more general level, we can say that art informel, as its name suggests, attempts to bring us to some primal moment that marks the birth of form out of formlessness (or what, in psychoanalytic theory, would be called the Real). Dalle Vacche implicitly notes this—minus the reference to the Real—when she notes how the primal materials that comprise, for example, Dubuffet's canvases (blood, feces, mud) bring us to a point where "death blends with life."[5]

The most famous of *Red Desert*'s stains is the bright yellow burning poisonous gas that erupts from the chimney of the plant, and which is prominent in both the first and last sequences of the film. The reason why this is such a summarizing image is the way in which the stain here shows its pure formlessness, its purely illusory nature, its "nothingness"—it is an emptiness that at the same time has the power to completely fill up the diegesis of the film, to pollute or poison everything. As such it exemplifies most clearly the nature of all the points of anamorphosis in Antonioni's images: they are the point of the gaze as object *a.* It holds the place of a limit, the place where the regime of images reaches the point of unimaginability: in short, where the "beautiful" gives way to the sublime.

Red Desert is postmodern insofar as the terrain of the sublime has shifted from nature to the technological. In *L'avventura,* the sublime of nature was still possible, in the mysterious waterspout and in the storm that carries Anna mysteriously away; but significantly, Antonioni had to go to Sicily, to the terrain of the *Odyssey,* in order to find it. In contrast, in *Red Desert* there is a scene in which Ugo and Corrado walk outside the plant, and suddenly, from the side of a wall, a frightening and powerful cloud of steam erupts with a force that is quite unimagin-

18
Red Desert:
the eruption
of primary
color

19
Red Desert:
the yellow
poisonous gas

able. A few scenes later, Giuliana walks among a circle of huge, red, steel structures that curve up to some imaginary point in the sky. A worker tells her that the structure is a device for listening to "the noise made by the stars." This is our first indication that sound—audible or inaudible—will be linked in the film to the decentered gaze: in fact, a sequence to be discussed shortly revolves precisely around whether or not a scream was heard.

Throughout *Red Desert,* the question that torments Giuliana is the question she cries out to Corrado in the hut by the sea: "What should I do with my eyes? What should I watch?" This is but one of the indications Antonioni gives us that he is indeed concerned with the eye and the gaze; others occur in relation to Giuliana's young son. The son's hobbies—from the indications we get seeing his bedroom—are bound up in science and technology; in one scene, he and his father Ugo are looking at microbes in a microscope, and on a shelf in the background, there is a large anatomical model of an eye. The son has a robot that, in an earlier scene late at night, Giuliana discovers moving backward and forward in the sleeping son's room, its "eyes" two points of yellow light visible from the hallway where Giuliana stands. Even after she turns the robot off, the eyes continue to "stare" through the open door into the hallway. Because the robot's eyes are obviously a simulation, the film gives us here a perfect metaphor for the gaze that, as in *L'eclisse,* continually "watches over" the mise-en-scène.

Žižek notes how the automaton is the perfect filmic representation of drive: the "terminator," for example, clearly exhibits pure demand beyond any question of desire.[6] In *Red Desert,* the uncanny back-and-forth movements of the robot suggest the same thing, a frightening appearance of pure drive; this is underscored later when the son—in what is perhaps a hysterical symptom, but is definitely a narrative inversion of the robot's movement—suffers a sudden paralysis of the legs. Since the paralysis and the recovery from it are separated by the famous sequence in which Giuliana recounts the fantasy of the girl on the island, the boy's recovery is often attributed to that fantasy. Yet there is a layering of details in the sequences here that adds complexity to what is going on: namely, the emergence of the signifier in the form of the news media. For, right after the son announces his paralysis, the maid notices a magazine on the floor in the corner; when she picks it up and puts it on the table, she notices a lurid photo-story about children with polio. A few sequences later—after the phantasmatic island sequence, and after the lapse of an indeterminate time period—the maid enters the hallway announcing the arrival of the newspapers, which she hands over to Giuliana. It is immediately after that Giuliana looks through the open door into her son's room—from almost the exact place where she earlier saw the robot—and notices that he is walking around. I don't want to suggest here a simplified, schematic, or symptomatic reading. On the contrary, I am pointing to a complexity of the structuring of these sequences in which we see, one, the signifier as object of exchange, and two, the *beyond* of that intersubjective circuit, and finally, fantasy as precisely that which mediates the two levels; this is the organizing logic not simply of this episode of the boy's paralysis, but indeed of the entire film itself.

In *L'eclisse,* we can recall how the newspaper functions to announce the dimension of the sublime, at the beginning of the final sequence in which we arrive at the "eclipse." In *Red Desert,* the newspapers framing the episode of paralysis are clearly a part of an intersubjective network of exchange—that is, what constitutes the Symbolic order as such. But earlier in the film, in a much-commented-upon shot, Giuliana and Corrado encounter a page of the newspaper blowing in the empty street

20
Red Desert: the
newspaper arrest-
ing Giuliana's
motion

outside Giuliana's shop in the old city center; the paper becomes en-
tangled in Giuliana's legs and then is blown away. Here, the newspaper
(the "agency of the letter," we could say) subtly connects Giuliana to
what happens later with her son, for it temporarily *stops her mobility* by
wrapping itself around her body. We can also note how the sheet of
newspaper and later the magazine on the floor have in common the fact
that they are both *out of place,* thus functioning as stains. In the case of
Giuliana on the empty street, the newspaper is clearly litter, garbage
(and thus is linked not only formally to the objects that pollute the land
around her husband's plant, but, psychoanalytically, to shit). Within
Red Desert, thus, the Symbolic order (in the form of the print media
that daily are framing the reality of the new Italy of the postmiracle) is
presented as radically "ex-centric" to Giuliana, while at the same time
inscribing its effects upon both body and world.[7]

What has often been overlooked in the Lacanian schema of Imagi-
nary/Symbolic is the way that the gaze is what performs the crucial
function of breaking the deadlock of imaginary doubling or mirroring:
as such, the gaze falls on the side of the Symbolic (of the Other). For
example, the hysteric's theater would make no sense without there being a gaze of an audience, a virtual point where the hysteric "sees himself being seen."[8] Žižek's coup has been to show how this point of the
gaze can be applied to the entire symbolic reality; when, for example,
everyday reality is reflected in satire, the very effect requires a virtual
point beyond either image, in order to allow the satiric effect to hit the
everyday. Normally, this virtual point remains unconscious;[9] it provides
the coordinates for the *fantasy space* that frames the subject's experience
of the world (or, in relation to the Symbolic system as a whole, for the
phantasmatic that "drives" it ideologically). But when the subject's re-

lation to the Symbolic is disrupted in some way, this virtual point emerges within the visual field as the uncanny stain.[10]

To return then to the sequences of the son's paralysis, what happens is that Giuliana "misses" the significance of the signifier, in the same way that earlier she didn't understand that it was wrapping itself around her. The son, completely at home in the discourses of the new, seems completely unperturbed when his body is deformed by the symbolic; for Giuliana, this marks him with a terrifying strangeness, the same kind of strangeness that Pasolini was later to identify in the monstrous children of the new, consumerist Italy.[11]

Fantasy and Temporal Disruption

The fantasy sequence, embedded within the episode of the son's paralysis, is marked off from the rest of the film in many important ways. At the most obvious level, it is marked off narratively, by the framing function of Giuliana's narrating voice and by the abrupt change of location to the (unspecified, but Sardinian) beach. Stylistically, the color is intensely saturated, in contrast to the desaturation of the images in the rest of the film.[12] And finally, within the sequence there emerges the voice that Michel Chion has called the *acousmatique,* pure voice unattached to any diegetic body.[13] This voice occurs only one other time in the film: significantly, in the film's opening credit sequence.

The story Giuliana tells is this. One day a girl who felt very alone discovered a beautiful beach, a beach of pink sand, transparent water, and no sound whatsoever. She began going to the beach every day. (The high-saturation images thus far show us the pink sand and intensely blue water. The girl is about twelve years old, dark—perhaps North African—and wears a brown bikini. At one point, she removes the bikini top—but inexplicably, as there is nothing in the images or in Giuliana's voice-over to explain the highly charged act, and in the shots following the removal of the clothes, the top is back on. We must note, then, a deliberately constructed *repression* around this act.) One morning she saw a sailboat; it was unlike any she had ever seen, and seemed to have traveled all the world, and even *"fuori del mondo,"* even beyond. (Here, the images present us with a very curious inversion: first we see in the far distance a sailboat with white sails; then, somewhat closer, a sailboat with red sails going in the opposite direction; then, two sailboats with red sails crossing one another; and finally, the original sailboat with white sails. Here, the odd sequencing seems to be to establish retro-actively a thought process: namely, that the boat was different from others the girl had seen, a fact Giuliana has already narrated.) As we see the girl swimming toward the boat, Giuliana says "from far away, it was magnificent; getting closer, it was mysterious." (This, it should be noted, is the logic of the Lacanian object-gaze; whether or not the gaze erupts as a stain in the field of the visual is dependent upon the angle, distance, or proximity of the point of view. As Žižek would interpret Lacan, we see the "stain" in the Holbein painting as more than a stain only by looking at it "awry.")[14] The girl comes to understand that its mysteriousness is connected to its having no one on board; it is thus "the ship of the dead."

The boat leaves as mysteriously as it arrived, and when the girl returns to the shore, she begins to hear the haunting melody of a disembodied voice. Once again, the issue of distance and proximity is raised, as Giuliana narrates that the voice seemed sometimes near, sometimes far away. The voice continues to sing, and in a series of over-head shots, we see the girl walking among the limestone rocks, worked by the sea into smoothly shaped, variegated, almost organic forms; Giuliana narrates that the rocks seemed "like flesh." The mesmerizing voice continues as Giuliana's son asks, "Who was singing?" Giuliana responds, "Everyone was singing" ["Tutti cantavano"] and with this, we return to the room where Giuliana is narrating to her bedridden son. There follows a cut to an indefinite point in the future, with Giuliana in another room seeing a boat coming into harbor from the window look-ing out into the sea. (Boats, in fact, are central iconographic motifs throughout the film, a point to which we will come shortly.) It is at this point that the maid interrupts Giuliana with the delivery of the news-papers; this scene is followed by Giuliana's discovery of her son walking. It is this terrifying discovery of her son's radical "otherness"—what Pasolini might describe as his monstrous foreignness, but which for Giuliana indicates that her son "doesn't need" her—that throws Giu-liana into the disastrous sexual encounter with Corrado, at the end of which the room is suffused with the same pink hue as the flesh-like rocks in the fantasy.

We have already noted the ways in which the fantasy sequence marks itself off from the rest of the film. The sequence in fact marks itself as absolutely crucial to the overall narrative structure of the film. But *how*? And *why* is it so crucial? To start with, there is an inversion involved in the relationship between the overall narrative and this sequence: this

21
Red Desert's fantasy
sequence: the rocks
becoming flesh

sequence literally turns the film inside out. If at first it seems as though the fantasy sequence has been inserted into a larger narrative frame, it soon becomes clear that it is rather the *fantasy* sequence that is framing the rest of the film. And *this,* we can argue, is what explains the aesthetics of color in the film, how color has become the primary vehicle for the stain, for marking the point of the gaze. It is as if this lush, technicolor fantasy sequence had "exploded," leaving shards of color scattered through the desaturated mise-en-scène of the industrial landscape. This paradox or inversion of framing is precisely the mechanism of fantasy in the Lacanian sense. As Jacques-Alain Miller explains, the visual field achieves its sense of (symbolic) reality only through the extraction of object *a,* which then comes to *frame* the visual field. This frame is necessarily fantasmatic, insofar as the subject's relation to the object *a is* fantasy.[15] To put it in a less technical way: it is Giuliana's fantasy that continually intrudes in the film's diegesis; it intrudes precisely as the point of a gaze, the virtual point from which the film can break out of "the prison house of images." But this "breaking-out" can be achieved only at the cost of an eclipse—the inability to speak the disaster, the encounter with the sublime.

Methodologically, it is important to stress that here, psychoanalysis allows us to deduce a purely formal unity to the text, with no regard at all (yet) to the content of the fantasy sequence. Further, it permits us to speak of textual mechanisms without resorting to "psychologizing" Giuliana, which is in keeping with this textual system that resolutely refuses us the luxury of psychology. One can, of course, construct quite interesting interpretations that *do* construct a psychology; for example, P. Adams Sitney does a striking reading of this fantasy in terms of sexual repression. His argument centers on, first, the curiously charged shot in which the girl takes off her top, which goes unnarrated by Giuliana; and second, the figure of the siren as link between the "ship of the dead" and the disembodied voice. While these details do point toward a sexuality at once deadly and alluring (and hence repressed), Sitney then suggests that it is the onset of (presumably Giuliana's) puberty—in the specific form of menstruation—that lies at the origin of Giuliana's crisis. This is what Giuliana is reminded of in the soiled, polluted landscape of industrial Ravenna.[16] What is extremely interesting in Sitney's reading, from the point of view of ours, is the way in which he too situates the fantasy in relationship to that which "stains" the rest of the film. It is just that his argument must be turned around: what is primary is the *mechanism,* in light of which menstruation (for example) would acquire meaning only retroactively.[17]

Of central importance is the way the fantasy paints a world that is (always, already) riven; the ship discloses itself as a stain on the vast blueness of the sea. Like Lacan's sardine can,[18] the boat marks the point where meaning fails in the visual field, where meaning is "left unrevealed." It stands in for some unspecified trauma (perhaps the mysterious fate of its sailors); and as such, it ties together all the other many images of ships in the film. For Ugo and Giuliana live in a house built right on the coast, and often from the windows, we see ships passing in the distance. There is also the very famous shot—outside the hut where a party is given—when what looks like a forest of trees is suddenly "cut open" by a ship slowly entering the frame, presumably floating on a canal not visible from our point of view. This ship, too, becomes a ship of the dead, as it sends up the flag of the plague and marks itself contaminated by that which is unseen.

For Deleuze, the ship (generally) is an indicator of what he calls "the crystal image" (or "hyalosign"): the point where an actual image comes together with its virtual counterpart. This image, he argues, is deeply connected to the notion of nonchronological time. To follow his rather complex argument, we must begin with the mechanisms by which the cinematic images construct a world. There are essentially two ways of doing this, Deleuze argues: by extension (the method used by classical cinema) or by intension (that used by "modern" cinema). Extension characterizes the construction of the classical cinema insofar as our views of the world extend from particular characters performing actions upon that world. The modern cinema is constructed by intention, in that its characters are spectators of a world whose internal relations have been fundamentally ruptured: instead of action that extends us further into a "world," we get instead the contraction of the "image circuit" down to its internal limit. The result is that out of an actual image is constructed its virtual "double," and the two become locked in what we could call a "chiasmic exchange." Whenever, for example, the theater appears in film, there occurs a doubling whereby the "actual" gets drawn into the theatrical. The ship, Deleuze argues, divides space into the visible and the submerged, and this split "actualizes a kind of theater or dramaturgy." We see this, for example, in *The Lady from Shanghai* (1948), where the clarity of the above-board gradually yields to its double, the world of the predatory fish.[19] Ultimately, the point of Deleuze's argument is that the crystal image makes visible what he calls the most fundamental operation of time: "We see in the crystal the perpetual foundation of time, nonchronological time, Cronos and not Chronos. This is the powerful, nonorganic Life which grips the world."[20] This gives us a clue to the connection between the overarching narrative mirroring that characterizes Antonioni's work (which was discussed in chapter 5 in relation to Marsha Kinder's reading of *Blow-up*) and his inscription within the narrative of a kind of "redoubled" temporality, one that instigates the disruption of linearity and thus marks the film with trauma.

That Deleuze links this process to the crystal—and thus to the non-organic—provides us with a powerful link to the final images of the fantasy sequence. For in the fantasy, the pink limestone rocks begin to take the form of "flesh," of the organic, not only in Giuliana's voice-over but in the images as well. This, in fact, marks the point at which the fantasy approaches too closely the Real, which is why the fantasy soon disintegrates. The enveloping voice of the "siren" takes control of the image and effects the metamorphosis of rock into flesh; a condensation is effected, so that the entire world is seen in terms of the utter indifference of the life-force to any question of Being. This, according to Lacan, is Freud's "beyond" of the pleasure principle: pure drive, ultimately the death drive.

Finally, the inorganic makes another appearance earlier in the film, in what is a crucial detail. Corrado goes to visit Giuliana in her shop in the old city center of Ferrara. In fact, it is not yet a shop at all; Giuliana is still trying to figure out what she wants to do with it. The walls are painted with test swatches of various colors, as if Giuliana is trying to master in this private space the very dislocation that color provokes outside. At one point, Corrado asks Giuliana what she plans to sell, and Giuliana, not really sure, improvisationally comes up with the word "pottery."[21] Now "pottery" is hardly an innocent word here, and I

22
Red Desert: color
fields painted on
the wall

would argue that much more is happening than simply the representation of Giuliana's existential confusion. Pottery, that is to say, suggests
a primal moment, a moment shrouded in concealment, when the purely
inorganic is transformed into the objects of the human world. This opposition is familiar in Heidegger as the distinction between Earth and
World, and in his notion that the origin of the work of art lies in the *rift*
between the two, as the Real of substance is shaped into the meaning
of the Symbolic.[22] Jameson's reading of Heidegger is particularly suggestive in this regard: it is not simply that Earth and World are radically
incommensurable; it is that now (in the moment of the modern), the
"specific vocation" of art (as of philosophy) is to hold open this radical
tension rather than to try to close it.[23] So that Giuliana's casual free-
association brings us to the very heart of the logic of the film itself: the
inability to locate the inaugural moment, the "trauma," out of which
such an object world as we inhabit has emerged. This is the point, then,
at which the very historicity of Antonioni's filmmaking comes to light,
a point to which we will return in the final section of this chapter.

La Voix acousmatique

In what is sometimes called the "orgy scene" in *Red Desert*[24]—the scene
at the hut, described earlier, outside of which Giuliana sees the ship
cutting through the forest—the group is gathered in a tiny room whose
entire floor is a mattress. Suddenly, Giuliana is inexplicably startled; she
looks off, then glazes over in dissociation, only to end up smiling and
saying something stupidly lurid to the group. To say that Giuliana
looked as if she had heard something frightening is really a retroactive
critical construction: for the sound of the cry from the ship outside is
faint enough that even the attentive spectator/listener could doubt hav-

ing heard it.[25] It is only many minutes later, after the ship has hoisted the quarantine flag, that the issue comes up: Giuliana insists she heard a cry that no one else, save one other woman, had heard. It is around this ambiguity that something very interesting gets constructed around the style of free indirect discourse: namely, the fact that we, the audience, have already been taken account of in the scene (in an almost Hitchcockian way). Even after many viewings, a spectator can easily doubt that s/he has heard the sound we know is there. Sound, then, becomes the Archimedean point from which we break out of the enchainment to Giuliana's point of view: but only ironically, only through negation, only because *we can't remember* what Giuliana remembers perfectly.

In this sequence, the disembodied voice falls on the dividing line between audible and inaudible; as such, it illustrates the quality of "living death" that Michel Chion attributes to the cinema's *acousmêtres*—those disembodied voices consigned to the cinematic limbo of the off-screen.[26] This is the voice that will emerge in the fantasy sequence: a voice impossible to attach to any body, a voice of pure sound detached from any signifiers. In fact, voice *is* what is left over when speech is drained of signification; as such it attains the status of drive—invocatory drive— and thus a trance-like, hypnotic quality, that of sound in circulation and never "resting" in the finality of meaning. Marguerite Duras's *India Song* has become a privileged site in the critical discussion of the "acousmatic voice," insofar as it presents us with a film which, instead of being narrated from a voice anchored to a secure symbolic position, gives us heterogenous voices not attached to the bodies on screen. Joan Copjec explains how this makes the status of the acousmatic voice one of "living death": "These off-screen voices cannot be construed as mortal. They are . . . *intemporal voices;* they cannot be situated in—nor submitted to the ravages of—time or place. This is not to deny that the voices are associated with death, but to note that this death brings no expiry; rather, in them, death persists."[27] Copjec, in her study of film noir, has hit upon the same connection with which I began this chapter: namely, that in the cinema that we can provisionally call "modern," the disturbances in temporality are linked to disturbances in voice. (This, it should be noted, is my generalization; it is not overtly stated as such by Copjec.)

Since there is more at stake in this discussion than the interpretation of *Red Desert*'s fantasy sequence, a brief excursus is in order. There is an argument to be made that the period around 1960 marks a key "moment" in the cinema's construction of image/sound relations: and in particular, that it marks a turning point as the primacy of image gives way to the primacy of sound. For there is no doubt that a key stylistic trait of "postmodern," contemporary cinema is the dense "rendering" of sound that constructs a hyperreal acoustic space. This "sonic aquarium," as Chion calls it, not only tends to take over the function of establishing shots; it also blurs the distinction between the inside and the outside of the body, as sounds from both are mixed and indistinguishable.[28] Implicit, though unstated, in this argument is that in postmodern cinema we ought thus to see a destabilization in the image's relation to narrative temporality, as the image becomes unhooked from classical syntax. (In light of this, it might [for example] be fruitful to look at Jameson's characterization of postmodernity—particularly that it prioritizes space over time.) Within this schema, film noir—with its programmatic destabilizations of temporality and of body/voice relations—would be seen as the opening "move" (or "symptom") in a much larger development, often called the transition from modernity to postmodernity. Certainly, both technological developments in sound, and the dissemination of the televisual (which, as many have noted, prioritizes sound over image) lend at least a "mechanistic" credibility to this periodization. Finally, the period of the late fifties presents us with paradigmatic cases of disturbances of temporality and voice: *Kiss Me Deadly* (1955), *Rear Window* (1954), *Psycho* (1960), and the already discussed *Il grido* come immediately to mind.

But a purely mechanistic or technology-driven explanation ends up not really explaining much except the conditions for change; we must search for some "cultural logic" that drives or underlies the change. The by now standard Lacanian conception of this cultural logic is the historical move from *desire* to *drive* as the structuring mechanism of the subject's relation to the Other. Copjec lays out the argument most clearly in her essay on noir:

> Lacan has argued that this shift [from desire to drive] describes a general historical transition whose process we are still witnessing: the old modern order of desire, ruled over by an oedipal father, has begun to be replaced by a new order of the drive, in which we no longer have recourse to the protections against *jouissance* that the oedipal father once offered. These protections have been eroded by our society's fetishization of being, that is of *jouissance*. Which is to say: we have ceased being a society that attempts to preserve the individual

right to *jouissance,* to become a society that commands *jouissance* as a "civic" duty.

Copjec immediately adds that "civic" is perhaps not the right word, since it is the very domain of the "civic" that collapses as everyone retreats into their private domains of jouissance. This is why Copjec sees existentialism—which, we must recall, became film noir's contextualizing discourse—as a philosophy of drive par excellence, this because of "the difficulty of fathoming the Other, society itself, from the perspective of the drive."[29]

In the postmodern economy of drive, voice takes on particular significance, for voice has been seen as the locus of the superego ever since Freud's first conceptualization of that mental entity. Thus, without that Oedipal protection against jouissance, the superego itself, once an obstacle to enjoyment, paradoxically becomes an agency of enjoyment.[30] This is the inherent logic of the central apparatus of postmodernity, the televisual: whatever else it is doing at any given moment (and certainly it is working at many levels; I don't want to posit a totalizing function to television), it is always commanding enjoyment.

Curiously, then, *Red Desert*—so often seen as the epitome of the modernist work—is actually pointing forward toward the postmodern. For what erupts in *Red Desert* is always drive, never desire. The acousmatic voice of the siren in the fantasy is a manifestation of the pure invocatory drive. It is only the *desiring* voice—as Copjec notes in relation to Roland Barthes's essay—that activates in the listener a transference, a sense of some "X" to be fathomed, of some narrative to be traversed. When voice is pure drive, it marks "not some ideal point where the subject would finally be absorbed into [her] narrative; it materializes rather that which can never be incorporated into the narrative."[31]

Both voice and gaze, then, function for Antonioni as limit points to the very project of narrative. The fantasy sequence "explains" only insofar as it takes us to this limit: the limit visualized in the pink rocks metastasizing into the fleshy monuments[32] to the real of jouissance. This is what gazes at Giuliana everywhere she looks, prompting her agonizing question, "What should I do with my eyes?"

We can now recall that we have heard the acousmatic voice of the siren before: in the very credit sequence that opens *Red Desert*. Here, however, instead of the sharply registered images of the fantasy sequence, we are presented with a visual field *completely out of focus,* fuzzy shapes and colors whose objects are completely undifferentiated. This, we could say, is the gaze in the process of its emergence; this is Antonioni's answer to the fundamental problematic of neorealism, the relation of the seen to the unseen, of the object to the subject. For insofar as neorealism grounded itself in the phenomenologists' battle cry, "To the things themselves!" Lacan's reply is, "Beyond appearance there is not the Thing-in-itself, there is the gaze."[33]

History and Oedipus

The final question that remains to be answered is the question we started with: namely, how does the very form of the film manifest or signal the film's historicity? For we saw with *Il grido* how the economic miracle suddenly surfaces toward the end of the film, only to be withdrawn by the scream that conceals it. *Red Desert* is situated in a world totally and radically transformed by neocapitalism, a world that would have been unrecognizable only a decade or so before. This sudden—but unmarkable—transformation of the world of things—at once sublime and disastrous—is what pushes Antonioni toward his understanding of the split between eye and gaze: in the credit sequence, for example, where the visual field only comes into focus against the background of a radical *loss*.

In an essay that is central to the study of Italian cinema of this period, Cesare Casarino uncovers a logic in Pasolini's *Edipo re* (*Oedipus Rex,* 1967) which has crucial points of contact with our discussion of Antonioni; as such, it demands extended discussion.[34] Like *Red Desert,* Pasolini's film of the Oedipus myth is in many ways a pivotal film (although not as "purely" as *Red Desert*): for, with the major exception of the 1968 *Teorema,* Pasolini after *Edipo re* abandons contemporary Italy and moves to the terrain of the ancient, the preindustrial, the Third World. (Pasolini's flight from the here and now is of a kind similar to what we see in the trajectory of D. H. Lawrence, in his response to an earlier moment of economic modernization.) There is, then, something in Pasolini's telling of the Oedipal story that leads him to some kind of basic repudiation. But of what?

What first strikes us about *Edipo re* is its unusual narrative structure, predicated on a profound temporal *lapsus*. The "body" of the film is a telling of the myth "from within," so to speak; it images a diegesis that we take to be the terrain of the myth, of antiquity, of an inaugural moment. But this "body" has a prologue, set in the environs of 1922 (fascist) Bologna, and an epilogue, set in the post–economic miracle Bologna of 1967. (We can argue that the epilogue alludes to Oedipus at Colonnus, at least linguistically: for what characterizes the Bologna city center is the system of arcades that run through it.) At the heart of Casarino's argument is this: that Pasolini positions the myth precisely in the position of the "absent cause" (although he does not use this phrase), between the solidification of the fascist state in 1922 and the transformed Italy of 1967. That is to say—if I may freely argue from Casarino's position—in the movement from point A to point B, what "falls out" is precisely the Oedipal.

To understand what is at stake here, we need to review the ways in which Pasolini—and the Italian Left generally—periodized Italian history since fascism. For the Left, the end of the war and the victory of the American-backed Christian Democrats over the Left in 1948 does not represent the profound historical break that it is conventionally characterized as being. The transition from fascism to Christian Democracy was remarkably smooth and involved a reshuffling of the traditional power elites and not at all any radical transfer of power.[35] As Pasolini put it, the regime of the Christian Democrats was one of "clericofascism," hardly distinguishable from what came before it. But by the mid-sixties, Italy had been thoroughly transformed by neocapitalism into a culture of consumption. It is *this* transformation that constituted the radical break in Italian postwar history: from Pasolini's point of view, a move from the old "clericofascism" to a new (and for him more terrifying) fascism of the commodity.

Unlike the "fall" of fascism toward the end of the Second World War, which could be marked by visible and important events (thus reinforcing the illusion that a real historical break had occurred), Italy's economic transformation could not be so marked. This change might more accurately be characterized by—to alter a phrase Lyotard employs in discussing the postmodern sublime[36]—a sense that "'it' has happened," where the "it" is something that continually recedes from our grasp. Casarino uncovers an important essay from Pasolini's *Scritti corsari* that metaphorizes (in synecdoche) this ineffable change in the event of "the disappearance of fireflies." The fireflies had been wiped out due to increased air and water pollution, and Pasolini uses this "event" to stand in for the inexpressible event of modernization. In *Edipo re*, Casarino argues, it is the myth of Oedipus that stands in the position of the disappearance of fireflies, that marks the indefinable point of transformation.

For what, Casarino astutely asks, is being posited through a word like "disappearance"? Here Casarino deploys Ernst Bloch's notion of "nonsynchronism" to great effect. For Bloch, the very processes of modernization leave in their wake a panoply of heterogenous leftovers. In many respects, Bloch here comes close to Benjamin in the latter's notion of porosity (discussed in chapter 3); for both, residual structures coexist with emergent ones, in such a way that temporality itself becomes "multiply inscribed" in the social space. Indeed, for the early Pasolini, it was this very nonsynchronism of neocapitalism with itself, the very porosity of the urban space, that provided him with the leverage from which to mount a critique, within the very structure of the realist image.[37] But as Casarino notes, Bloch was writing from the time of a still-developing transformation (as was, we should note, Benjamin as well). *Edipo re,* in contrast, marks the last moment in this development; so that afterward, Pasolini could never connect the archaic or preindustrial to the present.[38] Fascism is now "in complete synchronism with itself, precisely because it is a decentered, fatherless fascism."[39] With this final mention of the absent father, Casarino's reading connects to the psychoanalytic view of postwar history as presented earlier by Copjec, insofar as it is the collapse of the Oedipal father that allows drive to overturn the regime of desire.

Finally, though—and here is where I would like to make an intervention in the overall argument, by way of a crucial shift—we must ask in what sense has the Oedipus been "exploded," whether in Pasolini's film or in the critical discourse that emerges from it. The ending of *Edipo re* in Bologna both invokes and retreats from *Oedipus at Colonnus,* to be sure: Pasolini's Oedipus returns to the very house where he was born, thus constructing a narrative circle by saying, "Life ends there, where it begins." And this containment contrasts with the "deterritorialization" we see at the end of Sophocles' tragedy, where Oedipus "evaporates" into the elements. But it can be argued—indeed, has been argued[40]—that this incomprehensible (sublime) event, the disappearance of Oedipus, is in fact the central truth of the myth. What is at stake in the Oedipal is (always, already) the very problematic of articulating history with narrative, of grounding speech in the world. This is the sense in which psychoanalysis is always "interminable," always approaching a primal scene shrouded in concealment.

In an important reading of *Oedipus rex,* Ned Lukacher argues that central to the play is a repudiation of what we might call "the political game" for the sake of a higher politics. He bases his argument on key details regarding the shepherd who "knows" the secrets of the past.

Sophocles presents us with details about the servant that allow us to conclude that Oedipus could easily have discredited the story and, by thus playing the political game, at least could have postponed his fate. Of course it isn't in the structure of tragedy that this could happen. But Lukacher's point is that Sophocles' inclusion of these details about the servant points to the reading that Oedipus forsakes the game of power for something larger: a "process of destruction" that is "the only way toward the new order."[41] Oedipus, then, becomes a model for "a certain kind of political impasse," one that Marx faced in the aftermath of the 1848 revolutions,[42] but which Pasolini perhaps also faced in the year before the politically charged 1968.

In the end, what all these readings (including the reading of *Red Desert*) move toward is the centrality of the notion of the primal scene to any possible narrativization of the event of modernization. As Lukacher argues, the radicality of both Freud and Heidegger lies in the way that, for both thinkers, the critical moment that marks the beginning is always a moment that hides, that shrouds itself in concealment as soon as it is approached. And this is what we've seen happens over and over in *Red Desert:* around the inapproachable disaster whose effects reverberate through Giuliana's world, the narrative can only circulate, can only miss the mark. At the same time, however, it makes visible the traces of the disaster, in its disruptions of gaze and voice, and ultimately, of temporality itself.

Thus, both Pasolini and Antonioni can only be fully understood in light of the fundamental trauma of modernization undergone by Italy. In *Edipo re,* Pasolini comes closest to Antonioni in the way he keeps open the site of trauma. But the distinction drawn in chapter 6, regarding the stances of the two toward the problematic of neorealism, still holds: between the culturalist position underlying Pasolini's stance and the formalist position underlying that of Antonioni. Both auteurs arrive at narrative's limit point, the point where temporality itself collapses in the face of historical trauma; but Pasolini's aesthetic solution rests on a kind of *embodiment,* whereas Antonioni's is one of disembodiment.

part IV

BOUNDARIES

*For the European observer
the process of artistic creation
in the underdeveloped world
is of interest only insofar as
it satisfies a nostalgia for
primitivism.*

—GLAUBER ROCHA

*Sono questi i figli del
lontano futuro disperato!*

—PIER PAOLO PASOLINI

THE EROTICS OF THE PERIPHERY 8

The narrative of Pasolini's murder plays itself out over a great spatial divide: on the one side, Stazione Termini in the center of Rome, where Pasolini picks up the "rent boy"; on the other, the squalid beach at Ostia, where Pasolini is brutally murdered under circumstances that still, after more than twenty years, remain a mystery. Pasolini's death—like his cinema—is played out along the opposition of center to periphery. This center/periphery divide is no pure binary opposition but reflects the kind of mutual contamination of terms that—again—was key to Pasolini's artistic practice.

For on the one hand, the narrative "begins" at Termini, that is, at the "terminus" or end point, the point in Rome to which all roads (or in this case, trains) lead. And the train station itself is a nodal point, what Michel Foucault would call a "heterotopia": it is a space that exists in relation to all the other spaces, "but in such a way as to suspect, neutralize, or invert the set of relations that they happen to designate, mirror, or reflect."[1] Like the more ancient city gates but vastly more complex, Termini is a point of permeability in the city's texture, the point of transition between inside and outside. But the liminal quality of Termini extends beyond the station itself and into the surrounding "zone" or neighborhood, where porno movie houses are the sites of transgressive sexual exchanges, where the ruins of the Baths of Diocletian are charged with the mystery and danger of desire.

And if we've seen in earlier chapters the way in which the beach functions generally as the site of the social totality of the "new Italy," then the real beach at Ostia presents us with the "other" of that totality: it is a space (in 1975) of great industrial pollution (to the extent that it is often dangerous to enter the water) and shanty town shacks built from the debris of the economic miracle. For this reason, the beach too becomes a space of liminality and transgression: for it fails to provide us with narrative closure regarding the death of Pasolini and instead opens up the possibility that the responsibility for the crime extends into the highest reaches of the power elite. This, of course, is a "conspiracy theory": the idea that the lone "rent boy" could have inflicted the kind of damage evidenced by Pasolini's corpse seems far-fetched to many, yet the involvement of others is unprovable. The beach, then—which in Pasolini's *Comizi d'amore* functioned not only as the site of the social totality, but more specifically a protofascist one, given the long speech by the Tuscan man about the centrality of the family to the national idea—now registers that fascist social totality by its absence, its invisibility. So that in a fully modernized and spectacularized Italy, the conspiracy emerges as the trope that expresses the final triumph of "appearance" over "reality," and thus of the unmappability of socioeconomic relations and patterns of exploitation in the era of globalized capitalism.[2] And in a final, queer twist to the conspiracy debate, we might note what is often cited by proponents of the "lone-boy" theory of the murder as definitive proof of their position: that the boy, when questioned after the murder by a psychiatrist, announced, "Voleva incularmi" ("He wanted to fuck me in the ass"). That such an excuse can so function to totally occlude the production of further discourse—after all, what kinds of battering shouldn't one expect when the issue is one of breaching the boundaries of the male body, even when the rent boy was seasoned enough to have undoubtedly received propositions of the like before?—attests most immediately to the ideological tenacity of homophobia. What is more interesting is the mechanism by which this social fantasy actually renders transparent its own logic, and incorporates within itself the very trace of conspiracy that it is attempting to refute. For psychoanalytically, the repression of the unconsciously fantasized penetration of the male body is precisely the mechanism underlying paranoia; so that—"fighting fire with fire"—the conspiracy theory is discredited by an unconscious invocation of paranoia.

To return to the issue of space, the interplay between center and periphery animated Pasolini's work as a filmmaker, especially in his early and late works. In the early sixties, when the engine of the economic miracle was running full steam, Pasolini could find in the squalid borgate surrounding central Rome the spatial realization of the contradictions in the emergent neocapitalism; at the same time, he could find in the alterity of the underclass boy the point where the erotic and the political could meet. Indeed, the only glimmer of hope in the otherwise very bleak *Accattone* is at the level of the enunciation, in the erotic solidarity between the camera and the character of Accattone. It order to better understand what is at stake politically in this erotics, it would be instructive to imagine, for a moment, the substitution of "the aesthetic" for "the erotic" as the term standing in relation to the political. For the linkage of the aesthetic to the political takes us—as Fred Jameson has uncovered—back to the moment of the French Revolution and the emergence of the modern democratic project. Jameson notes that for Schiller, the aesthetic becomes the *prerequisite* for a meaningful politics: as if not political rhetoric but art itself provides us with the fundamental experience of freedom out of which the political act can be projected. Jameson then uses this conceptual scheme to understand the refashioning of the concept of freedom by Herbert Marcuse, in light of the newly emergent "affluent society" of the sixties. For Marcuse, the liberations—sexual and otherwise—that emerged in the sixties were utterly imbricated in the emergence of unprecedented social controls and social organization: that is, an apparent wide expansion of freedom coincides paradoxically with an equally wide expansion of "velvet" social control. Within this order of things—the embourgoisement of the working class, the large-scale manufacture and then "satisfaction" of "needs"— the work previously performed by the aesthetic loses its utopian force, leaving us with the body as the potential figure for the experience of freedom. But of course, if the freedom to be achieved is to be anything more than "individual narcosis, . . . individual salvation only in the midst of the collective shipwreck," then the personal liberations accorded by the consumerist culture must be conceived of in a spirit of *negation*.[3] A very similar line of thought runs through Pasolini's work; perhaps not coincidentally, for he shared with Marcuse both a historical moment in the history of capitalism and a dismay at that historical moment's invention of "lifestyle" to replace lived experience (the *Erfahrung*" of Frankfurt school thought). For this reason, it was vitally important for Pasolini that homosexuality remain an alterity, remain outside the "repressive tolerance" of a consumerist bourgeoisie;[4] in this sense, Pasolini remains central to any theorization of "queerness."

By the seventies—and especially with *Fior delle mille e una notti (Arabian Nights,* 1974), the last film of the "Trilogy of Life"—the issue of center and periphery was recast at the level of the global and the historical. If, that is to say, Pasolini's early work was driven by the phantasmatic of the precapitalist space surviving in the midst of neocapitalism—with such a space providing the best hope for seeing the new order in its totality—then by the early seventies such a space had vanished from the Italian landscape.[5] This drove Pasolini toward other "peripheries"—the texts of the Middle Ages, and the space of the Islamic Third World.

Pasolini and Pedagogy

In 1996, the young Italian director Aurelio Grimaldi released *Nerolio,* an odd and fascinating film that is not a biography of Pasolini but rather a kind of tone poem composed around the figure and the life of Pasolini. The film is in three segments, although most of the screen time is taken up by the long second section, which is the story of an imagined encounter between Pasolini and a young student who wants him to read his novel. This section is bookended by two, much shorter sections: the first, an enactment of the sexual encounters between Pasolini and a group of *ragazzi* on a beach in Sicily; the last, a reenactment of the events on the night of Pasolini's murder. These two sections mirror each other, repeating the iconography of car and beach and the spatial strategy of a movement from center to periphery. In the first sequence, Pasolini spots a group of young men playing soccer in a piazza in the center of town; after he talks briefly with the oldest boy, we cut immediately to the beach at night, where one after another, the boys go up to Pasolini's car, strip, and have some sexual encounter with him. The highly charged eroticism of this sequence is in complete contrast to the grim encounter of the final sequence, which leads to Pasolini's murder. It is as if the final sequence is the brutal answer to the phantasmatic sexual utopia imagined at the film's beginning; and precisely because the film banishes the political from its conclusion, it is in this respect retrograde, unfortunately.

The fact that the length of the middle section is such that it constitutes the "body" of the film suggests that it might somehow provide the connection between the beginning and ending, perhaps almost in a "theorematic" fashion providing us with the middle term of a deduction. It begins when a college-age boy manages to gain entry to Pasolini's study one afternoon while Pasolini is at work. The boy has a manuscript he wants the irritated Pasolini to read, and when Pasolini presses him about his background, the boy, lying, tells Pasolini he is a student of a famous professor at the university. Pasolini discourages the boy regarding any potential he may have as an artist, while at the same time more than intimating that he might be good for a quick sexual fling. The boy remains deferential and eventually leaves, and when Pasolini calls the professor (whom the boy naively must have thought Pasolini didn't know), he discovers that the professor has no student fitting the description. A sudden cut to the boy's bedroom reveals him lying in bed masturbating, thus forcing the audience to begin to revise any notion we may have that the sexual dimension of the relationship was one-sided—and this is just the first in a series of abrupt revisions and reversals that will characterize the episode. Later, for example, the boy's mother is complaining about a disgusting and vulgar new film she's just seen (which must have been *Arabian Nights*), but when she finds out that the director might possibly be interested in her son's career, her appreciation of the film's aesthetic value is suddenly increased. In another scene, the boy's brother is talking with him in the kitchen and chiding him about his new mentor; suddenly, the boy arrogantly says that Pasolini is an ugly, washed-up artist whose work is completely out of date, and casually implies that he'd have no problems having sex with Pasolini if it would get him what he wanted (a publisher for his novel).

This is a point of stunning reversal in the episode, for if hitherto we had been able to view the boy, through our own ideological lenses, as naive and innocent, we are now forced to confront the fact that he is perhaps more cynical than his would-be "mentor"; that, in fact, Pasolini may have sensed the boy's manipulativeness all along. When the boy returns to Pasolini's study, Pasolini tells him that he thinks little of the boy's novel, and that he would show the novel to his publisher only if the boy had sex with him right there. The scene ends with a sordid sexual encounter in the corner of the study.

The process of rereading that this episode requires is precisely what makes it work in relation to the other two episodes in the film; that is, the "oddness" of this episode sandwiched between the other two forces us to consider the way in which it mediates between the first sexual encounters in Sicily and the final murder. After we see Pasolini's own cynical participation in a commodified sexual exchange, the first part of the film becomes retroactively infused with a kind of *nostalgia,* insofar as the world it presents—the world of the innocent, Mediterranean boy whose homosexual relations are not categorized as anything but sex— has irrevocably disappeared. Gone, too, is the entire, premodern space of mythology, the space of the world invested with erotic charge, a space that until the sixties still survived among certain classes and in certain regions of Italy.

In this sense, the film is faithful to Pasolini's own thinking. However, it remains to attend to the film's ultimate address: namely, the film's figuration of Pasolini as one who cynically *refuses* to assume the pedagogical mandate required of him when approached by the young boy. But Pasolini—himself a teacher in his early career—always assumed the rhetorical stance of the pedagogical in his own work, as evidenced especially by his *Lettere luterane,* a series of didactic lectures on politics and life in the new consumerist Italy, addressed to a *genariello,* or young Neapolitan boy.

Pedagogy of the Oppressed

From the fifties onward, the neorealist "imperative" was taken up in countries across the spectrum of the developing nations by filmmakers who saw its potential for political engagement with the issues of economic transformation within the nation.[6] To be sure, one of the reasons was neorealism's promise of the potential for truth claims to be made in the cinema; another was certainly neorealism's position as an alternative to the dominance of Hollywood enunciative schemes, which could be seen as a kind of nonviolent colonization. However, neorealism's commitment to the pedagogical was also critical to its appropriations, insofar as the pedagogical becomes the rhetorical mode for the ideological discourses surrounding the nation and to whom that nation belongs. This pedagogical mode functions even in forms—like advertising and television—where there is a high investment in textual pleasure, insofar as these forms disseminate (seemingly neutral but in fact ideologically charged) "information" about hygiene, work, leisure, and daily life generally.

Perhaps the most recent detailed analysis of appropriations of neorealism is made by Marsha Kinder, in the context of Spanish cinema's attempt in the fifties to articulate a speaking position outside of fascist discourse. In her analysis of *Muerte di un ciclista* (*Death of a Cyclist,* 1955), for example, she notes how the film juxtaposes the enunciative regime of Hollywood melodrama with that of neorealism to create a dialogic clash between the two; in a sense, the neorealist borrowings are used to "crack open" the enforced closure of fascist discourse.[7] A similar appropriation occurred in Brazil in the fifties, during the period of "developmentalism" under Kubitschek. This use of neorealism continued into the early days of the *cinema novo* movement during the first years of the sixties.[8]

It is beyond the scope of this work to chronicle in detail the extent of neorealism's diffusion worldwide. Rather, I want to focus on the ways in which, within these different national contexts, the developments we have seen in the Italian cinema of the sixties—the decentering of the gaze in Antonioni, the overall crisis in the camera's ability to register reality, the insistence in Pasolini of the body as guarantor of authenticity—begin to repeat themselves, thus raising the possibility of some fundamental relationship between economic development and the aesthetic of the photographed image. Indeed, such an inherence has been argued by Rey Chow in her remarkable study of Fifth Generation Chinese cinema: her idea is that modernization carries with it a process of translation, whereby the older (elite) culture of the written is systematically replaced by a newer (mass) culture of the image. She goes on to argue that what further complicates matters in postcolonial cinemas—now hot commodities on the international festival circuit—is a second level of translation, as images of, for example, "Chineseness" move across national boundaries.[9]

In the case of neorealist appropriations, a particularly interesting repetition occurs around the issue of pedagogy and the figure of the teenage boy, with a pattern of motifs recurrent enough that one could use them to characterize a new international genre—let's call it "the international youth film." The characteristics of this genre are as follows: first, the action occurs in a nation undergoing the economic modernization associated with third-stage (or global) capitalism. Here, the notion of uneven development is centrally inscribed within the spatial system of the films. Second, the films follow the various fates of groups of adolescent (or preadolescent) boys from the subproletariat—characters clearly doomed to victimization by the various state apparatuses undergirding the economic development.[10] Third, central to the narrative is the youths' encounter with some kind of *inversion* of the social order that inevitably ensnares some of the boys. This is usually figured as drug trafficking or prostitution: in other words, those margins of the social order that are themselves produced by that order and which function as a kind of Hegelian negation inherent in the posited order itself. Finally, while the particular story is driven by the narrative desire in the film (a desire pinned to the fate of one of the protagonists), the film also wants to make a documentary truth claim. Thus the films hybridize the drive of classical Hollywood cinema with the documentary techniques—location shooting, use of nonprofessional actors, and so on—of neorealism. Examples of this genre are many: they include *Pixote* (1981) from Brazil, *Macho Dancer* (1988) (and a number of spin-offs of it) from the Philippines; *Rodrigo D—No Future* (1990) from Colombia; *Collegas* ("Buddies," 1980) from Spain. And even in a highly developed country like Italy, the genre has been deployed across the chasm of uneven development within the nation in Marco Risi's 1990 film *Ragazzi fuori* ("Boys on the Outside," 1990).

The first question to be asked is, Why is it that such a privileged position is accorded the adolescent boy in these narratives? Of course, the most obvious answer is that the teenage boy is culturally positioned as the future of the nation—sons figured in a certain relation to the nation's "patrimony." (We might note in this regard that even in the United States, the problems of youth are often constructed around a discourse of an incipient lapse into a new barbarism.) On a related level, the figure of the adolescent provides the text with a complex set of tropes that can be put into play around the notions of development and underdevelopment.

Finally, though, the figure of the adolescent boy brings to the film a set of *pedagogical* functions, and this pedagogy runs through the conditions of production as well as the mechanisms of reception of the film. Here, a particularly telling example is director Hector Babenco's appearance as himself at the beginning of his film *Pixote*. Babenco appears on screen surrounded by his "boys," the nonprofessionals under his tutelage, against the backdrop of the horrendous shanty towns surrounding São Paulo that have produced these children. Babenco, in direct address to the audience, makes a claim for the film's status as document—and thus, as an instrument of pedagogy to the world that wants to push aside any engagement with the profound inequalities in the new Brazil.

It is at this point that we must introduce one last characteristic of this genre, a characteristic at the level of the enunciation: all of these films present us with a world seen through a homoeroticized gaze. Given the extensive reconsideration of the gaze in earlier chapters of this work, it should be clear that I do not want to assert here a model that reduces the gaze to the camera's looking at the boys with a certain desire. Rather, the gaze is that which—within the given picture of the world—holds that world together, renders possible a "reality effect" while at the same time is unlocatable. Insofar as the homoerotics of these films is this *object*—the gaze as object *a*—the homoerotics can be seen as a kind of *repressed* of the film's nominal diegesis (in exactly the same way it functioned in Pasolini's *Accattone,* which can be taken as the genre's "prototype"). It structures the film, but it vanishes as soon as we try to pin it down. For the boys, the homosexuality is never a matter of identity but of transaction and/or performance, while for the audience in the developed nations, it remains for us to discover what is at stake in this move. Even in Lino Brocka's *Macho Dancer*—the most direct of these films to depict homosexual acts in that the boys are working in the Manila sex trade—still there is a disjunction between the sexual performance and the look of the (Western, American) spectator (who is both in and out of the text).

This can best be seen by analyzing in detail the complex interplay of looks in a central early scene of Brocka's film. The main character Paul has recently arrived in Manila from the countryside, which he left when the American G.I. who had been supporting him (and had been his lover) returned to the United States. His friend takes him to a nightclub in Manila's red-light district, where Paul applies for a job. After his "interview"—which consists mainly of his having to expose his penis to the "queen mother" of all the boys who work the club—he and his friend go down to the club, where a masturbation show is just beginning. In this eleven-shot sequence, the space of the club is divided into three zones: one, the stage where the boys are masturbating; two, the back of the room where Paul and his friend stand watching; and three, the audience to the show that separates the other two zones. Brocka's camera, by initially restricting itself to long shots in depth, carefully delineates this division between spectacle, audience, and Paul; and except for the three medium-close shots of Paul alone, looking at the spectacle with an unreadable expression on his face, the audience is included in all the shots. Clearly, this continual presence of the audience forces a split in the spectator: on the one hand, the spectator (especially the "First World," consumerist spectator) is forced into a complicity with the sexual consumers among the audience; on the other hand, the identification with Paul forces us to distance ourselves from the proceedings, even though we don't know the extent to which Paul himself may be aroused by the spectacle. Where, then, should we locate the gaze that is organizing this scene? On the one hand, we can say the gaze is "moralistic" (or "parental"), insofar as Paul's (unreadable) reactions are strictly speaking the point of a *projection* on the part of the film viewer, who attends to Paul's expressions (or *affect*) for any moral compass on the scene unfolding. On the other hand, the scene is also organized around the violation of the taboo against presenting the erect penis, which can also be seen as the organizing principle of the scene's presentation, one that effectively destabilizes the visual organization of the shots. Brocka thus puts his film spectator into a complex net of identifications and disidentifications, as he/she struggles to "read" the face of the hero Paul. It is this fundamental ambiguity that makes the film so powerful a document. For Brocka, like Grimaldi in *Nerolio,* refuses to submit the scene to a simple logic of "victimization." And a few scenes later—when Paul becomes a full-fledged "macho dancer"—the camera finally moves onto the stage, effacing the on-screen audience. This maneuver (seemingly) removes the sexual exchange between Paul and his friend from the economy of sexual exchange, and marks the encounter as a profoundly human moment of bonding. But this response depends upon our disavowing the knowledge that both audience and camera are *there:* and so yet another paradox arises, namely, the fact that "authenticity" makes the sexual display even more valuable as a commodity.

It may thus be the case—as Rey Chow suggests—that one of the fundamental projects of cinema in the current postcolonial space is precisely to deconstruct any notion of "authenticity." Much of Chow's argument is a direct response to the widespread criticism that Fifth Generation Chinese cinema participates in the orientalizing gaze of the West, but what this ignores is the way in which "the primitive" is not only a matter of characterization imposed from without: that is, in fact, a structuring feature not only of official national discourse (of, say, Chinese intellectuals seeking to legitimate some notion of authentic national culture) but of its oppositional discourses as well (namely, the films themselves).[11] Of course, one must be cautious in "translating" Chow's argument onto a space as different from China as, say, the Philippines. But that Lino Brocka is effecting a similar critique of authenticity, and that it results in a similar problematic with regard to the "primitive," can be seen by comparing his work to Kidlat Tahimek's *The Perfumed Nightmare* (1977), in particular the scene that photographs a ritual circumcision. The images here much more closely conform to the terms Rey Chow has set out in relation to the "primitive" in Zhang Yimou's work: the circumcision can be seen as simultaneously locating authenticity within a "native" tradition, creating a distorted and complicitly orientalized image of the Filipino, and exhibitionistically presenting the Western gaze with its own fantasy, thereby revealing its fundamental violence.

To return to the festival genre of the international youth film, the particularity of its construction of the homoerotic gaze can be traced back to the early work of Pasolini, and especially his first feature, *Accattone*. In this film, Pasolini uses several strategies to make the peripheral central, not the least of which is its construction of space: the sordid story of Accattone's life plays itself out almost entirely in the peripheral shanty towns that sprang up as a result of the increased urbanization wrought by the economic miracle. The few times that Accattone enters central Rome, the scenes are marked by death. In the first of these forays into the central city, Accattone's body is made the site of erotic spectacle: his friends having challenged him to jump off the Ponte Sant'Angelo and into the Tiber, Accattone stands among Bernini's angels, his stripped body the center of everyone's rapt attention.

We've already seen how, for Pasolini, the body itself is of critical importance, as a way to negotiate the representational problems inherent in his revival of neorealism. For Pasolini, the body is brute fact, an inescapable mark of the Real. In *Accattone,* this concern manifests itself in Pasolini's attention to the precise distance the camera should maintain in relation to the subject. This is why, when the erotic emerges within the space of the film, it cannot be pinned down to any precise location but instead becomes a generalized gaze that subtends the reality of the film. The body presents us with a kind of "thereness" that makes it clear that we are dealing with something that is "in Accattone more than Accattone," to use a Lacanian formula.

We might conclude from this that the pedagogy involved in *Accattone* is based on an erotics—specifically, the confrontation of the real body of the player with the "hidden" body of the director. Thus, we are dealing with a *transaction:* the director provides the nonprofessional boys with a (at least temporary but sometimes permanent) way out of the subproletariat, precisely insofar as the boy is able to be "educated." And at the same time, the boy must retain his identification with the subproletariat for the sake of realism, even as he is giving it up at the behest of the master's professionalism. No wonder so few of the boys in this position are able to make it work for them—although certainly with Pasolini, we have the cases of the Citti brothers and Ninetto Davoli as the success stories.

To return, then, to a discussion of the genre itself, it remains to put these observations together in such a way as to make sense of its narrative structure, as well as its historical specificity. Here, an important passage in Fredric Jameson's *Geopolitical Aesthetic* provides a clue for the narrative transactions common to these films. Jameson, writing of the Taiwanese new wave, argues that in the early modernist work (such as Gide's *Counterfeiters*), there is still—despite the moral dislocation among the youth in the novel—the possibility of the *Bildung* so central to the genre of the youth novel. It is as if the old form of the bildungsroman were preserved as a residual form in the modernist novel. It is with postmodernity, argues Jameson, that the possibility for the Bildung drops out [12]—and this, we can argue, is precisely because of postmodernism's inability to create a totalizing picture of the world upon which a pedagogy could be based.

Now, while this may certainly be true for the Taiwanese films discussed by Jameson, I would propose that in the genre we are looking at here, it is precisely the homoerotics of the enunciation that becomes the placeholder of the Bildung. In a sense, then, the residual form still survives in this new genre, but in a curious way. The homoerotic gaze results from an encounter between director and player (or, in another sense, between audience and player); and insofar as this encounter is pervaded by a kind of nostalgia, the homoerotics is precisely what allows that nostalgia to take form. This is why the homoerotic gaze here is the object *a:* of course the charge will evaporate if any of the characters (unthinkable in the context of these films) were to assume a "gay identity." It is only homosexuality as repressed that can give us simultaneously the feeling that these boys are doomed by the social order and yet at the same time filled with "unknown possibility."

So ultimately, the pedagogy in these films runs in two directions— not only are the boys recruited for a project that potentially will take them beyond the hopelessly confining social order they are in (with all the double binds noted above in this project), but they are also figured as objects of nostalgia, so that the pedagogical function runs from *them* to *us. We* are the ones whose experience under late capitalism has become excessively mediated and profoundly attenuated. The boys become sites of an impossible turning back of history, toward an authenticity that is always a fiction, and the mark of this impossibility is the penis itself. Homoerotics and pedagogy thus become the figures of a lived paradox (one that we see replayed in different guise in the arguments between identity-based models of homosexuality and performative ones).

Real Estate

If the binary opposition between Pasolini and Antonioni could be oversimplified into one between "body" and "architecture," such a move would then suggest that the films of the Taiwanese new wave are playing out—again, of course, within an entirely new social space—the second of the formal moves developing out of the neorealist aesthetic. Certainly, neorealist impulses are evident throughout the work of Hou Hsiao-hsien in the eighties, but when we reach the work of Edward Yang and Tsai Ming-liang, those impulses have already been inflected in an "Antonioniesque" direction. The formal echoes of Antonioni—for example, "dead time" at the beginning or end of shots, the embedding of the human figure within tightly composed architectural grids, an attention to surface (or, better, to figure-ground relations), and so on—are strong enough that the connection has become part of the critical literature;[13] while specific iconographic elements in a film like Yang's *Terrorizer*—the photographic blow-ups, the oscillating fans, the zebra-striped crossing, the giant gas tank—are arguably direct citations of *L'eclisse, Red Desert,* and *Blow-up.*

To begin to understand what this may mean, it would be useful to first return to the Jameson essay cited earlier, for it is in fact an extended analysis of Yang's *Terrorizer.* One could argue that the occasioning impulse for Jameson's essay is the appearance of what—at least on the surface—seems to be the embrace of a "modernist" aesthetic in the Taiwanese new wave, which is one of the reasons Jameson links his essay so closely to a concomitant analysis of the high-modernist novel. More generally, the nineteenth-century novel had to face the problem that arose when plotting—that is, the formal condition for the work itself—forced the author into the production of fortuitous encounters among seemingly unrelated and independent "agents." While at one point in history such a device could seem to accord with lived experience because of a shared belief in some Grand Design (whether "God" or "History"), the later modernists were faced with the formal problems attendant upon its lack. It is at this point in Jameson's argument that—for our purposes—a startling connection is made: the impossibility of having direct experience of the synchronicities of the novel's plot is compared to the impossibility inherent in the mode of free indirect discourse.[14] It is here where we can make a deeper, structural connection to the work of Antonioni, precisely insofar as one of its principal formal features is, as Pasolini first noted, the cinematic use of free indirect discourse. This cinematic free indirect discourse itself embodies an experiential impossibility, the technique being such that the shot presents us with the character (Monica Vitti in *Red Desert,* for example) within an environment that is no longer "neutral" but instead suffused with the intensities (or the "poetry") of her own personal neurosis. This, then, becomes the reason why considerations of the gaze become so central to Antonioni's work generally. For while it is true that classical point-of-view editing is equally impossible experientially, classical découpage hides this impossibility by assigning to the gaze itself the function of "grand design." With Antonioni's free indirect discourse, in contrast, the gaze is decentered, and thus often erupts within the images themselves.[15]

The question that thus arises—in relation to both Taiwanese cinema but as well to the other cinemas discussed earlier—is this: What can it mean, within the postcolonial spaces of transnational capital, for the gaze to "erupt" as a destabilizing force: that is, for it to become disconnected from an omniscience or "design" that is prerequisite to the coherence of a subject in history? Here I propose to look at two films of the Taiwanese new wave, Tsai's *Vive l'amour* (1996) and Yang's *Terrorizer,* beginning from the premise that it is the vacant apartment itself—a motif that recurs beyond the two films discussed here—that detaches space from subjectivity in such a way as to produce an aesthetic similar to that of Antonioni. But as will become evident, it is more the Antonioni of *Blow-up* and after that is the relevant reference point, that is, the point where free indirect discourse is abandoned, and replaced by the visual field dominated by the simulacrum.

For while Antonioni's cinema is often characterized as a cinema of surfaces, it is only with *Blow-up* and *Zabriskie Point* that his surfaces become as luminously "blank" as those of the Taiwanese new wave. Before that, Antonioni's surfaces exude a tactile quality that grounds them in materiality (one thinks of the way one experiences the cracks and textures of the walls in Giuliana's shop in *Red Desert*) so that the visible world—its Schein—is still able to bring us to the question of Being. This, we could say, is the precondition for the device of free indirect discourse, and the very thing that produces within Antonioni's visual fields those uncanny points of anamorphosis. With both *Terrorizer* and *Vive l'amour,* the blank walls and tiles shimmer and glow with reflected light of various hues, in a kind of pure opticality that, in *Zabriskie Point,* could only lead to the apocalyptic fantasy in which the image has become the purest, most indestructible form of the commodity. It is as if dirt itself has been banished from the world, which could then be read allegorically (as Jameson might) as a capitalism in full synchronicity with itself, with no place left for residual modes of production or consciousness. One thinks of the scene in *Vive l'amour* when the "gay" character[16] carves holes in a melon and uses it as a bowling ball, which rolls down the corridor and splatters against the wall, the only dirt in an apartment so pristinely unmarked by human habitation that the mattresses are bare.

Vive l'amour is certainly the more accessible of the two films under consideration here. May, one of the three main characters, is a real estate agent, most of whose time is spent in the transitory zones of empty apartments and her car. She casually picks up Ah-jong, a man "without means"—who turns out to be a street vendor of presumably black-market merchandise—and brings him to an empty apartment for sex. In the meantime, a listless salesman of funeral urns has decided to use the vacant apartment for a half-hearted suicide attempt and ends up watching May and Ah-jong have sex. Ah-jong and the salesman eventually meet and form a tentative bond, but May has no idea of the salesman's existence (except, perhaps, at the very end of the film, although this is ambiguous). During May and Ah-jong's second sexual encounter, the salesman is hidden under the bed, where he masturbates. When May leaves for work, the salesman hesitantly slips into bed with the near-naked, sleeping Ah-jong, and slowly works up the nerve to kiss him (without awakening him)—and for all intents and purposes, this is the one "event" of the film. But meanwhile, May's car won't start, and we hear her footsteps in the apartment as the salesman kisses Ah-jong. Abruptly, there is a cut to an extremely long take of May walking across a park, sitting on a bench (in what seems like an amphitheater of benches), and sobbing.

The structuring idea of the film, then, is the missed encounter; but what is perhaps unique is the way that the organization of space concretizes this idea—not, as we would expect, through the use of parallel montage (a strategy adopted in *Terrorizer,* for example), but rather by positioning within the shot itself. It is as if the empty apartments—themselves interchangeable "slots" within the urban center—then introduce the notion of interchangeability and subdivision into each shot: one can be on the bed or under the bed, behind door one or behind door two, and so on. The narrative then presents us with analogies to its spatial technique, as when we see, in the office where the salesman works, all of his coworkers playing a children's game akin to musical chairs; or when the salesman takes Ah-jong to the "crypt" where one buys slots for storing one's ashes. This latter space—gleaming and spotless—is made to resemble a high-tech information bank, or a vault of safety deposit boxes. With this image, one might feel one has "cracked open" the underlying spatial logic of the film itself: insofar as the "slots" themselves—whether real or "virtual"—take over the role once assigned to the subject. The "subject" is always, already accounted for in the space, which is why the final emergence of "the event"—the kiss—is so pathetic: it announces a subjectivity in ruins.

This final point allows us to see the deeper affinities the film has to the work of Antonioni, and in particular to the decentering of the gaze. This is best seen in the astonishing shot early in the film in which we are first introduced to the character of Ah-jong. From a high-angle view, we see him walking in the aisles of a convenience store. As he approaches the aisle on the far right of the frame, we notice that the image of his body undergoes an anamorphic distortion. Then, as he moves back toward the center of the frame, the camera pans left slightly, to reveal to us that we have been looking at him through the distorting mirror of the security/surveillance system. Finally, he reaches a point just below the mirror, and looks up to study himself. What is remarkable here is the suggestion that, at the margins of visuality, of the surveillant eye, there emerges a distortion which might—if pursued in some way—open up the image to some "other scene," some hidden possibility for the viability of agency. But this possibility is suddenly removed once the camera reveals to us that this is a surveillance mirror: thus, there being "no exit," no point where something remains hidden, Ah-jong has nothing to do but to accede to his being "in the picture," fully present, fully "framed," fully taken into account.

Edward Yang's film of a decade earlier (*Terrorizer*) has been the subject of a dense and thorough textual analysis by Fredric Jameson, and to produce here an entire (re)reading of the film would risk repeating an argument much of which I'm in agreement with. My concern here is much more narrowly delineated: to understand (again) the significance of Yang's appropriations of Antonioni, which in *Terrorizer* are blatant enough to consider the film in some ways an *hommage*.

In the first place, we have a central character (one of the four main characters) who is a photographer and who fills the walls of his apartment (taken over from the criminals in the film's early shoot-out, who have vacated it) with blow-ups. One of the film's other main characters, the wife of the doctor, is a writer suffering from writer's block; thus the film is set against not only an obsessive production of images but also the very failure of writing. (We might contrast this with Hou's *City of Sadness,* where writing, in the form of the notes the deaf-mute brother writes to his wife, are accorded the power to totally eclipse both image and sound, as Hou intercuts the text of the notes into the shots themselves.) This at once reminds us of one of the suggestive premises of Rey Chow's book on the cinema of the People's Republic of China: namely, that the processes of modernization work to shift cultural authority away from the written and toward the visual. The most striking of the blow-ups in the photographer's apartment is a shot of the "White Chick" that has been subdivided by a grid, each rectangle of the grid being printed separatedly, the entire image then being reassembled on the wall. The most striking thing about this image is not simply the way it violates the "integrity" of the indexical sign, but also in the way that it registers the emergence of newer technologies: the televisual, the digital. For if the grid of blow-ups doesn't immediately remind us of a bank of video monitors, then an image appears later in the film that makes the connection for us: when the writer finishes her novel and is interviewed for television, we see her image multiplied across the video screens in the studio.

What emerges here in this suggestion of a contamination of the photographic by the digital or electronic is an issue of visuality similar to that posed by the early mirror shot in *Vive l'amour.* To see why, it would be useful to go back to the photographic blow-ups in the Antonioni film: there, the anamorphic stain (the glint of light) in the image points to a hallucinatory outside: [17] there is still the sense in which the subject is implicated in the picture, in which the subject is vitally at stake. But with this detail in *Terrorizer,* that stake is abolished. Television, as institution and as apparatus, might *seem* to promise us a revitalized connection to an enlarged public sphere; but it cannot, precisely because it abolishes the very possibility of existential *traversal* that the stained photograph still requires. (That is, in order to penetrate the "mystery" of the photographs, the photographer in *Blow-up* has to traverse physical and social space, though to the viewer, it becomes evident he would have done better to traverse psychic space, if that were in fact still possible.) So that in both *Terrorizer* and *Vive l'amour,* the stain in the image is either shown or alluded to, but is immediately retracted as a possibility.

To link all these observations together, it might be fruitful to return to the issue of "real estate" and the postcolonial urban space itself. For *Terrorizer* begins and ends with "crime scenes": at the beginning, a shoot-out between police and drug dealers, and at the end, two undecidable versions of a finale, the first a murder spree by the doctor, the second his suicide. The conundrum that emerges here is the meaning of a narrative trajectory that moves from gangsterism at the beginning to a fantasized *crime passionnel* at the end. It has been noted in the critical literature that the underworld is centrally present in Taiwanese cinema generally; [18] and it seems plausible that the specificities of Taiwanese history gives the trope of gangsterism a peculiarly strong resonance today, since the gang activities are invariably transnational and cross all sorts of borders, national and otherwise. Thus, there is lurking subtextually in *Terrorizer* the sense that, if only we were able to follow *those other characters,* we might be able to map out some understanding of the global order itself. But this is ruled out, and one asks to what extent this impossibility is related to the impossibility of subjectivity itself, or the eruption into the "diegesis" of the violent fantasy that—who knows?— might have been real.

Recent Italian Cinema

While it would be beyond the scope of this study to present a complete picture of Italian cinema since 1990, there have emerged full-force in recent Italian cinema many of the concerns that have been central to this work: questions of uneven development in the context of the center/periphery divide; questions of the disintegrating urban centers of the great southern cities of Naples and Palermo; questions of the character of Italy as a nation in a period that has seen increasing numbers of immigrants from North Africa, Asia, and postcommunist Europe. Here I propose to look at three key films, each of which addresses aspects of these questions: Francesco Rosi's *Dimenticare Palermo* (*The Palermo Connection,* 1990), Marco Risi's *Ragazzi fuori* ("Boys on the Outside," 1991), and Gianni Amelio's *Lamerica* (1995). Significantly, the films of Risi and Amelio, the two "new" directors, consciously reinvoke the traditions of the first two waves of neorealism, asserting once again the primacy of that tradition to films that address the question of the nation.

Ragazzi fuori takes as its subject the dead-end lives of a group of young men living in the "ruins" of central Palermo. The film was inspired by (and reenacts as an episode) an actual incident in which a policeman cold-bloodedly shoots dead a young man in broad daylight in the middle of a crowded piazza. Risi's film has many points of contact with the Pasolini of *Accattone,* and much of what was discussed regarding the homoerotics of that film can be applied to Risi's as well. In fact, *Ragazzi fuori* begins by self-consciously refashioning the beginning of *Accattone,* the scene where Accattone is challenged by his friends to jump off the Ponte Sant'Angelo. In Risi's film, the boys challenge the main character to strip naked and stand neck-deep in the cold, winter water of the Mediterranean, while they tease him about what the water will do to his penis.

A quick comparison of *Ragazzi fuori* to Risi's previous film, *Mery per sempre* (*Forever Mary,* 1989), reveals an interesting progression. The earlier film, also set among the youth of central Palermo, has for its moral center the figure of a teen-age transsexual, thus literalizing the marginality from which it asks us to view the film. However, the figure with which the audience is asked to identify is the anguished schoolteacher (played by Michele Placido) whose own sense of identity is thrown into crisis by his encounter with the lives of the youth he teaches. *Ragazzi fuori* dispenses with both the textual representative of the "normal" bourgeois viewer *and* the extreme marginality of the transsexual. While this move cost him a loss of audience (the film has never been released in the United States, for example), it represents an aesthetic advance by allowing for more complexity in positioning the audience in relation to the action. In this later film, the audience has no textual representative of its (bourgeois) class, nor does it have a "shocking" marginal to which it can ultimately extend its tolerance and sympathy. It has only the "boys on the outside," and it must deal with them.

What I would like to focus on in *Ragazzi fuori* is the way in which it handles the space of the city in postmodernity. In the genre of the youth film discussed earlier in the chapter, one of the advantages of having adolescent protagonists is that it foregrounds the very project of understanding one's place within the economy of the city. That is, this project is central to the adolescent's coming to terms with his future. But in *Ragazzi fuori,* the older, center/periphery model of the city has fallen apart as an organizing principle: the urban center itself has become, as Jameson might put it, the site of an incomprehensible economic reorganization. Palermo is shown to be a giant "market," where all transactions are subsumed by the economic. In this sense, the young people's theft and prostitution become just another way to enter the system of exchange.

The shots in *Ragazzi fuori* are claustrophobic: Palermo continually closes in on us. This, too, reflects Jameson's notion of the impossibility of creating cognitive maps from the postmodern city.[19] It is only in the film's final sequence that we get an organized map of Palermo. The police have been notified that one of the boys has been murdered, and that his body has been dumped in the hills surrounding the city, hills that now function as waste dumps. As the police cars leave the station in central Palermo, we see the movement from center to exurb from within the speeding car; and when we reach the boy's body, decaying amid piles of trash generated by the city, the camera cranes up to give us our only panorama of the city. Self-conscious and didactic as this mapping of Palermo is, it nevertheless presents us with powerful connections between the economy of the city and the plight of its "delinquents."

In Francesco Rosi's *Dimenticare Palermo,* the spatial mapping is more critically acute, presenting us with a Palermo that is a microcosm of the new international capital flows. This is metaphorized by the international drug trafficking that is the film's nominal subject; for Rosi, however, this drug economy is clearly presented as simply the mirror image of neocapitalism itself. The story begins in New York, where mayoral candidate Carmine Bonavia (Jim Belushi) beleaguered by sagging polls entertains ideas from his staff for getting his campaign moving. At this point, he rejects the idea of decriminalizing drug use in the city, and opts instead to make a grandly publicized trip to Palermo with his wife, in order to discover his "roots." Here, Rosi's acuity is especially evident: for we have already seen a New York ravaged by the effects of the drug traffic, yet the political campaign can only see decriminalization as a gimmick. But even at that, such a gimmick would have at the very least set the terms of the mayoral campaign as essentially political; instead, the handlers opt for the gimmick that is all "human interest," and completely devoid of any serious political engagement with the issues of the city.

Little does Carmine know that his encounter with Palermo will bring him face to face with the very politics he has tried to avoid: as the film's title indicates, one can leave Palermo, but one can never "forget

Palermo." Rosi presents us with a Palermo seen through the eyes of a tourist; yet at the same time, he charges his images with a rich, polyvalent depth. At Carmine's elegant hotel, for example, there lives a "Lampedusa-like" aristocrat who—mysteriously—can never leave the hotel because he "knows too much." And when Carmine tours a rundown but famous palazzo, the sight of the now-ragged ballroom becomes the occasion for the camera to begin suddenly to swirl across the room in elegant and precisely executed dolly shots, recreating with the camera alone Visconti's famous party sequence in his adaptation of Lampedusa's *Il gattopardo.*

That these allusions are lost on Carmine is part of the logic of the film. Carmine is continually reading the details of everyday life in Palermo in the folkloristic terms of the tourist, when in reality, an organized and conspiratorial group (that we can call "the mafia") is using those details to orchestrate a message to him. For Carmine is not so obtuse that he does not grasp the invisible connections that link the disintegrating urban structures of Palermo to those of New York; and gradually, he comes to the conclusion, now no longer a gimmick but a reasoned political stance, that he really ought to make decriminalization of drugs the central position in his campaign. When he returns to New York and wins the election, he picks a blighted area in which to hold the press conference where he will announce his program. But he is assassinated just as he is about to speak. And at this point, it becomes clear that the international drug traffic is simply the obverse of global neocapitalism, the two existing in symbiotic relation to each other.

Amelio's *Lamerica,* as its title suggests, is a complex meditation on the idea of the nation in the postmodern, globalized world. Set in a chaotic Albania in the immediate postcommunist period, the film tells the story of two cynical Italian businessmen who take advantage of an Italian-Albanian initiative for capital development in order to get money to build a shoe factory that they never intend to make prosper. From the very first, the Italians view Albania only as a colony to be exploited; they arrogantly assume they can buy their way around any government restrictions or controls. When the law requires that the proposed factory be headed by an Albanian national, they get some officials to take them into a horrid prison and release a man who had been imprisoned since the end of the war. The older of the two Italians returns to Italy, and as the political climate in Albania becomes more and more unstable, the younger Italian's position becomes increasingly precarious. Finally, the scam is exposed and the young Italian arrested. He is ordered out of the country, but when he asks for his passport, the Albanian official who has it refuses to give it to him. The film ends as the Italian and the former prisoner—both now "undocumented"—sit on a crowded boat filled with refugees from Albania. When the Italian coast is sighted in the distance, the old prisoner looks up and exclaims "*Lamerica!*"

In Amelio's film, neorealism functions as a kind of trace that emerges only intermittently: in the shots of chaotic flows of people that suggest the historical immediacy of the first wave of neorealism; in the occasional lingering on the nonnarrative detail, like the ironic motif of shoes that runs through the film. This evocation of neorealism as a "lost object" becomes a metaphor for the loss of historical sense (and moral sense as well) that the main characters exhibit. As the film progresses, there are hints that the old Albanian prisoner might actually be an Italian who was imprisoned by the communists at the end of the Second World War. He thus becomes the highly ironic embodiment of a radical historical revision of neorealism: the "dead father" haunted by his complicity with fascism.

The final sequence of the film presents us with a remarkable set of condensations. Italy, hallucinated as "America" by the old man, has actually become a kind of "America" for the Albanians fleeing the repression and poverty of their homeland. At the same time, the image reconstructs the reality of Italy of a hundred years earlier, when boats carried masses of Italians to a different "America." In the end, Amelio's film asserts that the nation has always been a phantasmatic construction, an "America" whose discovery is always in some sense a rediscovery.

Il postino

If this study has been in large part a study of the ways a national film tradition (and the theories of the image that grounded it) has interacted with, and been inflected by, history, then the film *Il postino* (*The Postman,* 1993) can provide us with a symptomatically rich—if distressing—summarizing moment. For *Il postino* is very much a postmodern hybrid where the boundaries of the nation have been blurred in both the text and the production: it is a French-Italian coproduction, directed by the British Michael Radford, one of whose stars is the French Phillippe Noiret, who in the film plays Pablo Neruda, the Spanish-speaking Chilean poet in exile in Italy. That "Europeanism," combined with a narrative that reifies personal experience at the same time as it renders both history and politics completely unintelligible, gives the film all the earmarks of the new European media "product," specifically designed to take back some of the market from an increasingly hegemonic Hollywood.

Certainly, this market strategy was to a great extent successful in the case of *Il postino:* while its $20.7 million U.S. box-office take could be considered modest by blockbuster standards, it is surprisingly high given the decreasing adventurousness of American filmgoing audiences today. Outside the U.S., box-office figures were more than double the American total, at $54.9 million. Because of these figures—and because of a recent trend among Academy members to honor "little" films—Miramax decided to mount a campaign among Academy members to get the film some award nominations. What was unusual in the case of *Il postino* is that it was not eligible for consideration as best foreign-language film, since the Italian industry did not submit it as an official nominee. Thus Miramax's campaign was to get it nominated in the "regular" categories; to this end, it sent Academy members not only tapes of the film, but also a CD tie-in, the love poems of Pablo Neruda read by a host of Hollywood actors, set against the "romantic" score of the film. The result was five nominations, including Best Picture, Best Director, Best Original Score, and Best Actor (Massimo Troisi, who finished the film despite a failing heart and who died shortly after the film wrapped).

One of the observations to be made from this story is that Hollywood in the nineties, while commercially dominated by the mentality of the globally marketed blockbuster, nevertheless wants to locate "art" in some other place: thus the prevalence of independent productions of all stripes in the award nominations of recent years. In a certain sense, "Italy" becomes the perfect locus for the signifier "art," and this in fact evokes the grand decades of the fifties and sixties when Cinecittà was in many ways the imaginary other of Hollywood. It is no surprise, then, that the nineties saw the Academy recognizing two great Italian directors—Fellini and Antonioni—with lifetime achievement awards. This evocation of a great past irrevocably lost is, we shall see, exactly the specter that haunts the film *Il postino.* In fact, the film that paved the way for this nostalgic interest in Italy was Tornatore's *Nuovo Cinema Paradiso* (*Cinema Paradiso,* 1988), in which loss is centrally inscribed in the conflict of the main character (a Sicilian transplanted to the hectic and meaningless chaos of Rome). The return to Sicily and thus to "roots" climaxes in a montage-hommage to the power of the image in classical Hollywood cinema, images wrenched from their narrative context in a postmodern blur of past and present.

Il postino is "historical" in the sense that it is set in 1952, but the adoption of what Foucault has dubbed the *mode rétro* is the film's overarching strategy for history's containment, insofar as history spreads itself out in the style and mise-en-scène while losing its narrative dimension. Yet however elided by the film, history cannot help but make itself felt symptomatically—and, as we will see, in precisely the forms associated with emergent postmodernism: namely, a disarticulation of voice and body, a predominance of sound over image, and the disruption of narrative temporality. These symptoms occur at the very end of the film, and culminate in a sequence that alludes to neorealism by adopting a documentary aesthetic.

Because *Il postino* is set in an island fishing community in the early fifties, it brings to mind Visconti's neorealist *La terra trema,* and a comparison of the ways in which the two works handle their political dimensions can be revealing. In Visconti's film, the political and economic forces are clearly articulated; indeed, the film would not be comprehensible without a clear understanding of the relationships between the fishermen and the mafia of petit-bourgeois middlemen who buy their catch, or of the vast psychological distance between the isolated village and the town where the bank (and thus capital) is located. In Visconti's film, relationships of power and exploitation are clearly delineated; and it is this delineation—rather than the presence of some textual representative of "politics" in the form of, say, a communist—that constitutes the film as political. The film thus exemplifies the neorealist conviction that it is through the rigorous examination of the everyday (*quotidianità*) that a political conviction can be forged.

The political is far from absent in *Il postino;* but it never leads to a coherent understanding, and perhaps it can be argued that it is precisely the historical *failure* of the Italian Left from the postwar to the present to effect the kinds of social transformation it had hoped to that *Il postino*'s political "memory" is so sketchy. The island's politics are embodied in a slickly dressed politico who frequents the bar where Mario (the postino) will meet his wife-to-be. This politico hints that economic favors will be handed out if the town votes the right way. And before a key election, he begins a large public works project that clearly benefits Mario and his new wife and mother-in-law; but no sooner is the election won than the politico puts the project on hold. Clearly, this politico is a representative of the Christian Democratic party in control of the national government, yet curiously, the film never mentions the party by name. The only party the film *does* mention is the Communist Party, but only in a way that renders it a mere signifier. Mario acquires his commitment to this party—and this itself is overstating the case, for until the end, the film presents us with no signs that the communists are a coherent and organized force—not from any strong political awareness but from his infatuation with Neruda. *Il postino,* then, allows us to see something very important about the ideological function of the contemporary American "three-act" screenplay structure (which is becoming more widely adopted in those European films seeking broader audiences). Namely, that this structure itself works to contain the political, by turning its every manifestation into "subplot," unimportant except insofar as it complicates the "real" narrative (the story of "poetry" and "love").

Our analysis must turn, then, to this narrative. Mario is a young man who is temperamentally unsuited to being a fisherman, a problem in a tiny village whose only economy comes from the sea. The village has recently lost its anonymity, we discover, as we see a newsreel in the local movie theater describing the immanent arrival of the renowned Chilean poet Pablo Neruda. Soon after, Mario notices an advertisement for a part-time postman—with a bicycle, the poster indicates, in a clear allusion to *Bicycle Thieves*—and gets the job, which turns out to entail delivering the mail to Neruda. Quickly, a transference relationship is established between Mario and Neruda; and when Mario is smitten by the young woman who works at her mother's bar, Neruda becomes a key figure in helping the awkward and underemployed Mario to successfully marry her.

The notion of metaphor becomes a running motif, not only during Mario's courtship, but through the film. After Neruda explains the concept to Mario, Mario asks a question to the effect of whether or not everything in the creation is a metaphor. This, of course, is *the* question of representation itself. And as noted in chapter 2, in relation to *Ossessione,* Visconti deliberately plays with this question in relation to the function of his images: the images are "charged" only until the law is transgressed, whereupon the phenomenal "things" no longer point toward a "noumenal" beyond. And in subsequent chapters, I traced the way this problem played itself out in postneorealist cinema, culminating in Antonioni's exploration of the gaze itself.

In *Il postino,* of central interest is the way that *sound recording* displaces the image precisely in relation to this question. Mario—who linguistically is only able to plagiarize the already written metaphor—decides to keep the tape recorder Neruda left behind, and Mario's "poetic gesture" becomes the recording of the sounds of the island—waves, wind, "the stars." Thus the question of the metaphor is displaced from language and narrative to sound—to the body (for at one point, Mario records the heartbeat of his son still in the womb) or the "world's body." So we are brought, remarkably, to a kind of Heideggerian inaugural moment, an uncovery of the impossible schism between sound and the signifier, or between body and cosmos, which metaphor functions precisely to conceal.

At this point in the film, there is nothing left for Mario but to disappear—which is exactly how the film deals with him. From the scenes of sound recording, we cut directly to a shot of Neruda and his wife revisiting the island, walking into the bar and finding the son Pablito, now five or six years old, playing. Mario's wife explains to Neruda that Mario has died, and the film gives way to a grainy, black-and-white newsreel of a communist rally in which Mario was to read a poem, and where he died as a result of a police confrontation. Clearly, this newsreel footage, with its aesthetic of immediacy, suggests neorealism; yet it is impossible for the film to capture anything of real import.

It is in this sense that the film renders history as archival, disconnected from narrative, while at the same time rendering politics as incomprehensible. For, as noted earlier, the film consistently presents communism as an isolated, whispered alterity—this in a period in Italian history when nearly one-forth of the Italian electorate was voting communist, and when probably an even larger percentage were sympathetic to the communists' role in the antifascist movement. But in the film, one can only wonder where all these hundreds of participants in the rally came from, given their utter invisibility throughout the film. And just as surprising is the sudden and violent police intervention. Of course, it is certainly true that, in the South especially, there were instances when communist rallies were violently disrupted—the massacre at Portella della Ginestra depicted in Rosi's *Salvatore Giuliano* is one such instance; but the film gives us no way of understanding the scope and extent of the political repression of the Left during the early fifties, which was indeed a reality.

If it is true that the moment of Italy's economic miracle marked the moment when capitalism finally achieved "full synchronism with itself,"[20] then one might jump to the conclusion that we have truly arrived at "the end of history," and this would inevitably color one's views of postmodern culture generally. Indeed, if "post-Marxism" means anything, then surely it means the abandonment of the traditional view that capitalism is always, constitutively, nonsynchronous, and thus inherently unbalanced. The political impasses thus produced are obvious, and become visible in the commodified culture of postmodernity. Yet this is precisely why the issues of space, of nation, and of visual culture central to the Italian cinema are still of such urgent importance. For the issues of representation that emerge throughout the history of Italian cinema provide us, potentially, with the very means by which to think through the impasses which that cinema itself uncovered.

1. Writing the National Cinema

1 P. Adams Sitney, *Vital Crises in Italian Cinema: Iconography, Stylistics, Politics* (Austin: University of Texas Press, 1995), ix; Dudley Andrews, *Mists of Regret: Culture and Sensibility in Classic French Film* (Princeton: Princeton University Press, 1995).

2 Robert Kolker, *The Altering Eye: Contemporary International Cinema* (New York: Oxford University Press, 1983), 16–17.

3 Richard Dienst, *Still Life in Real Time: Theory after Television* (Durham, N.C.: Duke University Press, 1994), 145–46.

4 Gérard Genette, *Narrative Discourse: An Essay in Method,* trans. Jane E. Lewin (Ithaca: Cornell University Press, 1980), 23.

5 Sitney, *Vital Crises,* 1–6.

6 One could argue that the French and Japanese New Waves were also dealing with modernization in roughly the same period. But there is certainly the case to be made that for the French New Wave, Italian cinema was already paradigmatic, not only for showing the possibilities for a cinematic *écriture* (which the French could discern in their own tradition, in Vigo, Renoir, Bresson) but, more important, in the way that it showed the viability of a cinema that deviated from the international style of classical Hollywood. And the key directors of the Japanese New Wave were in turn very much influenced by the French.

7 I am using "essentialist" in the sense developed by Clifford Geertz and deployed in James Hay's study, *Popular Film Culture in Fascist Italy* (Bloomington: Indiana University Press, 1987), 8.

8 An excellent study of both genre and auteur films and their audiences in Italy is Vittorio Spinazzola, *Cinema e pubblico: Lo spettacolo filmico in Italia, 1945–1965* (Milan: Bompiani, 1974).

9 I am arguing here against the structuralist analogy of nations as a differen-

tial system, as set forth, for example, in Andrew Higson, "The Concept of a National Cinema," *Screen* 30.4 (fall 1989): 36–47.

10   I hold this position in common with, for example, Millicent Marcus, in her *Italian Cinema in the Light of Neorealism* (Princeton: Princeton University Press, 1986).

11   Bazin, "An Aesthetic of Reality," *What Is Cinema?* 2 vols, trans. Hugh Gray (Berkeley: University of California Press, 1971), 2 : 20.

12   For Bazin, the time frame was "endless months" ("An Aesthetic," 20); more recent historians would say years, or even decades, depending of course on the political position from which they are viewing postwar Italy.

13   Angela Dalle Vacche's study of Italian cinema takes as one of its theses the centrality of history to Italian cinema. See *The Body in the Mirror* (Princeton: Princeton University Press, 1992).

14   Thomas Elsaesser, "What Does Žižek Want?" *Spectator* 16.2 (1996): 13.

15   Philip Rosen, "History, Textuality, Nation: Kracauer, Burch, and Some Problems in the Study of National Cinema," *Iris* 2.2 (1984): 71.

16   The psychoanalytic terms "gaze" and "trauma" here are the result of my inflection of Rosen's argument.

17   Walter Benjamin, "Theses on the Philosophy of History," *Illuminations,* ed. Hannah Arendt, trans. Harry Zohn (New York: Schocken, 1968), 253–64.

18   Jean-François Lyotard, *The Postmodern Condition: A Report on Knowledge,* trans. Geoff Bennington and Brian Massumi (Minneapolis: University of Minnesota Press, 1984), 3–5.

19   Armand Mattelart and Michèle Mattelart, *Rethinking Media Theory,* trans. James A. Cohen and Marina Urquidi (Minneapolis: University of Minnesota Press, 1992), 122–25.

20   Michel Pêcheux, quoted in Mattelart and Mattelart, *Rethinking,* 69.

21   Mattelart and Mattelart, *Rethinking,* 123. Italics mine.

22   Thomas Elsaesser, *New German Cinema: A History* (New York: Rutgers University Press, 1989); Marsha Kinder, *Blood Cinema: The Reconstruction of National Identity in Spain* (Berkeley: University of California Press, 1993). I have selected these two studies because they both make claims to comprehensiveness while neither is conceived or written as a "survey." That said, I must remark here that I consider Rey Chow's study of Fifth Generation Chinese cinema—*Primitive Passions*—to be superb. In fact, with its central concern with questions of visuality in both a national and transnational context, her study has many points of contact with my own, points that I will discuss in the final chapter of this book.

23   Thomas Elsaesser, "Primary Identification and the Historical Subject," *Cine-Tracts* 11 (fall 1980): 48–49; and *New German Cinema,* 60–63.

24   The notion that the subject's symbolic identification might be constituted by a resistance to the position carved out by his/her speech is not, I think, sufficiently appreciated in critical theory. The neurotic's position in relation

to "his/her" discourse, for example, can be understood in terms of the gap between the symbolic position carved out by that discourse, and the person the neurotic thinks him/herself to be. For the graph of desire in which Lacan develops this notion of symbolic identification, see "The Subversion of the Subject and the Dialectic of Desire," in Jacques Lacan, *Écrits: A Selection,* trans. Alan Sheridan (New York: Norton, 1977), 303–15.

25 Thus, although the psychoanalytic view of history may be of *longue durée,* it is not therefore justified to conclude that psychoanalysis is ahistorical.

26 Peter Brooks, *The Melodramatic Imagination: Balzac, Henry James, Melodrama and the Mode of Excess* (New York: Columbia University Press, 1985), 15.

27 The starting point for the arguments presented lies in Jacques Lacan, "Kant with Sade," *October* 40 (1987): 55–104. Its application to the idea of the nation can be found in Slavoj Žižek, *Looking Awry: An Introduction to Jacques Lacan through Popular Culture* (Cambridge, Mass.: MIT Press, 1992), 162–69; and Slavoj Žižek, *Tarrying with the Negative: Kant, Hegel, and the Critique of Ideology* (Durham: Duke University Press, 1993), 200–237.

28 Mattelart and Mattelart, *Rethinking,* 99–100.

29 Homi K. Bhabha, "DissemiNation: Time, Narrative and the Margins of the Modern Nation," in *Nation and Narration,* ed. Homi Bhabha (New York: Routledge, 1993), 291–322.

30 Žižek, *Tarrying,* 202.

31 Žižek, *Tarrying,* 202.

32 A central psychoanalytic tenet since Freud's *Three Essays on the Theory of Sexuality,* which differentiates between the drive's aim and its object. Sigmund Freud, *Three Essays on the Theory of Sexuality,* ed. and trans. James Strachey (New York: Avon, 1972).

33 Fredric Jameson, "Imaginary and Symbolic in Lacan," in *The Ideologies of Theory: Essays, 1971–1986,* 2 vols. (London: Routledge, 1988), 1:106.

34 Dudley Andrew, *Mists of Regret: Culture and Sensibility in Classic French Film* (Princeton: Princeton University Press, 1995), 17.

35 Max Horkheimer and Theodor W. Adorno, *Dialectic of Enlightenment,* trans. John Cumming (New York: Continuum Publishing Company, 1997), 148; quoted in Fredric Jameson, *Signatures of the Visible* (New York: Routledge, 1990), 155.

36 Eric J. Hobsbawm, *Nations and Nationalism since 1870: Programme, Myth, Reality* (Cambridge: Cambridge University Press, 1990), 25.

37 Antonio Gramsci, "Notes on Italian History," in *Prison Notebooks,* ed. and trans. Quintin Hoare and Geoffrey Nowell-Smith (New York: International Publishers, 1971), 52–120.

38 Hay, *Popular Film Culture,* chaps. 3–4. The *Strapaese* ("Supercountry") was a defined and organized movement during the fascist period promoting

small town life and rural values. *Stracittà* ("Supercity") valorized the urban and the modern, and in fascist cinema was exemplified by such cycles as the "Grand Hotel" films.

39 Mira Liehm, *Passion and Defiance: Film in Italy from 1942 to the Present* (Berkeley: University of California Press, 1984), 57.

40 In Sigmund Freud, *Civilization and Its Discontents* ed. and trans. James Strachey (New York: Norton, 1961), 16–18.

41 Pierre Sorlin, in *European Cinemas, European Societies,* has made one of the few contributions so far to the discussion of this opposition in Italian cinema. See Pierre Sorlin, *European Cinemas, European Societies, 1939–1990* (New York: Routledge, 1991), 117–30.

2. Neorealism and the Stain

1 Millicent Marcus, *Italian Film in the Light of Neo-Realism* (Princeton: Princeton University Press, 1986), 3.

2 Fredric Jameson, "The Vanishing Mediator; or, Max Weber as Storyteller," *The Ideologies of Theory: Essays, 1971–1986,* 2 vols. (London: Routledge, 1988), 2:3–34.

3 Vittorio Spinazzola, *Cinema e pubblico: Lo spettacolo filmico in Italia, 1945–1965* (Milan: Bompiani, 1974), 101–21.

4 See Mira Liehm, *Passion and Defiance: Film in Italy from 1942 to the Present* (Berkeley: University of California Press, 1984), 91.

5 Benedict Andersen, *Imagined Communities: Reflections on the Origin and Spread of Nationalism* (New York: Verso, 1993), chap. 1.

6 Peter Brunette, *Roberto Rossellini* (New York: Oxford University Press, 1987), 43–45.

7 See the section entitled "Narrative Technique" in "An Aesthetic of Reality," in André Bazin, *What Is Cinema?* 2 vols., trans. Hugh Gray (Berkeley: University of California Press, 1971), 2:30–38.

8 For a discussion of the concept of coralità and its use by Italian commentators on neorealism, see P. Adams Sitney, *Vital Crises in Italian Cinema: Iconography, Stylistics, Politics* (Austin: University of Texas Press, 1995), 30–31.

9 According to Bazin, this is achieved most fully by the work of De Sica. Bazin, *What Is Cinema?* 2:60.

10 The use of the telephone as device in *Roma* is discussed by Vincent Rocchio in his psychoanalytic study of neorealism. Vincent Rocchio, *Cinema of Anxiety: A Psychoanalysis of Italian Neorealism* (Austin: University of Texas Press, 1999), 33, 37.

11 The influx of American films into Italian theaters in the immediate postwar period was so great that it prompted legislative moves in 1948 to enact pro-

tective barriers. See Spinazzola, *Cinema e pubblico,* 8; Liehm, *Passion and Defiance,* 90–91.

12 See Paul Ginsborg, *A History of Contemporary Italy: Society and Politics, 1943–1988* (New York: Penguin, 1990), 39–42, 56–57.

13 Sitney notes the importance of both monuments and the sounds of gunfire in this episode of the film. Sitney, *Vital Crises,* 51–52.

14 Tucker's film, through the dictaphone and the phone lines, also uses sound to uncover the network of corruption in the city. However, the film being "silent," the film must indicate all this visually.

15 Liehm, *Passion and Defiance,* 51–53.

16 The notion is from George Steiner and is discussed in relation to Pasolini by Naomi Greene, *Pier Paolo Pasolini: Cinema as Heresy* (Princeton: Princeton University Press, 1990), 50–52.

17 The dialectic between the seen and unseen is uncovered by Gilles Deleuze, *Cinema 1: The Movement-Image,* trans. Hugh Tomlinson and Barbara Habberjam (Minneapolis: University of Minnesota Press, 1989), 30; it is discussed in Greene, *Pier Paolo Pasolini,* 46.

18 Peter Brooks, *The Melodramatic Imagination: Balzac, Henry James, Melodrama and the Mode of Excess* (New York: Columbia University Press, 1985), 16–22.

19 Contemporary psychoanalysis gives a name to this insubstantial entity that gives to the world its sense of fullness: object *a.*

20 Angela Dalle Vacche, *Cinema and Painting: How Art Is Used in Film* (Austin: University of Texas Press, 1996), 50.

21 See Spinazzola, *Cinema e pubblico,* chap. 9.

22 For an excellent discussion of the Marxist positions on cultural practice in Italy in the fifties, see Greene, *Pier Paolo Pasolini,* 31–35.

23 Bazin, *What Is Cinema?* 2 : 83–92.

24 Gilles Deleuze, *Cinema 2: The Time-Image,* trans. Hugh Tomlinson and Robert Galeta (Minneapolis: University of Minnesota Press, 1989), 88.

25 See the scene in Tornatore's *Nuovo Cinema Paradiso* when *La dolce vita* is first projected in the small Sicilian town.

26 P. Adams Sitney has noted the importance of Spinazzola's term. However, Sitney, I believe, makes a mistake in including the work of Antonioni within this category. It is true that Spinazzola suggests that even the work of Antonioni was able to capture a larger audience in this period; but this was limited by Antonioni's resistance to a concession to spectacle. See Sitney, *Vital Crises,* 111–12; Spinazzola, *Cinema e pubblico,* 238, 242.

27 Sitney, *Vital Crises,* 113.

28 Sitney, *Vital Crises,* 116.

29 See, for example, David Harvey, *The Condition of Postmodernity* (Oxford: Blackwell, 1989); Fredric Jameson, *The Geopolitical Aesthetic: Cinema and*

Space in the World System (Bloomington: Indiana University Press, 1995); and Edward Soja, *Postmodern Geographies: The Reassertion of Space in Critical Theory* (New York: Verso, 1993).

30 Interestingly, one of Jacques Lacan's only pronouncements on the cinema had to do with the final sequences of *La dolce vita*, where he mentions, among other things, the status of the sea creature as the Thing. Jacques Lacan, *Seminar VII: The Ethics of Psychoanalysis*, ed. Jacques-Alain Miller, trans. Dennis Porter (New York: Norton, 1992), 253. The concept of *das Ding*—elaborated by Lacan in Seminar 7—has received considerable theoretical attention in recent years, as has Lacan's concomitant shift of attention from desire to the drives. See, for example, Slavoj Žižek, *The Sublime Object of Ideology* (New York: Verso, 1989), 201–31 (on the philosophical dimensions of the Thing); Žižek, *The Metastases of Enjoyment* (New York: Verso, 1994), 89–112 (an analysis of the discussion of courtly love in Lacan's Seminar 7); Joan Copjec, *Read My Desire: Lacan against the Historicists* (Cambridge, Mass.: MIT Press, 1995), 175–200 (on the move from desire to drive).

31 Which Sitney more accurately traces to the character of Matelda in the *Purgatorio*. Sitney, *Vital Crises*, 117–18.

32 Sitney, *Vital Crises*, 117–18.

33 Michel Chion, "Quiet Revolution . . . and Rigid Stagnation," *October* 58 (1991), 69–80.

3. Tropes of Modernization: The Bandit and the Road

1 See Gian Piero Brunetta, *Cent'anni di cinema italiano* (Rome: Editori Laterza, 1991), chap. 27.

2 All data taken from the "Statistical Appendix" to Paul Ginsborg, *A History of Contemporary Italy: Society and Politics, 1943–1988* (New York: Penguin, 1990), 427–55.

3 Brunetta, *Cent'anni*, 588–89.

4 Eric J. Hobsbawm, *Bandits* (New York: Pantheon, 1981), 19.

5 Hobsbawm, *Bandits*, 23.

6 Martin Clark, *Modern Italy, 1871–1982*, Longman History of Italy 7 (New York: Longman, 1984), 369.

7 Marsha Kinder, "Subversive Potential of the Pseudo-Iterative," *Film Quarterly* 43.2 (1989): 2–16.

8 The word "lament" comes up here because it is part of the title of a Spanish bandit film from the same period: Carlos Saura's *Llanto por un bandido*.

9 Cesare Zavattini, "A Thesis on Neorealism," in *Springtime in Italy: A Reader on Neorealism*, ed. David Overbey (Hamden, Conn.: Archon Books, 1979), 67–77.

10 P. Adams Sitney suggests that this last victim could be the unnamed mafia liaison in the plot to assassinate Giuliano, although he later notes that "the

shot deliberately hedges a clear identification." See Sitney, *Vital Crises in Italian Cinema: Iconography, Stylistics, Politics* (Austin: University of Texas Press, 1955), 203–5. Recently I was able to view a pristine 35mm print of the film, and there, the body of the victim was clearly identifiable as the mafia liaison.

11 See, for example, Homi K. Bhabha, "DissemiNation," in *Nation and Narration* ed. Homi K. Bhabha (New York: Routledge, 1993), 291–321.

12 Sitney, *Vital Crises,* 173–84; Naomi Greene, *Pier Paolo Pasolini: Cinema as Heresy* (Princeton: Princeton University Press, 1990), 39–52; Maurizio Viano, *A Certain Realism: Making Sense of Pasolini's Film Theory and Practice* (Berkeley: University of California Press, 1993), 68–83.

13 Sitney, *Vital Crises,* 178–79.

14 Pier Paolo Pasolini, "The Cinema of Poetry," in *Heretical Empiricism,* trans. Ben Lawton and Kate L. Barnett (Bloomington: Indiana University Press, 1988), 167–86.

15 The complexities attendant to the concept of the dialectical image in part result from the aphoristic quality of Benjamin's writing. Most discussions of the dialectical image begin from a reading of "Theses on the Philosophy of History," while the recently translated Arcades Project provides many instances illustrating how Benjamin may have meant the dialectical image to be understood. Walter Benjamin, *The Arcades Project,* trans. Howard Eiland and Kevin McLaughlin (Cambridge, Mass.: Harvard University Press, 1999), passim. Much of Susan Buck-Morss's *The Dialectics of Seeing: Walter Benjamin and the Arcades Project* (Cambridge, Mass.: MIT Press, 1991) is devoted to exploring the nature of the dialectical image. For a discussion of the dialectical image in Antonioni, see Joan Esposito, "Antonioni and Benjamin: Dialectical Imagery in Eclipse," *Film Criticism* 9.1 (1984): 25–37.

16 Gilles Deleuze, *Cinema 2: The Time-Image,* trans. Hugh Tomlinson and Robert Galeta (Minneapolis: Univeristy of Minnesota Press, 1989), 20–21.

17 Deleuze, *The Time-Image,* 2.

18 In Italy in 1990, a major media story concerned "Le strage di sabato sera" ["Saturday Night Carnage"—playing on the film title *Saturday Night Fever*]. Young people were driving literally hundreds of kilometers on Saturday evenings, just to be at the "right" discotheque, which resulted in a rash of drunken-driving accidents the following morning.

19 Fredric Jameson, *The Political Unconscious: Narrative as a Socially Symbolic Act* (Ithaca: Cornell University Press, 1991), 166–68.

4. Spatial Transformations: Mapping the New Italy

1 Slavoj Žižek, *The Sublime Object of Ideology* (New York: Verso, 1989), 87–100, 136–44. See also Žižek, *Enjoy Your Symptom! Jacques Lacan in Hollywood and Out* (New York: Routledge, 1992), chap. 3.

2 Henri Lefebvre, *The Production of Space,* trans. Donald Nicholson-Smith (Cambridge, Mass.: Blackwell, 1991), 46.

3 To use a binary opposition whose clever phrasing was given to me by Lynn Spigel.

4 Giuliana Bruno, *Streetwalking on a Ruined Map: Cultural Theory and the City Films of Elvira Notari* (Princeton: Princeton University Press, 1993), 47–57.

5 Margaret Morse, "An Ontology of Everyday Distraction: the Freeway, the Mall, and Television," in *Logics of Television,* ed. Patricia Mellencamp (Bloomington: Indiana University Press, 1990), 193–221; for further discussion of these issues, see Anne Friedberg, "*Les Flâneurs du Mal(l):* Cinema and the Postmodern Condition," *PMLA* 106.3 (1991): 419–31; Jean Baudrillard, "The System of Objects," in *Selected Writings,* ed. Mark Poster (Stanford: Stanford University Press, 1988), 10–28.

6 Lefebvre, *Production of Space,* 125.

7 Walter Benjamin, "Naples," in *Reflections,* trans. Hannah Arendt (New York: Schocken, 1978), 165–71. See also Susan Buck-Morss, *The Dialectics of Seeing: Walter Benjamin and the Arcades Project* (Cambridge, Mass.: MIT Press, 1989), esp. chap. 2.

8 This particular truffa is taken from personal experience. Benjamin discusses this Neapolitan practice in his essay "Naples"; and for an exhaustive and witty catalogue of *truffe,* see Luciano DeCrescenzo, *Thus Spake Bellavista: Naples, Love, and Liberty,* trans. Avril Bardoni (New York: Grove Press, 1988).

9 Victor Burgin, "The City in Pieces," *In/Different Spaces: Place and Memory in Visual Culture* (Berkeley: University of California Press, 1996), 139–60.

10 Lefebvre, *Production of Space,* 58.

11 At this point, it would be interesting to speculate on the extent to which Italian geography has shaped the post-1980 economic structures of the highly prosperous "Third Italy" (the area centered on Emilia-Romagna); in this region there evolved a kind of entrepreneurship based upon the family and centered in the home or its immediate environs. Certainly this model of capitalist development is seemingly at odds with the increasing economic concentrations we see elsewhere; at the same time, these family industries are fully plugged into the global economic system, often serving as middle points between the production of raw material in the underdeveloped world and the sale of finished product in the developed.

12 Fredric Jameson, "Architecture and the Critique of Ideology," in *The Ideologies of Theory: Essays, 1971–1986,* 2 vols. (London: Routledge, 1988), 2: 35–60.

13 Donald Sassoon, *Contemporary Italy: Politics, Economy and Society since 1945* (New York: Longman, 1986), 152–63.

14 Pier Paolo Pasolini, "New Linguistic Questions," has been translated and

appears in the collection *Heretical Empiricism,* trans. Ben Lawton and Kate L. Barnett (Bloomington: Indiana University Press, 1988), 3–22.

15 Pasolini, "New Linguistic Questions." Also Pier Paolo Pasolini, "L'italiano è ancora in fasce," *L'Espresso,* 7 February 1965.

16 Sassoon, *Contemporary Italy,* 57–58.

17 Andrea Barbato, "Una Faluca per Pasolini," *L'Espresso,* 14 February 1965. My translation.

18 Given the subject of this chapter, it should be noted here the important role that the army (and universal male military service) played in the construction of a new national subjectivity—something centrally inscribed in the 1977 film of the Taviani brothers, *Padre padrone.* It is not only that the army brought together the disparate regions under the language of "standard Italian"; it also provided the regions with an "infrastructure" of men skilled in low-level technologies, necessary for the coming explosion of consumer durables.

19 That the Italian cinema of the sixties was exporting the signifier "Italy as fashion"—especially to American audiences—can be seen in an episode of *I Love Lucy* from the early sixties. In it, the Riccardos and the Mertzes have just returned from seeing the latest Italian film; and while the husbands seemed to have enjoyed it, it is the wives, Lucy and Ethel, who are transported into dreamy and romantic reveries. These end up taking form in Lucy's desire for the smart new Italian hairstyle the actress was wearing. Interestingly, the TV show takes an odd narrative turn by informing husband Ricky of Lucy's planned *truffa,* thus eliminating from the episode the potentially subversive elements of deception, masquerade, and transgressive sexual desire mobilized by the prospect of an "anonymous" sexual encounter between Ricky and his unrecognized wife.

20 This exact sexual dynamic is seen in Bertolucci's *Conformist* (1971), where the political intrigues of the men are always somewhat ridiculous in the face of the women's "masquerade." This is most evident in the scene in the dance hall, when the camera cuts outside the hall to photograph Marcello and Quadri through the window, upon which is tacked up a photograph of Laurel and Hardy.

21 Fredric Jameson, "Surrealism without the Unconscious," in *Postmodernism, or, The Cultural Logic of Late Capitalism* (Durham, N.C.: Duke University Press, 1991), 77.

22 For this distinction, see Michel deCerteau, *The Practice of Everyday Life,* trans. S. Rendall (Berkeley: University of California Press, 1984), 34–39.

23 Michael Bommes and Patrick Wright, "'Charms of Residence': the Public and the Past," in *Making Histories: Studies in History, Writing, and Politics,* ed. R. Johnson et al. (London: Hutchinson, 1982), 290.

24 For the relationship between the car and "postmodern geography" generally, see Morse, "Ontology of Everyday Distraction," 195–201.

25 James Hay, "Invisible Cities/Visible Geographies: Toward a Cultural Geography of Italian Television in the 90s," *Quarterly Review of Film and Video* 14.3 (April 1993): 41.

26 Jean Baudrillard, "Consumer Society," *Selected Writings,* ed. Mark Poster (Stanford: Stanford University Press, 1988), 29–56.

5. Pasolini and the Limits of Resistance

1 That Pasolini was aware of the processes by which his work was recuperated is evident in his essay "Il mio *Accattone* in tv dopo il genocidio," in *Lettere luterane* (Torino: Einaudi, 1976), 152–58. On the subject of sex and modernity, see Michel Foucault, *The History of Sexuality,* vol. 1, trans. Robert Hurley (New York Vintage, 1980), passim.

2 It must be stressed here that I do not hold to a strictly historicist or "Foucauldian" notion of the constructedness of sexuality. Psychoanalysis maintains that sex is itself a manifestation of the impossible/Real, however much discourse circulates around this Real. See the crucial essay by Joan Copjec, "Sex and the Euthanasia of Reason," in *Supposing the Subject,* ed. Joan Copjec (New York: Verso, 1994), 16–44.

3 The centrality of the body to Pasolini's work was noted at the beginning of this chapter. There is, we should note, important work on the importance of bodily affect as guarantor of truth in Pasolini's poetry; and on Pasolini's iconographic borrowings from early Renaissance painting, which privileges frontality and "gravity," in his films. Maurizio Viano, *A Certain Realism: Making Use of Pasolini's Film Theory and Practice* (Berkeley: University of California Press, 1993), 14–15, 239; Naomi Greene, *Cinema as Heresy: Pier Paolo Pasolini* (Princeton: Princeton University Press, 1990), 44–45.

4 Joan Copjec, "The Phenomenal Nonphenomenal," in *Shades of Noir,* ed. Joan Copjec (New York: Verso, 1993), 184.

5 Bill Nichols, *Representing Reality: Issues and Concepts in Documentary* (Bloomington: Indiana University Press, 1991), 249–54.

6 Slavoj Žižek, *The Sublime Object of Ideology* (New York: Verso, 1989), 21–26.

7 Michel Foucault, *The History of Sexuality,* vol. 1, trans. Robert Hurley (New York: Vintage, 1980), 147.

8 Foucault, *History of Sexuality,* 104–5.

9 *L'Espresso,* 23 May 1965, 30 May 1965.

10 Foucault, *History of Sexuality,* 43.

11 Here my argument is methodologically indebted to Fredric Jameson's semiotic mapping of space in *North by Northwest.* See Fredric Jameson, "Spatial Systems in *North by Northwest*" in *Everything You Always Wanted to Know about Lacan, but Were Afraid to Ask Hitchcock,* ed. Slavoj Žižek (New York: Verso, 1992), 47–72.

12 Arguably, *Porcile* examines the upper bourgeoisie, but in a broadly parodic way.

13 Maurizio Viano notes the importance of the newsreel footage in setting up the terms of the film. I concur with his reading that the opening strategy marks the film with a "crisis of signs" that the film then attempts "theorematically" to solve. I don't agree with his implication that the "unanswered question" of the television interview is somehow left unclear: in fact, the question to be answered is, what happens when the worker becomes bourgeois? This question becomes in Pasolini's later work, what happens when the worker becomes a consumer? Maurizio Viano, *A Certain Realism: Making Use of Pasolini's Film Theory and Practice* (Berkeley: University of California Press, 1993), 200–206, 212.

14 Thomas Elsaesser, "Tales of Sound and Fury: Observations on the Family Melodrama," in *Film Theory and Criticism,* 4th ed., ed. Gerald Mast, Marshall Cohen, and Leo Braudy (New York: Oxford University Press, 1992), 529.

15 It is important to note that Deleuze is engaged in a classification of cinematic images from an aesthetic (and even "epistemological") ground, and so does not present or subscribe to a chronological view of history. Thus, prewar films by Dreyer can anticipate traits of "modern" cinema, while a recent blockbuster can be thoroughly "classical" in its image organization.

16 This is my own condensation of an argument that arches through Deleuze's two volumes. Gilles Deleuze, *Cinema 1: The Movement-Image,* trans. Hugh Tomlinson and Barbara Habberjam (Minneapolis: University of Minnesota Press, 1989), and *Cinema 2: The Time-Image,* trans. Hugh Tomlinson and Robert Galata (Minneapolis: University of Minnesota Press, 1989).

17 Deleuze, *The Time-Image* 174–75. For an excellent discussion of the relationship between Kant's reflective judgment and Deleuze's emergences of the new, see Gregory Flaxman's introduction to *The Brain Is the Screen: Deleuze and the Philosophy of Cinema,* ed. Gregory Flaxman (Minneapolis: University of Minnesota Press, 2000) 38–39.

6. The Object Antonioni

1 Antonioni's remark is quoted in Sam Rohdie, *Antonioni* (London: British Film Institute, 1990), 39.

2 Peter Brunette's book on Antonioni addresses the issue of the economic boom in relation to Antonioni's work. In addition, his introduction discusses the way the critical literature has—with a few important exceptions—failed to connect the formal to the sociopolitical in Antonioni's work. See Peter Brunette, *The Films of Michelangelo Antonioni* (New York: Cambridge University Press, 1998).

3 For the political history of the immediate postwar period and the events of

1948, see Paul Ginsborg, *A History of Contemporary Italy: Society and Politics, 1943–1988* (New York: Penguin, 1990), chap. 3.

4 Sam Rohdie provides an excellent account of the critical reception of *Gente del Po*. Rohdie, *Antonioni*, 28–29.

5 See Peter Brunette, *Roberto Rossellini* (New York: Oxford University Press, 1987), 123–27, 168–70, for an excellent discussion of these moments.

6 This is precisely the quality that Bazin and later phenomenologists used to argue in favor of the possibility for transcendence, via the camera's implacable presentation of the "thingness" of the world.

7 Žižek's analysis of the Bergman/Rossellini films is short but brilliant. He notes, "Every one of [Rossellini's] films is an ultimately failed attempt to come to terms with the Real of some traumatic encounter." See Slavoj Žižek, *Enjoy Your Symptom!* (New York: Routledge, 1992), 60.

8 The sequence starts with cross-cut point-of-view shots of Katherine crying out to Alex as she is swept away by the crowd, and Alex moving forward to try to reach her. The sequence abruptly cuts to an overhead shot: when looked at on the moviola, one can see that Alex indeed reaches Katherine in this distant shot; but in the actual experience of a viewing, one cannot make out this action. Thus, the final shot of the two of them coming together seems to be a jump cut.

9 The notorious bad blood between Rossellini and Sanders can be traced back to Rossellini's insistence that Sanders "open himself up" to the camera's observation; i.e., that he not "act." See Brunette, *Roberto Rossellini*, 157.

10 See, for example, "An Aesthetic of Reality" and "In Defense of Rossellini" in André Bazin, *What Is Cinema?* 2 vols., trans. Hugh Gray (Berkeley: University of California Press, 1971), 2:30–38, 2:93–101.

11 Dudley Andrew develops this notion further, in his essay "The Gravity of *Sunrise*," *Quarterly Review of Film* 2.3 (1977): 356–77.

12 Pier Paolo Pasolini, "The Cinema of Poetry," in *Heretical Empiricism* 167–86. Antonioni is one of three directors Pasolini discusses in relation to free indirect discourse; the other two are Godard and Bertolucci.

13 Italian film scholar Lorenzo Cuccu has argued that Antonioni's work is best seen as an examination of the conditions of visuality. He sees Antonioni's work as moving from a "cinema of images" to a "critique of images" to a "critique of the Look/the Gaze" (in Italian, *lo Sguardo,* which can mean both look and gaze). Cuccu sees the films from *Blow-up* to *The Passenger* as those films in which Antonioni moves to the examination of the gaze, whereas I am arguing that this process begins much earlier in Antonioni's work. Cuccu doesn't, however, deploy the Lacanian notion of the gaze (as "seeing oneself being seen") except in a few suggestive remarks on *The Passenger*. See Lorenzo Cuccu, *Antonioni: Il discorso dello sguardo e altri saggi* (Pisa: Edizioni ETS, 1997), esp. 209–17.

14 I should point out that the Lacanian references in this chapter title — to both

object *a* and capital A (Other) —are also intentional, and will be addressed directly.

15 Jacques Lacan, *Seminar XI: The Four Fundamental Concepts of Psychoanalysis,* ed. Jacques-Alain Miller, trans. Alan Sheridan (New York: Norton, 1977), 274.

16 This issue is the subject of some debate in analytic circles. I would note that in the definitive reference by Laplanche and Pontalis, the authors note the ways in which Freud clearly differentiates between the two terms. J. Laplanche and J.-B. Pontalis, *The Language of Psychoanalysis,* trans. Donald Nicholson-Smith (New York: Norton, 1973), 214.

17 See Lacan, *Fundamental Concepts,* 149–73. For an excellent discussion of the drives, see also Maire Jaanus, "The *Démontage* of the Drive," in *Reading Seminar XI,* ed. Richard Feldstein et al. (Albany: SUNY Press, 1995), 119–36.

18 Which is why Lacan speaks of the *démontage* of the drives. See Lacan, *Fundamental Concepts,* 161–73. See also Jaanus 119–36; Eric Laurent, "Alienation and Separation," in *Reading Seminar XI,* ed. Feldstein et al., 26–28.

19 Lacan, *Fundamental Concepts,* 67–119.

20 See Žižek, *Looking Awry: An Introduction to Jacques Lacan through Popular Culture* (Cambridge, Mass.: MIT Press, 1992), 94–96; *Enjoy Your Symptom!* 113–24.

21 "The gaze" has been a concept at play in film theory since the psychoanalytic turn in the 1970s, although it can certainly be argued that it was so often oversimplified (by conflation with a panoptic, Foucauldian notion of the gaze that anchors it to a conscious agency) that the problems that arose subsequently were erroneously attributed to the Lacanian notion itself rather than its oversimplifications. A turning point came with the publication of Joan Copjec's "The Orthopyschic Subject" in the journal *October* in 1989 (reprinted in *Read My Desire: Lacan against the Historicists* (Cambridge, Mass.: MIT Press, 1995), 15–38, followed by Žižek's *Looking Awry.* Later in the nineties, Hal Foster wrote a number of essays for *October* that continued to argue for a more complex, decentered conception of the gaze, in essays such as "Obscene, Abject, Traumatic," *October* 78 (1996). See also Renata Salecl and Slavoj Žižek, eds., *Gaze and Voice as Love Objects* (Durham, N.C.: Duke University Press, 1996); and Kaja Silverman, *Threshold of the Visible World* (New York: Routledge, 1996).

22 Gilles Deleuze, *Cinema 1: Movement-Image,* trans. Hugh Tomlinson and Barbara Habberjam (Minneapolis: University of Minnesota Press, 1989), 56–66.

23 In Pasolini, *Heretical Empiricism,* trans. Ben Lawton and Karl L. Barnett (Bloomington: Indiana University Press, 1988), 233–37.

24 Deleuze both understands and criticizes Pasolini's use of the term "mimesis." He understands that Pasolini retains the word because of its connec-

tion to the sacred quality of the act, but argues that Pasolini really isn't talking about imitation, but rather about "correlation between two asymmetrical proceedings." Deleuze, *Movement-Image*, 73.

25 This is of course Kant's position.

26 See Žižek for a discussion of this phenomenon. Žižek, *Enjoy Your Sympton!* 165–86.

27 This is the weakness in what I take to be Žižek's oversimplified reading of the film. See *Looking Awry*, 145.

28 Marsha Kinder, "Antonioni in Transit," in *Focus on* Blow-up, ed. Roy Huss (Englewood Cliffs, N.J.: Prentice-Hall, 1971), 78–88.

29 Fredric Jameson, "The Existence of Italy," in *Signatures of the Visible* (New York: Routledge, 1992), 194–97.

30 Jean Baudrillard, "Consumer Society," in *Selected Writings*, ed. Mark Poster (Stanford: Stanford University Press, 1988), 29–56.

31 The critical discussions of Antonioni's general aesthetic orientation are summarized throughout Seymour Chatman, *Antonioni, or The Surface of the World* (Berkeley: University of California Press, 1985).

32 Angela Dalle Vacche, *Cinema and Painting: How Art Is Used in Film* (Austin: University of Texas Press, 1996), 48–49.

33 For an excellent discussion of the Lacanian gaze, see, Žižek, *Enjoy Your Symptom!* 94–95, 107–22.

34 Hal Foster, "Obscene, Abject, Traumatic," *October* 78 (1996): 107. (I have removed italics.)

35 As does Kaja Silverman. See her *Threshold of the Visible World* (New York: Routledge, 1996), 18–19 and passim.

36 "Analogon" is a concept from Jean-Paul Sartre and is defined by Fredric Jameson as follows: "that structural nexus in our reading or viewing experience, in our operations of decoding or aesthetic reception, which can then do double duty and stand as the substitute and the representative within the aesthetic object of a phenomenon on the outside which cannot in the very nature of things be 'rendered' directly." Fredric Jameson, *Signatures of the Visible*, 53.

37 Here I am borrowing from Deleuze in both the vocabulary I'm using and the conceptual scheme I'm adopting.

38 As Gregory Flaxman astutely notes in his introduction to *The Brain Is the Screen*, Deleuze adopts a kind of neo-Kantianism when he suggests that the move from classical to modern cinema is a move from determinate judgment (and hence "metaphor") to reflective judgment. Flaxman, *The Brain Is the Screen: Deleuze and the Philosophy of Cinema* (Minneapolis: University of Minnesota Press, 2000), 38.

39 Again, suggesting the process of Kant's "reflective judgment" as set forth in his *Critique of Judgment*.

40 Kevin Z. Moore, "Eclipsing the Commonplace: The Logic of Alienation in Antonioni's Cinema," *Film Quarterly* 48.4 (1995): 22–34.

41 Thus, the stakes in this debate for the current state of film studies are high: for in the last decade at least, we've seen a widespread attack on "theory" within the discipline. A director like Antonioni in this climate would appear to be a last bastion to be taken by those with empiricist claims; so it is doubly important to insist on the deconstructive force of Antonioni's work—"deconstruction" taken here in its strict, Heideggerian sense.

42 Roger Caillois, "Mimicry and Legendary Psychasthenia," quoted in Foster, "Obscene, Abject, Traumatic," 121.

43 Foster's gloss on Caillois, in "Obscene, Abject, Traumatic."

7. The Sublime and the Disaster

1 Sam Rohdie identifies this moment in the film and provides an interesting discussion of the problem of acting that it presents. Rohdie, *Antonioni* (London: British Film Institute, 1990), 110, 117.

2 Pier Paolo Pasolini, "The Cinema of Poetry." In *Heretical Empiricism,* trans. Ben Lawton and Kate L. Barrett (Bloomington: Indiana University Press, 1988), 167–86. See chapter 6 for an extended discussion of this essay.

3 Angela Dalle Vacche notes how Antonioni's decors play with the bravura of Italian industrial design. One of the most interesting points she makes, along with Andrea Branzi, in this regard is that Italian industrial design benefitted from "the advantage of delay": that the delayed economic modernization in Italy allowed residual, artisinal modes to inflect the modernization process itself. This has interesting points of contact with this study's discussion of uneven development and the porosity of the Italian urban space, in chapter 4 above. Dalle Vacche, *Cinema and Painting: How Art Is Used in Film* (Austin: University of Texas Press, 1996), 55–56.

4 Dalle Vacche, *Cinema and Painting,* 70.

5 Dalle Vacche, *Cinema and Painting,* 72.

6 Slavoj Žižek, *Looking Awry: An Introduction to Jacques Lacan through Popular Culture* (Cambridge, Mass.: MIT Press, 1992), 22; *Tarrying with the Negative: Kant, Hegel, and the Critique of Ideology* (Durham, N.C.: Duke University Press, 1993), chap. 1.

7 At this point, I must address a possible misunderstanding of the textual strategy involved in my reading. For when I presented a sketch of this material in a conference paper, some listeners were troubled by what they perceived as an argument based on analogy or metaphor. Perhaps this is a natural misunderstanding, for traditional textual analysis often works by positing a metaphoric value to a particular repeated phrase, image, or structure in the work (in which case, for example, "psychoanalysis" is being "ap-

plied to" the text). I am not doing "applied psychoanalysis" here. That is to say: the newspapers are not "symbols" of the order of the signifier; they *are* the order of the signifier, in the same way that Giuliana is a woman, or her son is a boy.

8 In Lacan, the locus classicus of this notion is the *écrit* "Subversion of the Subject and the Dialectic of Desire" (*Ecrits: A Selection,* chap 9), trans. Alan Sheridan (New York: Norton, 1977), along with the "companion" seminar on desire, three sessions of which are available as "Desire and the Interpretation of Desire in *Hamlet,*" trans. J. Hulbert, *Yale French Studies* 55–56 (1977): 11–52.

9 Hence, one of Žižek's contributions to ideological analysis is the necessity for uncovering this virtual point within ideological discourse. He uses the example of the Frankfurt school analysis of the "authoritarian personality"; the virtual point breaks the deadlock of the binary opposition between authoritarian and democratic personalities, showing how the first is the repressed truth of the second. See Slavoj Žižek, *For They Know Not What They Do: Enjoyment as a Political Factor* (New York: Verso, 1991), 7–20.

10 Thus for example Hamlet's visual world is anamorphically distorted by "phallic stains"; the phallus potentially appears in every object, including Ophelia ("O phallos"). Lacan, "*Hamlet,*" 20–24.

11 See Pier Paolo Pasolini, *Lettere luterane* (Turin: Einaudi, 1976), 53–56, 152–58.

12 Some critics have likened the quality of this color saturation to that of a travelogue; this is unconvincing to me, for reasons that will become clearer as the argument proceeds. The important thing at this point is the stylistic shift that marks difference per se.

13 Michel Chion, *La Voix au cinéma* (Paris: Cahiers du cinéma, 1982) chap. 1.

14 See the discussion of the Holbein painting in Jacques Lacan, *The Four Fundamental Concepts of Psychoanalysis,* Seminar XI, ed. Jacques-Alain Miller, trans. Alan Sheridan (New York: Norton, 1977), 88–89. See also Žižek, *Looking Awry.*

15 Jacques-Alain Miller, "Montré à premontré," quoted in Žižek, *Looking Awry,* 94–95.

16 P. Adams Sitney, *Vital Crises in Italian Cinema: Iconography, Stylistics, Politics* (Austin: University of Texas Press, 1995), 215–16.

17 This might provide the best occasion to elaborate the psychoanalytic methodology of this book; and in particular, its usefulness in dealing with conflicting interpretive claims made upon texts. I see psychoanalytic theory first and foremost as applicable to the *dynamics* of a textual *economy,* which, while manifested in certain particular "content," ultimately speaks more to the form the work takes. I use the resulting understanding of the formal properties of the text to address particular interpretations of specific

content, so that while those interpretations may on the surface seem to be instances of "reading in"—the menstruation in Sitney's analysis, the self-transformation of Vittoria in Moore's analysis of *L'eclisse* discussed in the previous chapter—they can now be seen as valid but partial articulations of one or another aspect of the form.

18 Lacan, *Four Fundamental Concepts,* 95. Here Lacan chooses to illustrate his theory of the gaze through an anecdote involving a sardine can spotted from a fishing boat. In the episode, the glint of light from a floating sardine can—itself a "throw-away" object—derails any notion we may have that the world constructed through vision is unproblematically "objective," but rather opens up to the unconscious desire that "stains" that presumed objectivity. Thus Joan Copjec can note that this anecdote is a "send-up of the broadly expansive Hegelian epic form"; see *Read My Desire: Lacan against the Historicists* (Cambridge, Mass.: MIT Press, 1995), 30. I discuss Lacan's notion of the gaze in detail in chapter 6 of this book.

19 Gilles Deleuze, *Cinema 2: The Time-Image,* trans. Hugh Tomlinson and Robert Galeta (Minneapolis: University of Minnesota Press, 1989), 68, 72–73.

20 Deleuze, *The Time-Image,* 81.

21 Giuliana says "*ceramiche,*" here, which could be translated as "ceramics," but that the word has primal resonances with "pottery" can be seen by considering its Greek root: *keramos,* "potter's clay, pottery."

22 Heidegger, "The Origin of the Work of Art," in *Basic Writings,* ed. David Krell, trans. Albert Hofstadter (San Francisco: Harper, 1977), 149–87.

23 Fredric Jameson, "The Synoptic Chandler" in *Shades of Noir,* ed. Joan Copjec, (New York: Verso, 1993), 49.

24 The use of the word "orgy" has an interesting history in relation to the reception of Italian film in the United States. Fellini's *La dolce vita*—which was billed here as a "shocking" look at contemporary Roman life—seems to have been the first of the Italian imports to give us an "orgy." Given what actually happens in these "orgies," the word seems rather overblown (although probably only a reception study could give us the view of the spectator of 1960); but it did work to characterize Italian cinema as "daring," as dealing with "adult" material often elided in Hollywood cinema. The same historical period also saw a number of epics set in ancient Rome, thus playing upon the popular association of Rome with decadence. Vincente Minelli's *Two Weeks in Another Town,* which was consciously intended to outdo Fellini's film, also included a Roman "orgy," but the studio cut the scene so badly that Minelli disowned the final product.

25 The sound is there on the soundtrack; something that the prevalence of video makes it easy to verify today.

26 Michel Chion, "The Impossible Embodiment," in Slavoj Žižek, ed., *Every-*

thing You Always Wanted to Know about Lacan, but Were Afraid to Ask Hitchcock (New York: Verso, 1992), 195–207.

27 Joan Copjec, "The Phenomenal Nonphenomenal," in *Shades of Noir,* 185.

28 Michel Chion, *La voix aux cinéma* (Paris: Cahiers du cinéma, 1982), 116–23; also Žižek, *Looking Awry,* 82–83.

29 Copjec, "Phenomal Nonphenomenal," 182, 186.

30 This concept, first articulated by Lacan in "Kant with Sade" and in the ethics seminar (Seminar VII: *The Ethics of Psychoanalysis,* ed. J.-A. Miller, trans. D. Porter [New York: Norton, 1992]), is central to recent Lacanian theories of ideology. Žižek's work has been crucial in this development.

31 Copjec, "Phenomenal Nonphenomenal," 188. See also Roland Barthes, "The Grain of the Voice," *Image/Music/Text,* trans. Stephen Heath (New York: Hill and Wang, 1977), 179–89.

32 For the connection between monuments and the materialization of jouissance, see Žižek, "In His Bold Gaze My Ruin Writ Large," in Žižek, ed., *Everything,* 215.

33 *Four Fundamental Concepts,* 103. The phrasing of the quote is Žižek's (*Everything,* 257); the English translation in *Four Fundamental Concepts* actually reads "if beyond appearance there is nothing in itself, there is the gaze."

34 Cesare Casarino, "Oedipus Exploded: Pasolini and the Myth of Modernization," *October* 59 (1992): 27–47.

35 In fact, this same "reshuffling" is what characterized the postwar dominance of the so-called Penta-partito, so that under the seeming instability of constant changes of government, there was always a continuity of power based on a coalition that froze out the Communist Party. It was when this ruling coalition was faced with bringing in the communists—in the so-called *compromesso storico*—that the profound social antagonisms of the post-1968 period erupted in the terrorism of the neofascists and the extra-parliamentary Left.

36 Jean-François Lyotard, "The Sublime and the Avant-garde," in *The Lyotard Reader,* ed. Andrew Benjamin, trans. Lisa Liebmann (Cambridge: Blackwell, 1989), 196–211.

37 See chapters 3–4 of this study. This is not a part of Casarino's particular argument.

38 Casarino, "Oedipus Exploded," 35.

39 Casarino, "Oedipus Exploded," 47.

40 See Shoshana Felman, "Beyond Oedipus: the Specimen Story of Psychoanalysis," in *Lacan and Narration,* ed. Robert Con Davis (Baltimore: Johns Hopkins University Press, 1983), 1021–53.

41 Ned Lukacher, *Primal Scenes: Literature, Philosophy, Psychoanalysis* (Ithaca: Cornell University Press, 1986), 244.

42 Lukacher, *Primal Scenes,* 245.

8. The Erotics of the Periphery

1   Michel Foucault, "Of Other Spaces," *Diacritics* 16.1 (1986): 22–27.

2   For an extended discussion of the social fantasy of "conspiracy" as it functions in recent American cinema, see Fredric Jameson, *The Geopolitical Aesthetic: Cinema and Space in the World System* (Bloomington: Indiana University Press, 1995), 9–84.

3   See Fredric Jameson, *Marxism and Form* (Princeton: Princeton University Press, 1971), 83–116. Herbert Marcuse, *One Dimensional Man: Studies in Ideology of Advanced Industrial Society* (Boston: Beacon Press, 1992).

4   A point well made by Patrick Rumble, in his *Allegories of Contamination: Pier Paolo Pasolini's* Trilogy of Life (Toronto: University of Toronto Press, 1996), 140.

5   As Pasolini himself noted.

6   This is widely noted enough to be a film-historical commonplace. The key references are Roy Armes, *Patterns of Realism* (New York: A. S. Barnes, 1971), and his *Third World Filmmaking and the West* (Berkeley: University of California Press, 1987). See also Robert Kolker, *The Altering Eye: Contemporary International Cinema* (New York: Oxford University Press, 1983).

7   Kinder, *Blood Cinema: The Reconstruction of National Identity in Spain* (Berkeley: University of California Press, 1993), 73–86.

8   See Johnson and Stam, *Brazilian Cinema,* 30–33.

9   Rey Chow, *Primitive Passions: Visuality, Sexuality, Ethnography, and Contemporary Chinese Cinema* (New York: Columbia University Press, 1995), parts 1 and 3.

10 As recently as 1996, newspapers still report the existence of private police forces that function as a death squad to the displaced youth living on the streets of the major cities of Brazil.

11 Rey Chow, *Primitive Passions: Visuality, Sexuality, Ethnography, and Contemporary Chinese Cinema* (New York: Columbia University Press, 1995), 22–23, 48–52.

12 Jameson, *Geopolitical Aesthetic,* 124–33.

13 See, for example, Jonathan Rosenbaum's excellent overview of Edward Yang's work, "Exiles in Modernity: The Films of Edward Yang," accessed at ⟨http://www.chicagoreader.com⟩.

14 Jameson, "Remapping Taipei," in *The Geopolitical Aesthetic,* 115. Jameson refers here to Ann Banfield, *Unspeakable Sentences: Narration and Representation in the Language of Fiction* (Boston: Routledge & Kegan Paul, 1982).

15 See part 3 of this study for a detailed discussion of the gaze.

16 While promotional literature for this film calls the character "gay," I find the film to be ambiguous on this point.

17 Here I disagree with Jameson's reading of the "punctum" in the photograph in *Blow-up*. Jameson, "Remapping Taipei," 141.

18 See June Yip, "Constructing a Nation: Taiwanese History and the Films of Hou Hsiao-hsien," in *Transnational Chinese Cinemas: Identity, Nationhood, Gender,* ed. Sheldon Hsiao-peng Lu (Honolulu: University of Hawaii Press, 1997), 139–68; and Rosenbaum, "Exiles in Modernity."

19 Fredric Jameson, "The Cultural Logic of Late Capitalism," in *Postmodernism, or The Cultural Logic of Late Capitalism* (Durham, N.C.: Duke University Press, 1991), 38–54.

20 See chapter 7 of this study.

Anderson, Benedict. *Imagined Communities: Reflections on the Origin and Spread of Nationalism*. New York: Verso, 1993.

Andrew, Dudley. "The Gravity of *Sunrise*." *Quarterly Review of Film* 2.3 (August 1977): 356–377.

———. *Mists of Regret: Culture and Sensibility in Classic French Film*. Princeton: Princeton University Press, 1995.

Armes, Roy. *Patterns of Realism*. New York: A. S. Barnes, 1971.

———. *Third World Filmmaking and the West*. Berkeley: University of California Press, 1987.

Barbato, Andrea. "Una Faluca per Pasolini." *L'Espresso*. 14 February 1965.

Barthes, Roland. *Image/Music/Text*. Trans. Stephen Heath. New York: Hill and Wang, 1977.

Baudrillard, Jean. *Selected Writings*. Ed. Mark Poster. Stanford: Stanford University Press, 1988.

Bazin, André. *What Is Cinema?* 2 vols. Trans. Hugh Gray. Berkeley: University of California Press, 1971.

Benjamin, Walter. *The Arcades Project*. Trans. Howard Eiland and Kevin McLaughlin. Cambridge, Mass.: Harvard University Press, 1999.

———. *Illuminations*. Ed. Hannah Arendt, trans. Harry Zohn. New York: Schocken, 1968.

———. *Reflections: Essays, Aphorisms, Autobiographical Writings*. Ed. P. Demetz, trans. E. Jephcott. New York: Harcourt, Brace, Jovanovich, 1978.

Bentham, Jeremy. *The Panopticon Writings*. Ed. Miran Bozovic. New York: Verso, 1995.

Bhabha, Homi K., ed. *Nation and Narration*. New York: Routledge, 1993.

Bommes, Michael, and Patrick Wright. "'Charms of Residence': The Public and the Past." In *Making Histories: Studies In History-Writing and Politics*, ed. R. Johnson et al. London: Hutchinson, 1982.

Bondanella, Peter. *Italian Cinema: From Neo-Realism to the Present*. New York: Frederick Ungar, 1983.

Bozovic, Miran. "An Utterly Dark Spot." Introduction to *The Panopticon Writings*, by Jeremy Bentham. New York: Verso, 1995.

Brooks, Peter. *The Melodramatic Imagination: Balzac, Henry James, Melodrama and the Mode of Excess*. New York: Columbia University Press, 1985.

Brunetta, Gian Piero. *Cent'anni di cinema italiano*. Rome: Editori Laterza, 1991.

Brunette, Peter. *Roberto Rossellini*. New York: Oxford University Press, 1987.

———. *The Films of Michelangelo Antonioni*. New York: Cambridge University Press, 1998.

Bruno, Giuliana. *Streetwalking on a Ruined Map: Cultural Theory and the City Films of Elvira Notari*. Princeton: Princeton University Press, 1993.

Buck-Morss, Susan. *The Dialectics of Seeing: Walter Benjamin and the Arcades Project*. Cambridge, Mass.: MIT Press, 1991.

Burch, Noel. *To the Distant Observer: Form and Meaning in the Japanese Cinema*. Ed. Annette Michelson. Berkeley: University of California Press, 1979.

Burgin, Victor. *In/Different Spaces: Place and Memory in Visual Culture*. Berkeley: University of California Press, 1996.

Burgoyne, Robert. *Bertolucci's 1900*. Detroit: Wayne State University Press, 1991

Buscombe, Edward. "Nationhood, Culture and Media Boundaries: Britain." *Quarterly Review of Film and Video* 14.3 (April 1993): 25–34.

Casarino, Cesare. "Oedipus Exploded: Pasolini and the Myth of Modernization." *October* 59 (1992): 27–47.

Champagne, John. *The Ethics of Marginality: A New Approach to Gay Studies*. Minneapolis: University of Minnesota Press, 1995.

Chatman, Seymour. *Antonioni, or The Surface of the World*. Berkeley: University of California Press, 1985.

Chion, Michel. *La Voix au cinéma*. Paris: Cahiers du cinéma, 1982.

———. "The Impossible Embodiment." In *Everything You Always Wanted to Know about Lacan, but Were Afraid to Ask Hitchcock*, ed. Slavoj Žižek. New York: Verso, 1992.

———. "Quiet Revolution . . . and Rigid Stagnation." *October* 58 (1991) 69–80.

Chow, Rey. *Primitive Passions: Visuality, Sexuality, Ethnography, and Contemporary Chinese Cinema*. New York: Columbia University Press, 1995.

Clark, Martin. *Modern Italy, 1871–1982*. Longman History of Italy 7. New York: Longman, 1984.

Copjec, Joan. "The Orthopsychic Subject: Film Theory and the Reception of Lacan." *October* 56 (1989): 53–71.

———. "The Phenomenal Nonphenomenal: Private Space in Film Noir." In *Shades of Noir*, ed. Joan Copjec. New York: Verso, 1993.

———. *Read My Desire: Lacan against the Historicists*. Cambridge, Mass.: MIT Press, 1995.

———. "Sex and the Euthanasia of Reason." In *Supposing the Subject,* ed. Joan Copjec. New York: Verso, 1994.

Cuccu, Lorenzo. *Antonioni: Il discorso dello sguardo e altri saggi.* Pisa: Edizioni ETS, 1997.

Dalle Vacche, Angela. *The Body in the Mirror.* Princeton: Princeton University Press, 1992.

———. *Cinema and Painting: How Art Is Used in Film.* Austin: University of Texas Press, 1996.

DeCerteau, Michel. *The Practice of Everyday Life.* Trans. S. Rendall. Berkeley: University of California Press, 1984.

DeCrescenzo, Luciano. *Thus Spake Bellavista: Naples, Love, and Liberty.* Trans. Avril Bardoni. New York: Grove Press, 1988.

Deleuze, Gilles. *Cinema 1: The Movement-Image.* Trans. Hugh Tomlinson and Barbara Habberjam. Minneapolis: University of Minnesota Press, 1989.

———. *Cinema 2: The Time-Image.* Trans. Hugh Tomlinson and Robert Galeta. Minneapolis: University of Minnesota Press, 1989.

Dienst, Richard. *Still Life in Real Time: Theory after Television.* Durham, N.C.: Duke University Press, 1994.

Elsaesser, Thomas. *New German Cinema: A History.* New York: Rutgers University Press, 1989.

———. "Primary Identification and the Historical Subject." *Cine-Tracts* 11 (fall 1980): 43–52.

———. "Tales of Sound and Fury: Observations on the Family Melodrama." In *Film Theory and Criticism,* 4th ed, ed. Gerald Mast, Marshall Cohen, and Leo Braudy, 512–35. New York: Oxford University Press, 1992.

———. "What Does Žižek Want?" *Spectator* 16.2 (1996): 9–23.

Esposito, Joan. "Antonioni and Benjamin: Dialectical Imagery in Eclipse." *Film Criticism* 9.1 (1984): 25–37.

Feldstein, Richard, et al. *Reading Seminar XI.* Albany: State University of New York Press, 1995.

Felman, Shoshana. "Beyond Oedipus: The Specimen Story of Psychoanalysis." In *Lacan and Narration,* ed. Robert Con Davis, 1021–1053. Baltimore: Johns Hopkins University Press, 1983.

Flaxman, Gregory, ed. *The Brain Is the Screen: Deleuze and the Philosophy of Cinema.* Minneapolis: University of Minnesota Press, 2000.

Foster, Hal. "Obscene, Abject, Traumatic," *October* 78 (1996) 107–124.

Foucault, Michel. *The History of Sexuality.* Vol. 1. Trans. Robert Hurley. New York: Pantheon, 1978.

———. "Of Other Spaces." *Diacritics* 16.1 (1986): 22–27.

Freud, Sigmund. *Civilization and Its Discontents.* Ed. and trans. James Strachey. New York: Norton, 1961.

———. *General Psychological Theory: Papers on Metapsychology.* The Collected Papers of Sigmund Freud. Ed. Phillip Rieff. New York: Collier, 1963.

———. *Group Psychology and the Analysis of the Ego.* Ed. and trans. James Strachey. New York: Norton, 1959.

———. *Three Essays on the Theory of Sexuality.* Ed. and trans. James Strachey. New York: Avon, 1972.

———. *Totem and Taboo.* Trans. A. Brill. New York: Vintage, 1946.

Friedberg, Anne. "*Les Flâneurs du Mal(l):* Cinema and the Postmodern Condition." *PMLA* 106.3 (May 1991): 419–31.

Genette, Gérard. *Narrative Discourse: An Essay in Method.* Ithaca: Cornell University Press, 1990.

Ginsborg, Paul. *A History of Contemporary Italy: Society and Politics, 1943–1988.* New York: Penguin, 1990.

Gramsci, Antonio. *Prison Notebooks.* Ed. and trans. Quintin Hoare and Goeffrey Nowell-Smith. New York: International Publishers, 1971.

———. *Selections from Cultural Writings.* Ed. David Forgacs and Geoffrey Nowell-Smith; trans. William Boelhower. Cambridge, Mass.: Harvard University Press, 1985.

Greene, Naomi. *Pier Paolo Pasolini: Cinema as Heresy.* Princeton: Princeton University Press, 1990.

Harvey, David. *The Condition of Postmodernity.* Oxford: Blackwell, 1989.

Hay, James. "Invisible Cities/Visible Geographies: Toward a Cultural Geography of Italian Television in the 90s." *Quarterly Review of Film and Video,* 14.3 (1993): 35–48.

———. *Popular Film Culture in Fascist Italy.* Bloomington: Indiana University Press, 1987.

Hebdige, Dick. *Hiding in the Light.* New York: Routledge, 1988.

Heidegger, Martin. "The Origin of the Work of Art." In *Basic Writings,* ed. David Krell; trans. Albert Hofstadter, 149–187. San Francisco: Harper, 1977.

Higson, Andrew. "The Concept of a National Cinema." *Screen.* 30.4 (1989): 36–47.

Hobsbawm, Eric J. *Bandits.* New York: Pantheon, 1981.

———. "Introduction: Inventing Tradition" and "Mass-Producing Traditions: Europe, 1870–1914." In *The Invention of Tradition,* ed. Eric Hobsbawm and T. Ranger, Cambridge: Cambridge University Press, 1983.

———. *Nations and Nationalism since 1870: Programme, Myth, Reality.* Cambridge: Cambridge University Press, 1990.

Jaanus, Maire. "The Démontage of the Drives." *Reading Seminar XI.* Eds. Richard Feldstein, Bruce Fink, Maire Jaanus. Albany: State University of New York Press, 1995.

Jameson, Fredric. *The Geopolitical Aesthetic: Cinema and Space in the World System.* Bloomington: Indiana University Press, 1995.

———. *The Ideologies of Theory: Essays, 1971–1986.* 2 vols. London: Routledge, 1988.

———. *Marxism and Form*. Princeton: Princeton University Press, 1971.

———. *The Political Unconscious: Narrative as a Socially Symbolic Act*. Ithaca: Cornell University Press, 1981.

———. *Postmodernism, or, The Cultural Logic of Late Capitalism*. Durham, N.C.: Duke University Press, 1991.

———. *Signatures of the Visible*. New York: Routledge, 1990.

———. "Spatial Systems in *North by Northwest*." In *Everything You Always Wanted to Know about Lacan, but Were Afraid to Ask Hitchcock*, ed. Slavoj Žižek. New York: Verso, 1992.

———. "The Synoptic Chandler." In *Shades of Noir*, ed. Joan Copjec. New York: Verso, 1993.

Jay, Martin. *The Dialectical Imagination: A History of the Frankfurt School and the Institute of Social Research, 1923–1950*. Berkeley: University of California Press, 1973.

Johnson, Randall, and Robert Stam, eds. *Brazilian Cinema*. East Brunswick, N.J.: Associated University Presses, 1982.

Kinder, Marsha. "Antonioni in Transit." In *Focus on* Blow-up, ed. Roy Huss, 78–88. Englewood Cliffs, N.J.: Prentice-Hall, 1971.

———. *Blood Cinema: The Reconstruction of National Identity in Spain*. Berkeley: University of California Press, 1993.

———. "Subversive Potential of the Pseudo-Iterative." *Film Quarterly* 43.2 (1989): 2–16.

Kinder, Marsha and Beverley Houston. *Self and Cinema: A Transformalist Perspective*. Pleasantville, N.Y.: Redgrave Publishing, 1980.

Kline, T. Jefferson. *Bertolucci's Dream Loom: A Psychoanalytic Study of Film*. Amherst: University of Massachusetts Press, 1987.

Kolker, Robert. *The Altering Eye: Contemporary International Cinema*. New York: Oxford University Press, 1983.

Kracauer, Siegfried. *From Caligari to Hitler: A Psychological History of the German Film*. Princeton: Princeton University Press, 1947.

L'Espresso. "Omosessuali si nasce?" 23 May 1965.

———. "La Paura della donna," 30 May 1965.

Lacan, Jacques. "Desire and the Interpretation of Desire in *Hamlet*." Trans. J. Hulbert. *Yale French Studies* 55–56 (1977): 11–52.

———. *Ecrits: A Selection*. Trans. Alan Sheridan. New York: Norton, 1977.

———. *The Four Fundamental Concepts of Psychoanalysis*. Seminar XI. Ed. Jacques-Alain Miller; trans. Alan Sheridan. New York: Norton, 1977.

———. "Kant with Sade." *October* 40 (1987): 55–104.

———. *Seminar VII: The Ethics of Psychoanalysis*. Ed. Jacques-Alain Miller; trans. Dennis Porter. New York: Norton, 1992.

Laplanche, J., and J.-B. Pontalis. *The Language of Psychoanalysis*. Trans. Donald Nicholson-Smith. New York: Norton, 1973.

Laurent, Eric. "Alienation and Separation." In *Reading Seminar XI*. Eds. Richard Feldstein, Bruce Fink, Maire Jaanus. Albany: State University of New York Press, 1995.

Lefebvre, Henri. *The Production of Space*. Trans. Donald Nicholson-Smith. Cambridge, Mass.: Blackwell, 1991.

Liehm, Mira. *Passion and Defiance: Film in Italy from 1942 to the Present*. Berkeley: University of California Press, 1984.

Lukacher, Ned. *Primal Scenes: Literature, Philosophy, Psychoanalysis*. Ithaca: Cornell University Press, 1986.

Lyotard, Jean-François. *The Lyotard Reader*. Ed. Andrew Benjamin; trans. Lisa Liebmann. Cambridge, Mass: Blackwell, 1989.

———. *The Postmodern Condition: A Report on Knowledge*. Trans. Geoff Bennington and Brian Massumi. Minneapolis: University Minnesota Press, 1984

Marcus, Millicent. *Italian Film in the Light of Neo-Realism*. Princeton: Princeton University Press, 1986.

Marcuse, Herbert. *One Dimensional Man: Studies in Ideology of Advanced Industrial Society*. 2nd ed. Boston: Beacon Press, 1992.

Mattelart, Armand, and Michèle Mattelart. *Rethinking Media Theory*. Trans. James A. Cohen and Marina Urquidi. Minneapolis: University of Minnesota Press, 1992.

Mellencamp, Patricia, ed. *Logics of Television* Bloomington: Indiana University Press, 1990.

Miccichè, Lino, ed. *Brasile: "Cinema novo" e dopo*. Quaderni della Mostra Internazionale del Nuovo Cinema (Pesaro Film Festival) 9. Venice: Marsilio Editori, 1981.

———, ed. *Il neorealismo cinematografico italiano*. Atti del convegno della X Mostra Internazionale del Nuovo Cinema (Pesaro Film Festival). Venice: Marsilio Editori, 1975.

Moore, Kevin Z. "Eclipsing the Commonplace: The Logic of Alienation in Antonioni's Cinema." *Film Quarterly* 48.4 (1995): 22–34.

Morley, David. "Where the Global Meets the Local: Notes from the Sitting Room." *Screen* 32.1 (1991): 1–15.

———. "Spaces of Identity." *Screen* 30.4 (1989): 10–35.

Morley, David, and Kevin Robins. "No Place like Heimat." *New Formations* 12 (1990): 1–24.

Morse, Margaret. "An Ontology of Everyday Distraction: The Freeway, the Mall, and Television." In *Logics of Television*, ed. Patricia Mellencamp. Bloomington: Indiana University Press, 1990.

Nichols, Bill. *Representing Reality: Issues and Concepts in Documentary*. Bloomington: Indiana University Press, 1991.

Overbey, David, ed. *Springtime in Italy: A Reader on Neo-Realism*. Hamden, Conn.: Archon Books, 1979.

Pasolini, Pier Paolo. *Le ceneri di Gramsci*. Milan: Garzanti, 1957.

———. *Heretical Empiricism,* trans. Ben Lawton and Kate L. Barnett. Bloomington: Indiana University Press, 1988. Translation of *Empirismo eretico* (Milan: Garzanti, 1972).

———. *Lettere luterane*. Turin: Einaudi, 1976.

Rocha, Glauber. "Aesthetic of Hunger." In *Brazilian Cinema*, ed. Randall Johnson and Robert Stann. New Brunswick: Associated University Presses, 1982.

Rocchio, Vincent. *Cinema of Anxiety: A Psychoanalysis of Italian Neorealism*. Austin: University of Texas Press, 1999.

Rohdie, Sam. *Antonioni*. London: British Film Institute, 1990.

Rondolino, Gianni. *Dizionario del cinema italiano, 1945–1969*. Turin: Einaudi, 1969.

Rosen, Philip. "History, Textuality, Nation: Kracauer, Burch, and Some Problems in the Study of National Cinema." *Iris* 2.2 (1984): 69–84.

Rosenbaum, Jonathan. "Exiles in Modernity: The Films of Edward Yang." Accessed at ⟨http://www.chicagoreader.com⟩.

Rumble, Patrick. *Allegories of Contamination: Pier Paolo Pasolini's* Trilogy of Life. Toronto: University of Toronto Press, 1996.

Rumble, Patrick, and Bart Testa. *Pier Paolo Pasolini: Contemporary Perspectives*. Toronto: University of Toronto Press, 1995.

Salecl, Renata, and Slavoj Žižek, eds. *Gaze and Voice as Love Objects*. Durham, N.C.: Duke University Press, 1996.

Sassoon, Donald. *Contemporary Italy: Politics, Economy and Society since 1945*. New York: Longman, 1986.

Schneider, Cynthia, and Brian Wallis, eds. *Global Television*. New York: Wedge Press, 1988.

Schwooch, James. "Cold War, Hegemony, Postmodernism: American Television and the World System, 1945–1992." *Quarterly Review of Film and Video* 14.3 (1993): 9–24.

Silverman, Kaja. *Threshold of the Visible World*. New York: Routledge, 1996.

Sitney, P. Adams. *Vital Crises in Italian Cinema: Iconography, Stylistics, Politics*. Austin: University of Texas Press, 1995.

Skovmand, Michael, and Kim Schroder, eds. *Media Cultures: Reappraising Transnational Media*. New York: Routledge, 1992.

Soja, Edward. *Postmodern Geographies: The Reassertion of Space in Critical Theory*. New York: Verso, 1993.

Sorlin, Pierre. *European Cinemas, European Societies*. New York: Routledge, 1991.

Spinazzola, Vittorio. *Cinema e pubblico: Lo spettacolo filmico in Italia, 1945–1965*. Milan: Bompiani, 1974.

Viano, Maurizio. *A Certain Realism: Making Use of Pasolini's Film Theory and Practice*. Berkeley: University of California Press, 1993.

Witcombe, R. T. *The New Italian Cinema*. New York: Oxford University Press, 1982.

Yip, June. "Constructing a Nation: Taiwanese History and the Films of Hou

Hsiao-hsien." In *Transnational Chinese Cinemas: Identity, Nationhood, Gender,* ed. Sheldon Hsiao-peng Lu. Honolulu: University Hawaii Press, 1997.

Žižek, Slavoj. *Enjoy Your Symptom!* New York: Routledge, 1992.

——, ed. *Everything You Always Wanted to Know about Lacan, but Were Afraid to Ask Hitchcock.* New York: Verso, 1992.

——. *For They Know Not What They Do: Enjoyment as a Political Factor.* New York: Verso, 1991.

——. *Looking Awry: An Introduction to Jacques Lacan through Popular Culture.* Cambridge, Mass.: MIT Press, 1992.

——. *The Metastases of Enjoyment.* New York: Verso, 1994.

——. *The Sublime Object of Ideology.* New York: Verso, 1989

——. *Tarrying with the Negative: Kant, Hegel, and the Critique of Ideology.* Durham, N.C.: Duke University Press, 1993.

Gaze (*continued*)
186 n.13, 187 n.21; and the Imaginary, 130–31, 135; luminence and, 104; perspective and, 104; and the phallus, 17–18, 110–11, 190 n.10; and the Real, 104–105; and the Symbolic, 103, 111–12, 129–30. *See also* Image; Perception; Visuality
Gender, 16, 59, 82
Genette, Gérard, 6
Giallo, 33
Global Space. *See* Space
Gospel According to St. Matthew, The, 77, 85. *See also* Pasolini, Pier Paolo
Gramsci, Antonio, 18, 36, 66, 67
Grand magasin. See Department stores
Grido, Il, 124, 125, 138, 140. *See also* Antonioni, Michelangelo
Grimaldi, Aurelio, 150, 156
Gulf Oil Company, 73

Harvey, David, 41
Hay, James, 18, 74
Hegemony, 4, 26, 45, 60–68, 72, 81, 169
Heidegger, Martin, 38, 114, 122, 136, 143
Hertz Rent-a-Car, 73
Historicity, 9, 13, 114, 125, 126, 136, 140
Historiography: and cultural studies, 13, 17; and "deep structure," 4–5, 13; desire in, 3; of national cinemas, 6, 10–18, 153, 156–57; periodization, 4, 8, 138; postmodernity and, 5, 12, 15; and symptomatic reading, 11
History of Sexuality, 80. *See also* Foucault, Michel
Hitchcock, Alfred, 137
Hobsbawm, Eric, 18, 48–49
Hollywood, 3, 4, 8, 9, 22, 25–27, 30,

65, 89, 103, 110, 152–54, 169–70
Homogenization (cultural), 28, 71, 76
Homosexuality, 21, 54, 62, 68, 87, 91; attitudes toward, 81–83; and male prostitution, 147–48, 155; Mediterranean, 81–83, 152; modernism and, 34; pedagogy and, 152–59; performative models of, 82–83, 159; representations of, 34, 58, 150–52, 155–56. *See also* Pasolini, Pier Paolo
Horkheimer, Max, 18
Hou Hsiao-hsien, 159, 163
Hyperspace. *See* Space

Identification, 14, 15, 17, 24, 81, 155–57
Ideology, 37, 99, 101
Image 4–6, 19–21, 72–73, 87–89, 100, 102–103, 120–23, 138, 142, 153, 166, 168, 170, 172; anamorphosis in, 95, 104, 110–11, 116–17, 125–27, 132–34, 160–63, 190 n.10, 191 n.18; circulation of, 21, 28–29, 36; and commodification, 63, 108, 114–15, 161; dialectical, 54–55; digital, 114, 163; faceting of, 38–39, 134–35; indeterminacy in, 55–56, 125–27; as indexical sign, 85, 98, 106–107, 163; as simulacrum, 40–42, 106, 115, 160; time-image, 4, 89, 134–35. *See also* Gaze; Perception; Visuality
Imaginary (Lacanian), 14, 28, 46, 63, 112, 128, 130, 169
Imitation of Life, 59
India Song, 137
Inferno (Dante), 41
I Soliti Ignoti, 9
Itineraries. *See* Space

James Bond, 108, 115
Jameson, Fredric, 17, 22, 41, 58, 60, 65–66, 73, 114, 149, 158, 159, 161, 162, 166, 188 n.36

the aesthetics of contamination, 53, 56; the body in the works of, 79–80, 157, 184 n.3; center/periphery in the works of, 53–55, 147–50; film theoretical writings of, 100–101, 106–107, 126; and homosexuality, 21, 54, 81–83, 91, 148–49, 157–59; influences of, outside Italy, 155–59; and language, 45, 67–68, 80; murder of, 147–49, 150; and neorealism, 8, 91; and neorealist revival, 48, 85; and pedagogy, 152, 157–59; political and cultural writings of, 36, 45, 67–68, 131; style of editing/montage, 78, 87–91

Passage à l'acte, 86

Passenger, The, 124, 125. *See also* Antonioni, Michelangelo

Pedagogy, 71, 150, 152–54, 157–59

Peplum films, 9

Perception, 89, 101, 120; anamorphosis in, 95, 104, 110–11, 116–17, 125–27, 132–34, 160–63, 190 n.10, 191 n.18; and appearance, 35, 37–38, 114, 140, 148, 160; and fantasy, 129–135; and phenomenology, 99–100, 105–107, 140; and reality-effect, 95, 105, 112, 155. *See also* Gaze; Image; Visuality

Performative, 13, 14, 16, 83, 159

Perfumed Nightmare, The, 156

Phallus, 17, 59, 90–91, 110, 125

Philippines, 156

Pilota ritorna, Un, 96

Pink neorealism, 23, 32, 35

Pixote, 154

Po Valley, 29, 33, 46, 96, 125

Point de capiton, 61, 71, 107, 125

Pop, 58, 108–109, 114–15

Porosity, 62–65, 76, 142

Portella della Ginestra, Massacre at, 51, 172

Postcolonial, 47, 67, 153, 156, 160, 164

Postino, Il, 168–72

Postman Always Rings Twice, 24

Postmodernity: aesthetics of, 41–42, 113, 119, 123, 137–40, 168–70; and historiography, 5, 12; and the image, 42, 76, 119, 123; and neocapitalism, 12, 48, 65, 76, 138–39, 142; and space, 5, 41, 53, 57, 61–65, 73, 76, 138, 165; and subjectivity, 7, 42, 61, 123, 138–39, 158; and the sublime, 113, 119, 127, 141

Primal scene, 111, 113, 142–43

Prison, 55, 56, 133, 167

Problema del Mezzogiorno, 47

Prostitution, 55, 80, 82, 83, 154, 166

Proust, Marcel, 6, 82

Psycho, 138

Psychoanalysis: and film theory, 7, 13, 61, 79, 187 n.21; and history, 13, 15, 103, 137–39, 142; interpretive methods and, 7, 61, 103, 133, 142, 189–90 n.7, 190–91 n.17. *See also* Gaze; Lacan, Jacques; Narrative; Real; Sound/image relations; Symbolic; Visuality

Public Space, 73, 118

Public sphere, 118, 163

Purgatorio (Dante), 42

Quel bowling sul Tevere, 95. *See also* Antonioni, Michelangelo

Ragazzi fuori, 154, 164–66

Real (Lacanian): the body as, 79, 124, 157; encountering, 86, 98, 135; formlessness, 38, 127, 136; and the Gaze, 104–105, 122; history as, 7, 10, 76; object *a*, 111; and Symbolic, 61, 97–98, 136; trauma, 78, 98, 124

Realism, 22, 23, 25, 26, 35, 38, 50, 54, 97–102, 119, 157

Reality effect, 95, 105, 111, 115. *See also* Visuality

Angelo Restivo is Assistant Professor of Film Studies in
the Department of English at East Carolina University.

Library of Congress Cataloging-in-Publication Data
Restivo, Angelo.
The cinema of economic miracles : visuality and modern-
ization in the Italian art film / Angelo Restivo.
p.   cm. — (Post-contemporary interventions)
Includes bibliographical references and index.
ISBN 0-8223-2787-2 (alk. paper)
ISBN 0-8223-2799-6 (pbk : alk. paper)
1. Pasolini, Pier Paolo, 1922–1975 — Criticism and inter-
pretation.   2. Antonioni, Michelangelo — Criticism and
interpretation.   3. Motion pictures — Italy — History.
I. Title.   II. Series.
PN1998.3.P367 R47 2002
791.463'0945'09046 — dc21   2001040683